READY, AIM, FIRE

Major James Francis Thomas

THE FOURTH VICTIM IN THE EXECUTION OF LIEUTENANT HARRY "BREAKER" MORANT

JAMES UNKLES

About the Author

James has been a lawyer for over 40 years, practising in criminal, administrative law and dispute resolution. He works as a lawyer and dispute resolution practitioner for a statutory authority in Melbourne. He was a former Police and Commonwealth Prosecutor. He is also a serving Officer in the Royal Australian Navy Reserve. His web site contains a history of his work to secure posthumous pardons for Lieutenants Harry 'Breaker' Morant, Peter Handcock and George Witton.

www.breakermorant.com

James' *pro bono* work is to see justice done on behalf of the descendants of these men.

Interests: Military history, music (plays drums, jazz / blues), veterans' hockey, cooking (not master chef standard!), advocating for Australian military veterans.

Published in Australia by Sid Harta Publishers Pty Ltd,
ABN: 46 119 415 842
23 Stirling Crescent, Glen Waverley, Victoria 3150 Australia

Telephone: +61 3 9560 9920, Facsimile: +61 3 9545 1742
E-mail: author@sidharta.com.au

First published in Australia 2018, This edition published 2018
Copyright © James Unkles 2018
Cover design, typesetting: WorkingType Studio

The right of James Unkles to be identified as the Author of the Work has been asserted in accordance with the Copyright, Designs and Patents Act 1988.

The Author of this book accepts all responsibility for the contents and absolves any other person or persons involved in its production from any responsibility or liability where the contents are concerned.

All rights reserved. No part of this publication may be reproduced, stored in a retrieval system, or transmitted, in any form or by any means without the prior written permission of the publisher, nor be otherwise circulated in any form of binding or cover other than that in which it is published and without a similar condition being imposed on the subsequent purchaser.

ISBN: 978-1-925230-50-5
pp236

Reviews

"This comprehensive scintillating examination of Major James Thomas of Tenterfield and the Transvaal is long overdue. Too often the heavy lifters in historical sagas get overlooked. This book goes to the core of the Breaker Morant trial and the role of Major Thomas, a brave dedicated man who deserves this testament as he stepped up for justice against the diktats of Kitchener. He also made his contribution to to the NSW regional community of Tenterfield, and to State and Nation."
— Tim Fischer AC. Ex Deputy PM , Former Ambassador and author.

"It is an awesome responsibility for a defence lawyer to try to save the life of a client – as I know from my own death row practice. This fascinating book tells the story of a country solicitor called upon at the last moment to defend three Australian soldiers facing a British military establishment determined to execute them and to cover up its own failings. The trial was outrageously unfair by today's standards, and even by rules of the time, but Major James Thomas did his best — which is all you can do. A worthy contribution to literature on miscarriage of justice."
— Geoffrey Ronald Robertson, AO, QC

Abusing the Power to Withhold Using Power
"Each year the Australian community commemorates Gallipoli for the ardent and dedicated role of our soldiers, and only some are mindful of how sacrificially and dismissively they were treated by the British Command.

This book comprehensively outlines with clarity and gravitas the egregious display of shameless arrogance by Lord Kitchener as to how he treated perceived military and political "expendables" in prioritising his own self-polished reputation — and contrasts that with the simple respectful behaviour of one man in defending military men whose superiors had mortally turned on them without humanity.

Few people understand or know how shocking it is in Australia's history that our soldiers in support of the British Boer War effort could be executed for following Orders in an expected guerrilla-war way - summarily shot within hours of a rigged court's outcome, and the plenary disregard for appeal rights, the rules of court, procedural fairness, and due process.

This book tells the story of how the nobility of a great and decent man, Major Thomas, was also shot in February 1902, and how his life thereafter declined with the emotional attrition and trauma of it all. It has the impact of recognition."

— **MG in the Macedon Ranges**

Australian history an injustice revealed
"*Ready, Aim, Fire* is a well researched and compelling account of the country lawyer who unwittingly was caught up in Australia's most controversial military trial. The mistrial and execution of Lieutenants Breaker Morant and Peter Handcock and imprisonment of George Witton was controversial and still is some 120 years after the event. Unkles offers an inside view of what Major J.F. Thomas was faced with defending half a dozen men on capital charges with one day's notice to prepare. The book highlights many of the legal issues with the trial process and how Thomas fought gamely, but unsuccessfully to save his clients from a politicised trial'.

'The book also charts the sad decline of Thomas after the war, traumatised and haunted to his last day by his experiences in a bitter war between the British and the Boer Republics in South Africa. A dark chapter in Australia's history that must be addressed and a long overdue salute to one of Australia's finest."

— **Nick from Sydney**

Military justice gone wrong. One man against an Empire
"I recommend this book to everyone. You will learn firsthand the plight Major James Francis Thomas faced in his attempt to get justice for three Australian Soldiers, with himself becoming the fourth victim. Our Australian soldiers 'were' Scapegoats of the British Empire, and now 118 years

later, the fight continues for justice. Author and Historian James Unkles, has given voice to Major James Francis Thomas by telling his story of the trials and tribulations he faced in representing our three 'already condemned' soldiers and fellow Australians. If you are one for Military history and one for Justice, this book is for you... I could not be prouder to be an Australian, of our lost soldiers and those who believe and fight for their justice."

Respect at last
"I am the great nephew of Major Thomas and on behalf of the Thomas clan; I would like to commend James Unkles for his determination and perseverance in recognising Major Thomas' place in Australian history. The Thomas family has always celebrated Major Thomas' role as a leading community figure in the development of Tenterfield and his dedicated service during the Boer war, including his decision to represent Lieutenants Morant, Handcock and Witton. His advocacy was commendable and met the high standards of the legal profession. Unfortunately, it was a service that later wreaked havoc in his life and he suffered as a result. For the first time, this book brings to the public's attention the life, the successes and sufferings of a country solicitor, a gentleman and proud Australian. I highly recommend the book to anyone who wishes to reflect on James Francis Thomas and appreciate the enormous responsibility he had to try secure trials according to law and save two of his clients from the firing squad. This book skilfully explores the military law of 1902, exposes the serious defects in the trials that were politically motivated and the gross injustices done to the accused. The author also discusses his skilful work to bring justice 117 years later to a cause that alluded Major Thomas. Bravo".
— **Proud GRW Descendent from Boonah QLD**

"I had the pleasure of recently launching the book *"Ready, Aim, Fire"* by James Unkles. The book tells the story of Major James Francis Thomas, defence lawyer in the 1902 Breaker Morant trial. Himself a military lawyer, James Unkles wrote it acknowledge Thomas' sacrifice in taking on the case. Which detrimentally affected his life and reputation for years afterwards. A great read for anyone with an interest in the military, law, and this remarkable period in Australia's history."

— **Senator Jim Molan AO DSC**

"This book will appeal to lawyers as it delves into military law and generally for presenting a side to the British Empire which is less gilded than the perceptions of many Australians. Concentration camps for civilians, destroying farms, a clear take no prisoners policy. This is a compelling read."

— **Roger Mendelson Lawyer and author-Law Institute of Victoria Review Aug 2019**

"Although this book gives the impression that it is a biographical study, the biography of Major James Francis Thomas (the fourth 'victim' in the Breaker Morant saga), is woven round the true centerpiece of the author's focus: the trial of Harry Morant and Peter Handcock'. Understandably, it is too, a sympathetic record of a hard-working country lawyer from Tenterfield who was placed in a difficult environment to do a job where the odds were undoubtedly stacked against him from the very outset."

— **Rob Droogleever, Anglo Boer War Study Group**

"I love Australian military history and enjoyed the story telling about a country lawyer who served his country but suffered as a result, a great read!"

— **History buff from Boronia**

Foreword

ALEXANDER STREET SC, QC, CMDR (RANR)
JUDGE OF THE FEDERAL CIRCUIT COURT OF AUSTRALIA

Australian legends are made in adversity. There could be no more challenging environment than South Africa during the second Boer War for a military lawyer to face, than to be trying to defend three Australian Bushveldt Carbineer volunteers, Lieutenants Harry 'Breaker' Morant, Peter Handcock and George Witton in a combination of unfair trials. The looming prospect of immediate capital punishment became a reality. The trials involved the adducing of false evidence from the prosecution witness, Lord Kitchener's second in command, denying the existence of orders made by Lord Kitchener to take no prisoners alive. This order made by Lord Kitchener, lawful at that time under British military law, and at that time lawful under the international laws of armed conflict, was a central plank of the defence case. Major James Francis Thomas valiantly defended these innocent Australian volunteers who were arraigned for trial on orders signed by Lord Kitchener, wrongly convicted and unlawfully executed Morant and Handcock upon pre-emptory orders also signed by Lord Kitchener. George Witton was sentenced to life imprisonment, but should also have been acquitted.

Sir Laurence Whistler Street, AC, KCMG, KStJ, QC with his son Alexander Street, QC

Just as Breaker Morant's and Peter Handcock's wrongful execution calls for posthumous pardons, this book serves to advance the true recognition, courage, valour and dedication of an Australian legendary military lawyer. Major Thomas valiantly and in accordance with his highest duty as a servant of the rule of law, raised proper objections and defences for his two innocent Australian clients, who were the subject of unfair trials and a most serious miscarriage of military justice. The conduct of Lord Kitchener in proceeding with the improper and unjust executions, contrary to undertakings given to the Australian Government and to frustrate the legal endeavours of their courageous Australian military lawyer Major Thomas, is an indictment that this book properly brings to public account.

Major Thomas, in his incredible battle for military justice for these two wrongly convicted courageous Australian volunteers, is himself an Australian legend. It has taken almost equal courage and determination, by this author James Unkles CMDR (RANR) to rectify the inadequate and missing recognition of this great Australian legend. Thomas, the Aussie military lawyer, from Tenterfield, defended, to the utmost of his ability and forensic skills, and with remarkable tenacity within the constraints of ethical propriety, the wrongful convictions and unlawful execution of 'Breaker' Morant and Peter Handcock.

Alexander Street SC, QC, CMDR (RANR)
Judge of the Federal Circuit Court of Australia

Dedication

To Marie Unkles,
for her abiding tolerance and support.

Acknowledgement

This author's thanks to Nick Bleszinski, author of *Shoot Straight, You Bastards! The truth behind the killing of "Breaker" Morant* 2nd Edition. His contributions have made this book possible. The journey has been stimulating, rewarding and continuing.

This author also expresses thanks to Ted Robl, Ex Royal Australian Navy, married and residing in Seymour, who commenced research into "Breaker" Morant in 1980 and has authored a book *A Backblock Bard* in 2002 featuring many of Morant's poems and short stories. His interest in this aspect of Australian history has resulted in a further two volumes currently underway on Morant containing newly discovered material not previously seen.

Contents

Preface		1
1	Why This author?	6
2	The Fourth Victim	7
3	Major James Francis Thomas	15
4	Newspaper Proprietor	23
5	A Marksman and More!	25
6	Military Career	29
7	War! What War? — 1880 — 1902	30
8	Australia Fights	48
9	Tenterfield and Beyond	51
10	And So Fate	58
11	Brief to appear far from home	71
12	Protest Upon Protest	95
13	Reflection	115
14	Social and Political Reformer	130
15	The Tragic Final Years	133
16	Decline into professional disrepute	144
17	The Thomas Family Speaks	155
18	A final salute	161
Epilogue		165
Chronology & Summary of Major James Francis Thomas		173

Appendixes

A	NSW Parliamentary Debates and letters from Thomas	178
B	Opinions of Senior Lawyers, Judicial Officers and Community Leaders	184
C	Courts Martial Charges	190
D	Parliamentary Motion and transcript of addresses made by MPs	196

E	Speech by George Christensen to the Australian Parliament	203
F	Letter from George Christensen to Hon Darren Chester MP	205
G	Letter and Statement of Major James Thomas to the Premier of Western Australia, and other responses	208
H	Press Reports	215
I	Law Society Press Release	233
J	Mayoral Minute, Tenterfield Council	234
L	Letter from Mayor of Tenterfield	237
Endnotes		239

Preface

'I was present at the burial and helped to carry them and placed the Australian flag on their grave. I have a photograph of this somewhere. It is not true as stated in Bushman and Buccaneer that the burial was not fully and properly conducted, for it was. All that I wrote in that letter is true and much more might have been written and may yet be written for the full facts have never been made known, also I have the whole proceedings of the courts martial held at Pietersburg, correspondence etc. The whole affair is a tragedy and might form a tragedy if written for one.'[1]

Matters of justice confront Governments in the Commonwealth. Our histories are riddled with cases of abuse of power, and remedies that seek justice, reparation and apology for injustices done.

The respect for law illustrates the defining principle of trial according to law, a fair hearing that defines values that embrace judicial values. This has been the cornerstone of law revered and practised in Commonwealth jurisdictions and defined by British statutory and common law.

However, there is one case that should be singled out for particular attention that remains one of Australia's and Britain's most enduring military and political controversies. For 116 years, the issue of whether Lieutenants Harry "Breaker" Morant and his fellow Australians, Peter Handcock and George Witton, were tried according to British law and treated fairly when convicted and sentenced for shooting Boer prisoners during the Anglo Boer War has been disputed. Since 2009, a *dogged war* of a legal nature has been waged by this author in an effort to persuade the British and Australian Governments to comprehensively review the case.

The execution of Morant and Handcock on the 27th of February 1902 and the sentencing of Witton to life imprisonment continues to ignite passionate debate in Britain, South Africa and amongst the descendants of these men.

The brutality of this episode in British military history is one that many, particularly in London, would rather forget. In the midst of the Boer War, the trial of these three Australian volunteers highlighted reprehensible tactics ordered by British officers, including reprisal through summary execution, as a legitimate means of prosecuting the war.

It is argued that the three Australians who shot 12 Boer combatants did so while acting under orders that they believed were lawful according to Military law of 1900 issued by senior British Regular Army Officers, including the Commander In Chief, Lord Kitchener. Put simply, the accused were not afforded the rights of a person facing serious criminal charges enshrined in military law of 1902, were denied their right of appeal to the King and to state a redress of grievance according to military law.

A focus of this author's career has been the study of injustices, the intriguing aspects of politics, social interactions, the abuse of power and those who have been sacrificed in the process. Thomas is one such victim and it's this author's mission to understand Thomas' rightful place in history by understanding his endeavours, character and contribution to Australian history.

Recognised or Forgotten?

Thomas has been recognised by a few historians in various writings, essays, publications and web sites. The contrasts have fluctuated between criticism, scepticism, ignorance, understanding and respect.

For example, the Australian Light Horse Association contains a reflection about Thomas, his life and exploits, including his service in the Boer War and his service to the community of Tenterfield.[2]

However, a lack of recognition of Thomas is aptly identified in a book that explores the history of the Australian Army's Legal Corps.[3] This book edited by Oswald and Waddell celebrates the history of the legal corps and highlights its creation and development from the beginning of the 21st Century to 2014. While the book recognises the Boer War and identified Major Thomas, (although incorrectly citing Thomas initials as JT instead of JF), it pays scant recognition of Thomas as an effective legal officer.

In a few lines, Colonel Jim Waddell cited critical comment of Dr John Bennett to summarise Thomas' contribution as Australia's first military lawyer:

> 'The first lawyers involved in the Australian Army were officers with legal qualifications who served in the Boer War. Among them was Major J.T. Thomas, a Tenterfield solicitor. He defended Morant, Handcock and Witton at their courts martial in 1902. Morant and Handcock were executed for shooting Boer prisoners and a German missionary. Colonel Waddell cites a view propounded by Dr John Bennett that the failure of the defence case can be attributed in large measure to Thomas' ineptitude and inexperience.'[4]

This author refers to aspects of Bennett's assessment further in this book.[5]

Colonel Waddell's view was also reflected by His Honour, Chief Justice Robert French, AC when he addressed guests at the launch of the book, Justice In Arms. His honour stated:[6]

> 'A high-profile practitioner of the legal arts during the Boer War, whose contribution was thought in some circles to be rather questionable, was Major Thomas, who had previously practiced as a solicitor at Tenterfield. He unsuccessfully defended Breaker Morant. One unkind commentator has suggested that his incompetence helped Morant to an early grave at the hands of the firing squad. Major Thomas' reputation was not enhanced when, after his return to practice at Tenterfield, he was struck off for misconduct involving trust moneys.

With due respect to Colonel Waddell and His Honour, Chief Justice French, the minimalist view of Thomas by reliance on a distorted conclusion by Bennett that Thomas was a failure as an advocate in the Morant trials is disputed.

Thomas' efforts to represent his clients in a professional manner was the subject of favourable comment by author F.M. Cutlack in his book, *Breaker Morant*[7]. He noted the evidence adduced by Thomas in the defence of Morant, Handcock and Witton, believing they had lawful orders to extract reprisal against Boer combatants. Cutlack's opinion was that it was this advocacy that resulted in the trial officers citing extenuating circumstances and strong recommendations for mercy, recommendations that were only considered in favour of Witton (Appendix C).

A similar assessment was noted by G.A. Embleton in the forward to Witton's book.[8] Embleton's opinion was that although Thomas was a very capable solicitor in Tenterfield, he was not an experienced barrister capable of representing men who were facing capital offences for which the penalty was death. Despite this, he stated:

> 'He had little practical courtroom experience and very little knowledge of the intricate military procedure connected with a court martial. Yet with very limited time to prepare his case, he managed to get the men acquitted of many of the charges.'[9]

Perhaps the most accurate assessment of Thomas' performance comes from Witton himself. Witton had applied and paid for his own copy of the trial transcripts received from the Judge Advocate General's Office in 1903. The record shows his copy was sent to his brother Ernest in Melbourne to assist him to instruct barrister, Isaac Isaacs to prepare a legal case to petition the Crown for George Witton's release.[10] After Witton was eventually released from prison and returned to Australia he had access to the trial transcripts sent to his brother.

Witton's book contains many references to verbatim quotes from the proceedings, including submissions made by Thomas, the prosecutor and the Judge Advocate.

Witton quoted from extracts of submissions made by Thomas, including on issues such as criminal liability, standard of proof for charges of murder, being accessories before the fact, the right of the accused to make unsworn statements (which they did) and principles of military law, including the principle of reprisal (a defence known in law of 1902).[11]

Witton quoted one example of Thomas' ability to address the court on legal issues. Thomas directed the court on the customs of war as per the Manual of Military Law, 1899[12] and its application to obedience to orders;[13]

'The first duty of a citizen is to defend his country, but this defence must be conducted according to the Customs of War. Further, War must be conducted by persons acting under the control of some recognised Government, having power to put an end to hostilities, in order that the enemy may know the authority to which he may resort when desirous of making peace. Under ordinary circumstances, therefore, persons committing acts of hostility who do not belong to an organised body, authorised by some recognised Government, and do not wear a military uniform, or some conspicuous dress or mark, showing them to be part of an organised military body, incur the risk of being treated as marauders and punished accordingly.

Persons, other than regular troops in uniform, whose dress shows their character, committing acts of hostility against an enemy, must, if they expect when captured to be treated as prisoners of war, be organised in such a manner, or fight under such circumstances, as to give their opponents due notice that they are open enemies from whom resistance is to be expected."

Retaliation is military vengeance; it takes place where an outrage committed on one side is avenged by the commission of a similar act on the other.'

Any dismissive assessment of Thomas is challenged by this author. Thomas was Australia's first identified military legal officer serving in an operational environment in Australia's first conflict after Federation in 1901. Despite Bennett's conclusion, Thomas' stoic dedication to his service as an advocate achieved a standard that modern day military lawyers should respect.

It should also be acknowledged that Thomas finished his service in South Africa highly decorated with three "Mentioned in Dispatches", the Queen's Medal with four clasps and was promoted to the rank of Major.

As this author explains, Thomas' credible and ethical work as an advocate for Morant, Handcock and Witton should be acknowledged given the oppressive circumstances that confronted him in a conflict far from Australia with no support of Australian authorities.

Chapter 1

Why This author?

In 2009, this author had been posted on military duty to Canberra to work at Australian Defence Force Academy. ADFA is Australia's centre for training Australia's officers. Amidst this elite centre of military learning, the Centre of Leadership and Ethics was to be his home for several months. This author's duties included assisting in the study of ethics in the profession of arms.

Little did he realise that over the next 10 years he would be confronting Australian and British Governments for a review into the manner in which Lieutenants Morant, Handcock and Witton were subjected to a brutal and illegal process that resulted in Morant and Handcock being executed and Witton sentenced to life imprisonment.

Ironically, against his study of warfare and ethics, this author was given the unique opportunity of investigating one of the most controversial cases of military history involving Australia's involvement in a war long ago at a time when Australia reached nationhood and immediately turned to support the British Crown in its war against the South African Boer.

This author travelled from Melbourne and resided at the Officers' Mess, Duntroon. Duntroon was approximate to ADFA and the Centre of Leadership and Ethics and the institutions that he would need to do his research, being the Australian War Memorial, the National Archives, and the National Library.

This author realised that in reviewing the case, he also had to examine the character and life of James Francis Thomas who defended these men.[14] It was an opportunity to unravel a mystery of history that had been the subject of so much speculation, debate, writings and film.[15]

Chapter 2

The Fourth Victim

'Thomas was given brown bread and barley soup by people worried about his starved condition soon before his death... a deserted Boer style cottage, its glowing rosewood and silky oak panelling infested with white ants, standing next to a goat paddock outside Tenterfield, is a neglected and little known memorial to the strange life of a man who defended "Breaker" Morant and who, it appears, was broken by Morant's execution. After the war his behaviour became increasingly strange. It is said he slept on a saddle in his office, and sometimes in the Tenterfield Cemetery and that he lived on raw onion... room in Tenterfield to "Boonoo Boonoo", and he died there that night.' [16, 17]

A word picture summarises the life of Thomas. A man desolate and abandoned! This author's intent in writing this book was to discover the life of Thomas who became entwined by a war, his devotion to King and Country, his work as a lawyer for Morant, Handcock and Witton, devotion to a country community and celebrated as community leader, but relegated to loneliness and misfortune.

Introduction

James Francis Thomas, (1861-1942). Thomas achieved a notable reputation as a lawyer who represented "Breaker" Morant — horse breaker, poet and soldier of fortune, Handcock, and Witton in South Africa during the Boer War. Morant and Handcock both paid the ultimate penalty on the charge of being accessories after the fact to murder, when they were both shot by a firing squad at the direction of British Commander-in-Chief, Lord Kitchener.

Thomas, however, had other significant parts to his life as he was a lawyer, local historian and citizen who contributed in major ways to the community of Tenterfield. It is challenging to summarise and assess the achievements of such an active, involved, and colourful character. Bachelor, poet, lawyer, soldier, war reporter, newspaper owner and editor, cheese maker, grazier, gardener, local historian, bankrupt, resident of Long Bay gaol for twenty months, lobbyist for Federation and for a new State of New England, advocate for Army veterans and notable citizen.

It is not so much an irony as a stubborn reality that one of life's main challenges is to find an outlet for our noblest energies and a home as it were for our best qualities of character. Well placed, these can lead onto success, misplaced, into tragedy. Thomas had some fine qualities, in his young adulthood he was poetic, patriotic, and professional. He had compassion and generosity for battlers, was buoyant and enthusiastic, a man of many words and lots of action. He supported Federation, the formation of a new State of New England and he wrote a history of Tenterfield. He promoted the erection of the Boer War and Great War Memorials and the War Memorial Hall in Tenterfield. He was articulate, energetic, and public spirited. Two episodes in his life, both related to court cases, combined to destroy his idealism and so his life plummeted downwards and he died at eighty-one, a lonely, malnourished, and stigmatised old bachelor, at the end surviving on his own home-grown raw onions and eking out a miserable existence in the shadows of Tenterfield which had once celebrated his position as a community leader.

Who was Thomas and has his life been recognised in Australian folk lore? Has his journey in one of the most controversial aspects of Australian military history been understood and respected? A history of a small-town county solicitor from Tenterfield whose dogged determination in legal advocacy for his clients pitted him against the might and dominance of the British Military and Government in a place and time so far from Australia and during a war as Australia emerged from colonialism to nationhood.

Thomas, who practised in wills, probate and contracts, found himself serving as an infantry officer and then by accident, as legal counsel desperately trying to represent three of his countrymen, Morant, Handcock and Witton. As a solicitor, Thomas handled a wide range of matters. For example, he sued a client for legal costs of £3, 5 shillings and 10 pence for drawing up a marriage settlement (reported 26 January, 1898), while of the 8th of January, 1915 he was reported as appearing for the defendant for alleged abusive language and successfully had the complaint dismissed. He appeared for the licensees of three Hotels on the renewal of their Liquor Licenses — Sandy Hills Hotel, Crown Hotel, Urbenville and Torrington Hotel, and he also appeared for an applicant for a Dredging Lease before the Warden's Court.

However, on 27 February 1902 when Thomas witnessed the execution of Morant and Handcock by firing squad and the imprisonment of Witton for life, his work as a country solicitor could not have prepared him for that experience in South Africa and the profound effect that it had on his life.

This book is an opportunity for this author to record history and to explore the life of Australia's first military lawyer. A man who ultimately paid the price of his health and sanity as he struggled against the might of the British Government and Military knowing that the fate of his clients was sealed from the moment of their arrest in November 1901.

The ultimate goal of this author's work has been to address the illegal manner in which Morant, Handcock, Witton were treated and to secure posthumous Crown pardons for these men and their descendants. Also, to recognise that the court martial process used was flawed and politically driven and that a gross injustice occurred to protect the real criminals, their British superiors.

The case this author has mounted has achieved some measure of success and continues to this day; however, he is compelled to review the life of Thomas, to understand his passions and contribution to the Tenterfield community. He is also determined to highlight Thomas' work as lawyer, the ethical manner in which he attempted to represent his clients in a county far from Australia without support of his Government as he pitted himself against the British Crown as it marshalled unlimited resources to prosecute and achieve a judicial outcome that was contrived and suited a political agenda to pacify a determined enemy, the Boers in a fight against the might of the British Military. Any injustice in time of war is compounded by inaction and denial by those who witness or are knowingly concerned with condoning those injustices that bring military standards our democratic principles and humanity into disrepute.

This is this author's story of Thomas and his destiny as an accidental advocate and how his loyalty proved to be the tragedy of his life.

When this author thinks back to where this all began in 2008 and what compelled him to invest ten years of his life in this project, he reflected on his determination to review the arrest, investigation, trial and sentencing of Morant, Handcock and Witton. As a military lawyer, this author was drawn to mystique surrounding Thomas and the little recognition that Thomas had received in military history. The photo of Thomas confirmed this author's decision to examine his life.

This author saw the haunting image of Thomas standing over the freshly dug grave of Morant and Handcock. The following photo had been rescued from a rubbish dump in Tamworth along with some other papers relating to 'The Breaker'.

Though the photograph is faded and sepia toned, it did not detract from the power of the image, giving it a surreal, dream-like starkness. It shows a tall, thin, dapper man standing over a freshly dug grave. The body language says it all. The deep regret caused him to stoop sorrowfully over their grave almost as though he was racked by some physical pain.

> 'The picture was of war graves, configured and numbered in military style. The officer-like bearing and dapper dress of the troubled subject in the weathered snapshot caught Cameron's eye: a sombre, reflective man, his tweeds offset by calf-length riding boots, baton and what appeared to be a military hat.'[18]
>
> 'It was a photograph consigned to the landfill of the waste disposal depot of the northern NSW city of Tamworth. A faded image rescued from the compactor as it was about to disappear forever into history's dustbin.
>
> 'After years of foraging through the rubbish dumped each day at the Tamworth tip, council worker Alan Cameron had become an adept practitioner of the adage, "One man's junk, another man's treasure".
>
> 'The picture was of war graves, configured and numbered in military

Chapter 2   *The Fourth Victim*

style. *The officer-like bearing and dapper dress of the troubled subject in the weathered snapshot caught Cameron's eye: a sombre, reflective man, his tweeds offset by calf-length riding boots, baton and what appeared to be a military hat.*

'Closer inspection of the photograph revealed a rear-side inscription: "J.F. Thomas at Morant's grave". On February 27, 1902, Second South Australian Mounted Rifleman Lieutenant Harry "Breaker" Morant and his farrier, Sgt. Peter Handcock, had been executed by firing squad following court martial for their role — while serving in an auxiliary guerrilla unit (the Bushveldt Carbineers)- in the summary execution of 12 Boer prisoners and a German missionary they claimed was an enemy spy.'[19]

The photo occupies a prominent place in this author's home library where he conducts his research on the "Breaker" case. While haunting, the photo remains the motivation to persevere, to bring a just outcome for Morant, Handcock and Witton, an outcome that eluded Thomas.

The trials of these men in South Africa between January and February 1902 ruined Thomas' life. Thomas might as well have been shot on the veldt with Morant and Handcock. At least their deaths were mercifully quick, but his was slow and lingering. His entire value system had been destroyed and it took him 40 years to die from the mortal emotional and physiological wounds he received in those Courts Martial. It is noted that people die of a broken heart and although it is not a recognised medical condition, in some cases there appears to be no other explanation. Something similar happened to Thomas, possibly Post Traumatic Stress Disorder from which he never recovered.

Jack Thompson's magnificent award-winning performance in the film, *Breaker Morant* [20] brought Thomas out of obscurity in more ways than one. Local newspaper articles revealed no one knew where he was laid to rest and some questioned if he was buried in Tenterfield at all. His modest grave was eventually found and is now a feature of the Tenterfield heritage trail.

However, as uplifting and inspiring as Jack Thompson's performance was, it was not entirely accurate. It was accurate insofar as it detailed the case Thomas made for the defence, but not in terms of the man himself. Where Thompson was physically and verbally robust, Thomas was slight in stature and quiet-spoken. Despite Bennet's assertion that he was *"impetuous, headstrong and self-opinionated"* and *"... adopted the role of lecturer, expatiating on subjects as if to an audience bound in ignorance"* there were no self- aggrandising tirades against the war, The Empire and the legal system — those were the preserve of Morant as he sensed the long shadows of the firing squad gathering in the courtyard. However, whilst *Breaker Morant* did pay long overdue homage to the courage with which Thomas single-handedly had taken on the might of the British Empire, the narrow scope of a film based around the court martial could not encompass the tragic effect this case had on his life.

Kit Denton's 1984 book *Closed File* did this in some measure, but only succeeded in substituting Thompson's identity of a man down on his luck who resorted to embezzlement and became a figure of ridicule and amusement as he waddled down the street with his colostomy bag[21]. This slight was expanded on by Arthur Davey[22] who incorrectly suggested that Thomas was dismissed from the army which tainted his conduct and called into question his version of events at the Courts Martial. [23]

Dr John Bennett in a history of lawyers and law in New England attempted what can only be described as a "hatchet job" on Thomas. He accused Thomas of being a "hack", yet in his nine-page diatribe he cannot find one redeeming feature in Thomas. This author will refer to Bennett's article as it is symptomatic of the erroneous historical analysis currently driving the Morant debate.

All this has left us with a distorted picture of Thomas, a Jack Thompson, a superman in his youth who ended up as Denton's and Bennet's sad and corrupt old man, bankrupt, disbarred and reclusive — a local figure of ridicule.

The whole story has not yet been told of the "fourth victim" — Major Thomas. This author says "fourth victim" as Thomas, along with Morant, Handcock and Witton, also received a life sentence at the Pietersburg Courts Martial — a terrible personal torment from which he would never be free. He performed heroics at the trials in difficult circumstances, but failed to save them or gain a reprieve in the eighteen hours between their sentence being announced and carried out. If Morant was the anti-hero, then Thomas was the hero.

> *'There are two great days in a person's life*
> *— the day we are born and the day we discover why.'*
> *— William Barclay* [24]

Chapter 3

Major James Francis Thomas

Life began so differently for Thomas. He was the first son born to James Henry and Sarah Eve Thomas (nee Dawson) — who was born in England — following their marriage two years earlier. His parents were dairy farmers. James junior was the eldest of their six sons.

James was born on the 25th of August, 1861 at St Mary's in Sydney's west on land which is now a busy multicultural suburb but was then a productive, diverse rural community.[25] The Thomas family were tenant farmers at nearby Bayley Park. It was common for people of that era to farm parts of larger estates. The Thomas family would have been reasonably well off, though they were neither gentry nor landowners.

Thomas' siblings were:

- Henry Percival Thomas, born 31st of December, 1862. Died 13th August, 1906, a surveyor, who had four children, Owen, Wilhelmina, Olga and Frank. Owen served in World War 1 and became a Solicitor like his Uncle Frank, as James Francis Thomas was known by his family. Percy died when Owen was only nine years old, and he was brought up by his Uncle Ernest.

- Hugh Ernest Thomas (called Ernest) born 4th of December, 1866, Bank Manager. Died Chatswood 1948; a bachelor. [26]

- Gilbert Stephen Thomas died 11th of January, 1896, a bachelor.

- William Beach Thomas, born 21st of March, 1868, for many years a Bank Manager at Wollongong. Married to Emily May Budden 1897[27], no children.

- Leslie Dawson Thomas, born the 11th of December, 1872. Anglican Minister died 1939.[28]

Thomas felt the burden of loss early in his young life. When he was only seven his sister, Ann, died aged two — just a month after the birth of his brother William, in April 1868. The inscription on her gravestone suggests that the Thomas family were a caring, God-fearing lot.

'Sacred to the memory of Ann, the third child of James Henry and Sarah Eve Dawson of Erskine Park. She is not dead the child of our affection, but gone unto that school, where she no longer needs our poor protection and Christ himself doth rule.'

To School

It must have dawned on the Thomas family that they had a gifted son who deserved more than a life on the land. Thomas was the only son to go to The Kings School, Parramatta, described as, *"the Premiere school in Australia"*. Thomas attended for four years from 1876 to 1879. The Kings School register records him as pupil number 1348 of School House, *'cadet, poet, army officer and solicitor.'*

Many years later at a meeting in Tenterfield with Perry John Alfred Ironside, an old school friend (Kings School, Sydney, 1876-79) in 2011, Thomas gave a candid explanation of his experiences in South Africa. According to Ironside, Thomas claimed that the execution of Morant and Handcock was a mistake and Lord Kitchener had attempted to silence the writings of a journalist who had attended the trial of Morant.[29]

The entry in the School magazine stated:

'On this trip I met an old pupil of the School in the person of J. F. Thomas. He attended under the Reverend G. F. Macarthur, and was in the sixth form with C. G. Wade and H. M. Baylis. Mr. Thomas was a man of great military spirit, and took part in the South African War, going over as a Captain, and afterwards attaining the rank of Major in Command

of the New South Wales• Citizens' Bushmen. He tells many interesting stories of that war, and is deeply convinced that the execution of Morant and Handcock was a mistake. He detailed to me how Lord Kitchener was, hoodwinked by a press-writer. This writer had written out a full account of the cases which led up to the execution, and this was taken by the military Press Censor to Lord Kitchener for his approval. The War-Lord glanced at the manuscript, which had taken some ten hours to write, and tore it to pieces. However, the writer, who was the Pretoria representative of a big London Press Agency, not to be outdone, set to work, re-wrote the article, and sent it away through an invalided returning Tommy Atkins, who hid it in his shirt, and subsequently duly delivered it in London, where it was promptly published by the leading dailies, thereby occasioning the sensation which it had been the business of the War Office to prevent. Mr. Thomas, however, says that what was published was far from being a full account of what really transpired, in. connection with these notable and painful cases. Even, the subsequent book by Lieut. Witton, entitled "Scapegoats of the Empire," he asserts is but a surface transcription.'

The content of the entry is consistent with Thomas' protest about the treatment of Morant, Handcock and Witton.

Thomas' school reports reveal that he was a keen sportsman and a good student, especially of English Literature. It extended to writing poetry and he paid homage to his *alma mater* in one of three poems published in *Australian Poets 1788-1888*. The foreword says of him, 'A native of New South Wales, born in 1861... educated at the old King's School. Has published no volume though he has written many fine poems'. Although it does not say when Thomas composed this verse it is clear that Kings had instilled him with certain qualities which reflected in the lines of, "On Revisiting The Kings School Parramatta":

'On Revisiting The Kings School, Parramatta,
Dear spot, my heart is bound to thee
By many a firm and tender tie

> 'Time cannot loosen; here were formed
> Sweet friendships that will never die;
> Here knowledge first her varied stores
> Displayed to charm our thoughtless youth;
> And here we learnt to love the paths
> Of honour, manliness, and truth.' [30]

School Photo of Thomas, undated

Of honour, manliness and truth were the qualities which Thomas aspired to until the end of his life. The other two poems are the typical musings of an adolescent youth, though to the voracious Bennett they are "*facile*" and not worthy of comparison with the great Banjo Patterson. They explore his Arcadian leanings and, if anything, reveal him to be both a romantic and sensitive soul.

By chance, the last stanza of a poem called *Tenterfield Star* reported appears on the same page as Thomas' first and is a chilling portent of the trials and tribulations Thomas would later endure:

> '... As nerves despair in need's oppressive hour
> He hurled them from the window of his cell
> Into the wide and rushing tide beneath.
> he saw them mingle in the roaring flood,

Chapter 3   Major James Francis Thomas

> *Borne swiftly even from his tearless eyes.*
> *And as the shipwrecked mariner beholds*
> *His fragile raft swept plank by plank away*
> *So gazed the Monk. Then kneeling down again*
> *he prayed the prayer of those who hope no more'.*

A local paper was not published until 1882 and local records reveal nothing about the Thomas family, so we can conclude that he probably grew up going to school and working on the farm — learning about life behind the plough. His country background also gave him the opportunity to become an accomplished horseman — a skill that would later come in very useful.

It was at Kings that he began his long association with the military, serving in the school's Cadet Corps.

Following his high school education, Thomas attended Sydney University and graduated, signing the Roll of Solicitors on the 28th of May, 1887. Like many young men with bright and inquiring minds he chose to go into the legal profession.

A career emerges

As a solicitor, Thomas started practising law in Emmaville, a bustling arsenic and tin mining town northwest of Glen Innes in northern NSW. Originally called Vegetable Creek after the Chinese market gardens that supported its population which in its heyday approached 7000, Emmaville was a privately owned town that was never officially gazetted and one that is now a picturesque village renowned for its neatness and abundance of leeches. On the other hand, Tenterfield, just 20 miles to the north of Emmaville, is regarded as one of the birthplaces of Federation, the place where on the 24th of October, 1889 Henry Parkes gave his famous oration urging for an independent Australia. Thomas, an ardent Federalist was one of the locals who organised the occasion and was present on that night to hear Parkes speak. Ironically in that speech Parkes foresaw an event that would come to consume Thomas' life.

Thomas moved the following year to the tough tin-mining town of Emmaville in New England and then to Tenterfield just short of the Queensland border in January 1890. Perhaps it was his farming background and his love of nature that drew him away from the "big smoke", or maybe he sensed an opportunity to make his own mark.

Denton stated:

'Thomas was obviously a good soldier and a good leader, as well as being a very capable country solicitor and a man interested and active in politics.'[31]

Thomas' interest in local affairs and politics encouraged him to purchase the *Tenterfield Star* newspaper which he owned for 16 years:

'By the outbreak of the Boer War, then James Francis Thomas was thirty-eight, a successful lawyer, a newspaper proprietor, a considerable figure in the local social and political life, and Commander of the district's Volunteer forces.'[32]

Only settled by sheep and stockmen some 50 years prior to his arrival, the discovery of gold and tin in the surrounding area had attracted prospectors and miners. Tenterfield was formally founded in 1851 and had just been connected to the Great Northern Railway network in 1886. A little later, on the completion of the Hawkesbury Bridge, it was linked to large metropolitan centres such as Brisbane, Sydney, Melbourne and Adelaide and later by the first rail link between the two states to Queensland.

Like many country towns of the day, Tenterfield's business was mainly agricultural in nature, cattle, sheep and cedar being its principal assets. Thomas' solicitor's duties consisted mostly of wills, business contracts and land and property transactions, rather than the murders, assaults and rapes which would have been the domain of a city lawyer. Conveyancing would be the modern equivalent. He combined this with some accounting work for local businesses and families.

Comparing the town today with archival photos of yesteryear, it still retains much of its 19th century charm, its bank, Federation style pub, the wooden church in which Banjo" Patterson married the daughter of a local landowner, the Tenterfield Saddler made famous by Peter *"The Boy From Oz"* Allen[33] and The School of Arts where (Sir) Henry Parkes delivered his historic Federation speech.

Parkes' speech took place in 1889, the year before Thomas arrived in Tenterfield and was an important turning-point for both Thomas and Australia. The New South Wales Premier was encouraged by a group of local citizens, including Thomas, to stop at Tenterfield on his way back from a meeting with political leaders in Queensland.

On the evening of 24th October, 1889, Parkes gave his historic speech in The Arts School to a banqueting audience of 80 persons. Likening Australia to the United States at the time of their Federation, he said the great question which they had to consider was whether the time had now arisen for the creation on this Australian continent of an Australian Parliament. He suggested a convention of leaders from all states to devise the constitution which would be necessary for bringing into existence a federal Government with a federal parliament for the conduct of national business.

Ironically, the issue which caused Parkes to ask the question was national defence. An Imperial General who had inspected the troops of the colony had recommended that the forces of Australia should be united into one Army and that the Imperial Parliament pass legislation to this effect. However, this would mean that the new Army would be under the control of the Imperial Government with the colonies having no power over it.

Parkes had shrewdly identified an issue which would become a real bone of contention in the next two decades as Australia staggered towards Federation and colonial jealousies propelled first Britain and then the world towards war. This subject would re-surface again and again as Britain recognised the need to have colonial units at its disposal to protect its vast Empire. Such was its importance that the British Government first tried to amend the Federation draft to make the Queen Commander-in-Chief of Australian forces and later entered a secret pact with the first Commander Australia's forces, General Hutton, who tried to persuade Prime Minister Barton to introduce legislation allowing Australian units to be used for Imperial business.

In the audience, Thomas may have grasped the significance of Parkes' argument, but could not have known that he would later play a part in resolving the issue of executive control through the Morant affair which provided both impetus and substance for the Defence Act of 1903.

Inspired by Parkes' vision, Thomas became a great supporter of the Federation movement and he later admitted that championing the cause was one of the main reasons he bought the local paper, the *Tenterfield Star*, from Messrs Taudevin and Laverty of Brisbane in 1898.

Chapter 4:
Newspaper Proprietor

Thomas owned the *Star* for sixteen and a half years making him its longest standing proprietor in its short and turbulent history which had seen it pass through many hands. Though mainly an outlet for local news, during his tenure Thomas used it to campaign for a number of issues close to his heart. He was a stout Labor man, supported the Federation of Australia and the formation of the Country party. The latter is evident because at fairly frequent intervals during his career as a journalist, he made a point of plugging what was even then the 'old cry' for decentralisation to get a better deal for the North. He deplored, *'the ever-increasing trend of the rural population to the cities'* and said that as soon as people can escape from the country they make off to the city. He also recognised, *'The voice of the small bush newspaper is very much that of one crying in the wilderness, but nevertheless, it's cry at all times should be directed against the blighting evil of city congestion'.* However spirited the editorials for the various causes he supported, there is little sign of the rampant egotism and self-aggrandisement which Bennett accuses him of.

While it is well known that Thomas owned the *Tenterfield Star*, less known is the fact that he also purchased the *Killarney Border Record*. Whilst Thomas lived in Tenterfield, the printing of the paper in Killarney was to be undertaken by Luke William Williamson who was also listed as being the publisher. The printing was to take place in Willow Street, Killarney.

As Thomas was building up his practice and becoming a pillar of the community local legend had it that a gentleman known as Harry "The Breaker" Morant stopped to work in at a cattle station called Barney Downs a few miles from Tenterfield where the infamous Bushranger "Thunderbolt" was once a stockman. It was the largest station in the Tenterfield area, work was casual and records few — other than what came in and went out. No records survive from that era and given his poor record of settling his debts, this author doubts that "The Breaker" ever paid taxes, far less his debtors as recalled in Will Ogilvie's *When The Breaker Heads for The South*.

Given the close proximity of Barney Downs to Tenterfield and the "Breaker's" celebrated fondness for grog and '... *trim set petticoat*' the chances are that he visited town. It is ironic to think that Morant and Thomas may have passed in the street, neither knowing their destinies would collide again a decade later in less happy circumstances half way round the world.

Tenterfield Life

Outside of his professional duties, Thomas also played an active part in the social life of Tenterfield. Amongst his many interests was history and he wrote some unpublished papers on the history of the town and had a long and distinguished association with the local defence force — the Tenterfield Mounted Rifles which Thomas joined as a 2nd Lieutenant on the 13th Feb 1891.

During the latter part of the 19th century there was a fear that Australia might be invaded by Russia and local volunteer forces were formed to provide a defence force. In October 1885, Major Chauvel was called upon to raise a Cavalry by the New South Wales Government. Two troops were formed, one at Tabulan and another at Cullendore, known as the Border Troop. In 1887, Casino superseded the Border Troop, and became No 2 Troop of the Upper Clarence Light Horse. The Tabulan Troop changed its name to Tabulan Mounted Rifles in 1888 with detachments at Tabulan, Fairfield and Tenterfield. Tenterfield consisted of No 1 Squadron, known as the Tenterfield Rifles, and was the foundation of all Mounted Rifle Regiments in NSW. This unit was one of the founders of the Australian Light Horse.

Chapter 5:

A Marksman and More!

Thomas was one of a number of famous soldiers from the Tenterfield district. It was at Tabulam on the 1st of October, 1885 that Major C.H.E. Chauvel was called upon by the New South Wales Government to raise a cavalry unit to be known as the Upper Clarence Light Horse which had a detachment in Tenterfield. In 1888, the NSW Mounted Infantry Regiment was formed and the Tenterfield detachment became half of A Company. Thomas was active in the local Troop from his earliest days in Tenterfield. On the 13th of February 1891 he was promoted to Second Lieutenant in the Tenterfield Company, Mounted Infantry Regiment. He was then aged 29 and the photo of him in his brand-new uniform, which is reproduced in many places including *Closed File*[34] was taken when he was promoted to Second Lieutenant. Three years later in 1894 he passed out of the Second Calvary School of Instruction and was promoted First Lieutenant and took over command of the Tenterfield Half-Company from Captain Charles Chauvel.

Hutton Shield Competition

Thomas was part of the Tenterfield team which won the Hutton Shield in 1893. The Hutton Shield was an annual competition which allowed the team to compete against other units. It was named after Major-General E.T.H. Hutton C.B A.D.C. to the Queen, Commanding NSW Military Forces who was responsible for organising and raising the first Australian Defence Units. The Shield was awarded to the best squadron or Company Team for shooting and riding.

It was to be held for one year by the Squadron or Company of the winning team, and to be finally held by the Squadron or Company winning it for three years in succession. The entrance fee was £20/- per team.

Two teams per Squadron of Cavalry or Company of Mounted Rifles

Major Thomas (middle row, third from left) and troopers, Hutton Shield winners

Thomas (centre) with unnamed troops of the Tenterfield Mounted Rifles

Capt. Thomas.

were allowed compete. The members of each team to be efficient for the current year.

The Shield competition consisted of the following:
Dress: Drill order.
Course: About 1-3/4 miles.
Target: As for Cavalry Section Attack, viz 4 x 6 as for volley.
Distances: Three firing points, 400, 600 and 300 yards approximately. Two or three obstacles — hurdles or ditches — between each firing point.
Rounds: Five rounds to be fired at each distance by the dismounted men.
Time: The team doing the course in the best time will receive 20 points; 5 points will be deducted from this total by each team completing the distance for every 30 seconds less than the best time.
Winning Teams: The teams making the highest aggregate total points for; (a) Shooting; (b) Style; (c) Time; (d) Turn Out will be the winners.

The match will be carried out on the lines laid down in Musketry Regulations, page 157 and Cavalry Drill see para 12,14 and following. The Lancer Teams will carry their lances, and will when dismounted stick them in the ground in front of their group of horses. There were three prizes; 1st £35, 2nd £10, 3rd £5.

In 1893, The Tenterfield Mounted Rifles won the Hutton Shield. The result was as follows:

Captain J.F. Thomas Tenterfield Mounted Rifles Time taken 11 minutes 14 seconds.
Total points: 226

The absence of records has led to some confusion as to whether Tenterfield did win it outright in 1893. In support of this, there is a copy of the order as stamped as received by the 4 Coy Tenterfield Mounted Rifles inviting them to Sydney to be presented with the Hutton Shield after they won it in 1895.

On the reverse of this order, Thomas has written indecipherable comments about the competition and his participation.

Chapter 6:
Military Career

Thomas became 1st Lieutenant in February 1894 and took over command of the Tenterfield Mounted Rifles in Nov. 1894. [35]His involvement in the local volunteer force was a sign of his growing social status in the town. To take up such a position one had to have disposable income as it was an established social tradition that the leader was expected to finance picnics for the ladies and kids and grog for the lads.

Thomas was a first class shot and an excellent soldier. In character, he was regarded by his superiors as non-excitable, principled and seen as a good leader. An extract from his record in 1894 says:

> 'A very high standard of efficiency has been reached by the Tenterfield Half Company and the excellent Military spirit which exists" and with extra work predicts that they will, "... achieve a standard of efficiency which should be second to none in the colony'.

That was proved the following year when they won the Hutton Shield outright under Thomas' leadership. This time there is a photograph of the victorious team with the Hutton shield and the team was as follows: Sergeant J. Mitchell, Private J. Grogan, Private Dan Sweeney, Private J. Donnelly, Private William Bender, Corporal Mick Toohey, Private F. Grogan, Private A. Holley, Private H. Lohse, Private P. Connolly, Private E.E. Elsworth, Private P. Kelly, and Private J. Kelly.

These skills, though not forged in the heat of battle, would be put to the test when the Empire sent out the call to the colonies for able-bodied young men to defend her honour when war was declared in South Africa in October 1899.

Chapter 7:
War! What War? — 1880 — 1902

'The Anglo-Boer War of 1899-1902 was the biggest, bloodiest, most expensive and most disastrous war involving people of European descent, from the Napoleonic wars, until World War I.'[36]

The southern part of the African continent was the focus of potential colonisers including Great Britain, Portugal and Germany. This part of the continent offered wealth by controlling the trade routes to India via the Cape of Good Hope, deposits of diamonds and gold in the Kimberley and the Transvaal and power over other countries who were racing to colonise much of the African continent.

From about 1880, the British attempted to annex the Transvaal and the Orange Free State and annexed Bechuanaland. Resentment amongst the Boer populations continued to grow as the British sought to extend its political and economic exploitation of South Africa.

Britain's Motive

Weber stated:

'For Britain's leaders, bringing the Boer republics under imperial rule seemed entirely logical and virtually pre-ordained. On the prevailing mind-set in London, historian Pakenham has written'.

'The independence of a Boer republic, bursting with gold and bristling with imported rifles, threatened Britain's status as a "paramount" power. British paramountcy (alias supremacy) was not a concept in international law. But most of the British thought it made practical sense ... Boer independence seemed worse than absurd; it was dangerous for world peace... The solution seemed to be to wrap the whole of South Africa in the Union Jack, the make the whole country a British dominion.'[37]

The Boers in Transvaal finally revolted and declared independence of Transvaal from the United Kingdom. What followed was two years of war between 1880 and 1881 with heavy losses on both sides. In 1881, an armistice was signed and a peace treaty saw self-Government for the Boers in the Transvaal. Peace was short lived with the discovery of the world's largest gold bearing deposit. With renewed British colonial intentions, tensions with the Boers quickly developed into hostilities.

The news of war travelled the length and breadth of the British Empire with a call to arms to support the mother country:

> 'So the fighting began and the news of it was followed eagerly in Britain and the colonies where by the turn of the year men began to volunteer for the Colours.'[38]

The call saw volunteers from the colonies support the war notwithstanding that the Australian population was also focused on the struggle for economic prosperity and Federation.

Guerrilla warfare

'War is always a struggle in which each contender tries to annihilate the other'
— *Ernesto Guevara*[39]

Weber's view of the Boer War was:

> 'The Anglo-Boer War of 1899-1902 was more than the first major military clash of the 20th century. Pitting as it did the might of the globe-girdling British Empire, backed by international finance, against a small pioneering nation of independent-minded farmers, ranchers and merchants in southern Africa who lived by the Bible and the rifle, its legacy continues to resonate today. The Boers' recourse to irregular warfare, and Britain's response in herding a hundred thousand women and

children into concentration camps foreshadowed the horrors of guerrilla warfare and mass detention of innocents that have become emblematic of the 20th century.'[40]

The conflict generated into a guerrilla war that the British, or indeed any Army would have preferred to avoid. While Lord Kitchener commanded a force of over 300,000 men and modern weaponry that achieved victory in open ground, there was nothing to be gained from using traditional methods of engagement, *'by solid formations, rigid drill lines against fast mounted hit and run raiders.'*[41] Despite conquering vast tracts of land, the British struggled against the Boers who were adept at living off the land and proficient in using commando style warfare.

> *'When is a War not a War? When it is carried on by methods of Barbarism in South Africa.'*[42]

Desperate Tactics to fight the Boers

> *'In a sense, the Anglo-Boer conflict was less a war between combatants than a military campaign against civilians.'*[43]

Lord Kitchener developed tactics to counter the Boers, including using a scorched earth policy, mass internment of civilians in concentration camps and destruction of farms that provided logistical support to Boer fighters:

> *'Kitchener's requirement was for mounted infantry units so that the Boer commandos could be fought by their own methods. It had already been shown that colonial troops of that kind from Canada, New Zealand and Australia were very good at that sort of warfare, they were largely men used to long and hard days in the saddle, men from outdoor occupations in places which were often barren as the rocky uplands above the veldt.'*[44]

Between 1900 and 1902, the war was characterised by guerrilla tactics on both sides. The war became tedious and adversely affected the morale of the British military and the public:

Chapter 7:   War! What War? — 1880 — 1902

'The elusive Boers were hard to hunt down. Kitchener's revised tactics demanded the troops act more and more like brigands. It became an environment which required a scorched earth policy, mental if not physical mistreatment of enemy supporters, summary execution of prisoners, in some circumstances, real or internationally perceived British atrocities, concentration camps with thousands of civilians dying and the raising of local irregular forces.'[45]

Britain's view of the dirty war was aptly summed up by Lord Roberts, Lord Kitchener's predecessor:[46]

'There are no more great battles to be won; the war has degenerated into guerrilla warfare'.

Lord Kitchener's inventiveness surpassed the weaknesses of Lord Roberts' pessimistic view of Britain securing a victory. Lord Kitchener eagerly and ruthlessly took a "new" fight to the Boers in a brutal manner to deal with an elusive enemy.

Barbaric war in a new age

Weber's view aptly expresses the *new fight* as follows:[47]

'Lord Kitchener, the new British commander, adopted tactics to "clean up" a war that many in Britain had considered already won. In waging ruthless war against an entire people, he ordered his troops to destroy livestock and crops, burn down farms, and herd women and children into "camps of refuge." Reports about these grim internment centers, which were soon called concentration camps, shocked the western world.

'Britain's new style of waging war was summarized in a report made in January 1902 by Jan Smuts, the 31-year-old Boer general (and future South African prime minister):

Lord Kitchener has begun to carry out a policy in both [Boer] republics of unbelievable barbarism and gruesomeness which violates the most elementary principles of the international rules of war.

'Almost all farmsteads and villages in both republics have been burned down and destroyed. All crops have been destroyed. All livestock which has fallen into the hands of the enemy has been killed or slaughtered.

'The basic principle behind Lord Kitchener's tactics has been to win, not so much through direct operations against fighting commandos, but rather indirectly by bringing the pressure of war against defenseless women and children.

'... This violation of every international law is really very characteristic of the nation which always plays the role of chosen judge over the customs and behavior of all other nations.'

Shooting Prisoners — *We Take No Prisoners Now*

The most outrageous element of Lord Kitchener's *new war* was orders to take no prisoners as a basis to justify retribution of Boer outrages but also to promote deterrence and the preservation of needed resources for British solders rather than Boer prisoners.

Private John Harris, of the Royal Welsh Regiment. Private J. Harris, number 5754, Royal Welsh Fusiliers served in the Boer War in 1901.[1] He reportedly wrote a letter to his parents describing the rules of engagement that he and other soldiers used to engage the enemy. His letter was reproduced in the *Express and Star* newspaper and stated:[2]

'WE TAKE NO PRISONERS NOW
'We take no prisoners now, One night this month some of our men lost their way and could not find the picket[.] They shouted out, "Where are you, lads?" The Boers answered, "Here we are," and the poor chaps went up to them and were made prisoners. Next morning we were looking for them when the Boers opened fire on us. It did not last long. We turned the guns on them, and we soon made them shift. There happened to be a few wounded Boers left. We put them through the mill. Everyone was

---

1 Soldiers of the Queen in the Second Anglo-Boer War 1899-1902, http://www.findmypast.co.uk/boer-war-register-search-start.action?product=BW&redef=1&submit=1
2 Wolverhampton *Express and Star newspaper* of January 12 1901, p.2

killed. About five Boers were brought in for not putting down their arms, and they all got shot the next day. I was on guard over them in the night, and you should have heard them praying when they knew they were to die next morning. They were taken out the next morning, made to dig their own graves, and two of the sections of my company went down about nine o'clock in the morning and shot them. The best thing to do with them is to serve them all alike.'

Political Condemnation

Radical politician John Dillon, an Irish Nationalist Member of Parliament and fierce critic of the Government's tactics in waging war in South Africa, spoke out against the British policy of shooting Boer prisoners of war. On February 26, 1901, he made public a letter by a British officer in the field. 'Here is the extract from the officer's letter :[48]

> 'The orders in this district from Lord Kitchener are to burn and destroy all provisions, forage, etc., and seize cattle, horses, and stock of all sorts wherever found, and to leave no food in the houses of the inhabitants. And the word has been passed round privately that no prisoners are to be taken. That is, all the men found fighting are to be shot. This order was given to me personally by a general, one of the highest in rank in South Africa. So there is no mistake about it. The instructions given to the columns closing round De Wet north of the Orange River are that all men are to be shot so that no tales may be told. Also, the troops are told to loot freely from every house, whether the men belonging to the house are fighting or not.'

Dillon also quoted from a letter signed by William Clyne, of the Liverpool Regiment, which was published in the Liverpool Courier.[49]

> 'Lord Kitchener has issued orders that no man has to bring in any Boer prisoners; if he does he has to give him half his rations for the prisoner's keep'.

Dillon also drew the House of Commons attention to three letters, published in the English press, one by a returned Liverpudlian foot soldier, another by a Welshman (Private Harris) who had served with Plumer and a third by a British infantryman.[50]

> 'Well, Sir. I turn now from this subject—this painful and humiliating subject—to another aspect of the war, which is full of mystery and sinister significance, and that is the charge made against Lord Kitchener, for which, while I am prepared to admit there is not complete evidence, I say there is sufficient evidence to demand from you an immediate, serious and searching investigation. ["Hear, hear!"] What is this charge? It is that Lord Kitchener has recently in the Transvaal repeated what he is alleged to have done on the eve of Omdurman— namely, that he conveyed to his officers secret instructions to take no prisoners. I will state the case frankly, and I claim that the evidence in support of the charge is sufficient to require the closest investigation.[51]

> 'First of all, let me say that this charge has been made, as I shall show, in an anonymous letter, but it is confirmed by the letters of two or three soldiers whose names I shall give, and who state in published letters that in accordance with the instructions they received they killed the wounded Boers and refused quarter. I wish to say, however, that this charge has been denied by Lord Kitchener himself, and also by the Secretary of State for War in this House; but the denial has been made by both in very extraordinary language. It was easy to them to treat these charges with contempt, and say they were unworthy to be taken notice of, but they did not adopt that course. They published a categorical denial of the charge, and it is remarkable that in the case both of Lord Kitchener and of the Secretary of State for War they do not deny the precise charges as made, but other charges that were never made. What was the denial, let me ask?

> 'Here are Lord Kitchener's words, telegraphed by him to the Attorney General at Cape Town— Instructions of the nature mentioned were never given or thought of. We treat the enemy surrendered with every consideration. That is Lord Kitchener's denial. The Secretary of State for

Chapter 7: War! What War? — 1880 — 1902

War most indignantly denied the charge, and said that Lord Kitchener had never given orders or ever intended to slaughter the prisoners in his possession. But that charge was never made. Before he could slaughter his prisoners he should capture them alive.

'The real charge made is that private instructions were issued to take no prisoners. That charge was first published in a letter in the Freeman's Journal, Dublin, and the second letter from the same officer was published by Mr. Stead. ["Oh !"and "Hear, hear !"] Hon. Gentlemen groan about that. Lord Roberts takes a totally different view of Mr. Stead, as you will see. Here is the extract from the officer's letter.

'So there is no mistake about it. The instructions given to the columns closing round De Wet north of the Orange River are that all men are to be shot, so that no tales may be told; I do not think they will in most cases go so far as some of their superiors would wish. I do not believe the soldiers or junior officers will carry out the intentions of their seniors, but in a great majority of cases outrages of all sorts will be committed under such a régime."

'Mr. Stead sent that letter to Lord Roberts, asking him for a contradiction, or a statement with reference to it, and Lord Roberts wrote to Mr. Stead the following most remarkable reply— I readily accept your statement that this officer is a man of good standing and undoubted repute. But Lord Roberts, who has known Mr. Stead for a long time, takes his word that this is a genuine letter from an officer serving in the Army. It entitles me to say that that adds considerable weight to the matter. So much for that letter.

'Now I come to the next piece of evidence, and you will take it for what it is worth. It is a letter signed by William Clyne, of the Liverpool Regiment, which was published in the Liverpool Courier. It contains this statement— Lord Kitchener has issued orders that no man has to bring in any Boer prisoners; if he does he has to give him half his rations for the prisoner's keep. Lord Roberts was too lenient with the Boers. De Wet sent in to General Knox asking for an armistice. Lord Kitchener told General Knox to keep on shelling him while he brought up reinforcements. That was the armistice he got.

> *'I turn to a letter from Private John Harris, of the Royal Welsh Regiment, published in the Wolverhampton Express and Star, which states:*
>
> *'We take no prisoners now. ... There happened to be a few wounded Boers left. We put them through the mill. Every one was killed. I give these letters for what they are worth. I wish to be perfectly frank in this matter, and not to put my evidence stronger than it is.'*

It would be easy to dismiss the claims as hearsay or a political beat-up. Dillon and other Irish MPs were fierce critics of the war in South Africa and the methods employed by Lord Kitchener in prosecuting it. They saw it as a mirror image of the Irish struggle. It would also be tempting to refute the claims of the soldiers as being those of a minority of disgruntled troops. What we have to remember is that speaking out against the Government and particularly the military at the turn of the 20th Century in Britain was unheard of. The country still maintained a profoundly potent class system and the military was to a certain extent the pinnacle of that system. In early 20th century Britain, to question authority was to challenge not only the status quo but in effect, that most sacred of British institutions, the monarchy. To be frank, there weren't a lot of whistle blowers seeking asylum in Uzbekistan in Edwardian England so for men to write letters of condemnation at their own risk it is reasonable to assume that they expected short military careers or did not fear being exposed for their superiors would be held accountable.

What Dillon failed to convey in that address to parliament was perhaps the most revealing part of the Private John Harris' letter that was relevant to the Morant defence.

Stephen Miller in his article *Duty or Crime, Acceptable Behavior in the British Army in South Africa* makes reference to unpublished letters and journals from the period. In one letter, H. Hayes wrote:[52]

> *'I would shoot everyone on first sight. All they have to do is come in and get a free pardon then nip out after they found all the tips and pop a few outposts off, but they don't always get off with the white flag trick now, for I saw 12 Boers put the rag up by Devils knuckles to the Aus-*

Chapter 7:   War! What War? — 1880 — 1902

tralian Mounted Infantry and they coolly walked up and bayoneted all the lot—no prisoners with them. They are a fine lot of chaps so are the Canadians the Boers detest them. Worst of all. For they don't believe in being shot all up the side of a hill and on getting to the top to see the white flag. They finish them off to a man.'

And it wasn't just the British writing letters. On the 10th of July 1901, long before the events in the Northern Transvaal a Lance Corporal Hughes of the NSW Bushman wrote:

'there is an order from Lord Kitchener that no quarter be given…and to take no prisoners, with the view to bringing the war to an early close.'

And Deneys Reitz, a Boer Commander who wrote the book *Commando* detailing his experiences during the war stated:[53]

'We could not believe that the British were resorting to the shooting of prisoners, and it was only after many had been executed that we learnt of Kitchener's proclamation [sic] ordering the death of all Boers caught in khaki. As far as I know no steps were ever taken by the Military to acquaint us of its contents.'

Breaker's Defence

The attitudes of the British newspapers and the address made by MPs, including Dillon are important in understanding the contempt that the British had for the Boers. The facts put forward by Dillon corroborated the defence made by Morant, Handcock and Witton. As members of an irregular unit, specifically formed to eliminate the enemy, fighting *"rebels"* and believing that the rules of warfare were suspended, they received orders from Captains Taylor and Hunt. They believed those orders were consistent with the type of warfare being waged by the British military as described by Dillon. Morant, Handcock and Witton exceeded those orders without fully understanding the constraints of military law and believing that they had orders that had to be obeyed. They were then refused any recognition of the existence of such orders and a defence at Court Martial of following orders, while no liability was attributed to other British officers, including Hunt and Taylor.

The "Breaker's" evidence during his trials that he had been given specific orders by Hunt to take no prisoners was corroborated by his claim that on occasions when he had captured prisoners he had been censured and warned not to care for them. In fact, Morant, Handcock, Witton, Picton, and other witnesses all testified that Hunt did not want prisoners brought in and reprimanding those who did. Hunt had told Morant that those orders were passed on to him by Colonel Hamilton, Lord Kitchener's Secretary and the orders had originated from the Commander in Chief. The order was verbal which makes it difficult to prove, but we do know that most orders that came from Lord Kitchener came that way. Strangely, during the Courts Martial Morant's assertion as to the source of the orders was suppressed and the court denied the defence an opportunity to call Lord Kitchener to be cross examined about this:

> 'Captain Hunt told the accused not to take prisoners. He (Morant) never questioned their validity. The prisoner was asked whether he knew who gave the orders, but the Judge Advocate protested against the question, and was upheld by the court after consultation.' [54]

A witness at the Court Martial involving the Visser death, Sergeant Robertson admitted in cross examination that Captain Hunt: [55]

> 'had given direct orders that no prisoners were to be taken and had on one occasion abused the witness for bringing in three prisoners without orders.'

Compelling Evidence of *take no prisoners*

The existence of orders not to take prisoners is contained in a legal opinion written by Colonel J. St Clair, Deputy Judge Advocate General in South Africa and addressed to Major General Kelly, Adjutant General. The opinion is dated 22nd November 1901 after St Clair had reviewed the

Chapter 7:   War! What War? — 1880 — 1902

report of the investigation into the incidents involving Morant, Handcock and Witton shooting Boer combatants.

James St Clair was an experienced jurist and military officer. He saw service in the Zulu War of 1879 serving as Adjutant to the 91st Highlanders. In 1891, James was called to the Barristers Bar, Lincoln's Inn, London.[56]

His legal and military experience made him ideal to review the outcomes of the two-month long investigation that recommended the prosecution of Morant, Handcock and Witton. St Clair's findings about Captain Taylor, a British Intelligence Officer, appointed personally by Lord Kitchener, and effectively the Officer Commanding in the Spelonken, senior to Morant, Handcock and Witton are compelling.

Whilst we know that he concurred with the findings of the Inquiry and agreed with prosecuting the officers charged, what seems to have been missing from the historical record are his detailed findings and recommendations for further action against Captain Taylor. In elegant cursive scrip in St Clair's *"minute"* case books which are held in the British Archives in London, is a series of entries regarding all thirteen cases that were brought against various members of the Bushveldtt Carbineers.

St Clair's findings recommended prosecution action against Morant as the "prime mover" and Handcock as the "principal executioner" of Boer prisoners. However, St Clair also made comment and recommendations regarding the culpability of Captain Taylor:

Case No 1 'I agree with the opinion of the Court of Inquiry, the order given by Captain Taylor that no prisoners were to be taken was against the usage of modern warfare in my opinion rendered him personally responsible for the shooting of these 6 Boers who were coming in to surrender, and who made no defence when fired on — As being an accessory before the fact he is liable to a charge of Murder.'

*Cases Nos 4 and 6. 'The verbal orders given by Captain Taylor to the officers and men of the BVC **at various times not to take prisoners** rendered him primarily responsible for these massacres and I think he is liable as an accessory before the fact'.*

'The shooting of Van den Berg without trial was an illegal act, however guilty he may have been, there appears no sufficient reason why this man should not have been made a prisoner and tried for his alleged offence. I think Captain Taylor has rendered himself liable to a charge of murder.'

'The idea that no prisoners were to be taken in the Spelonken appears to have been started by the late Captain Hunt and after his death continued by orders given personally by Captain Taylor.'[57]

St Clair's findings were not just confined to combatants. He also concerned himself with the execution of natives:

Case No 9. 'Captain Taylor should have been aware when he ordered these natives shot that he was exceeding his powers. It is possible however that he may have been acting in good faith in this instance.'

Case No 10. 'The summary shooting of these two natives as spies does not appear to have been warranted by the evidence against them, & Captn Taylor should have known that he was exceeding his powers in ordering them summary punishment. Some kind of investigation seems to have taken place & Capn Taylor may have acted in good faith.'

Clearly, St Clair was satisfied that Taylor implemented a "no prisoners" order for not just the six Boers case, but in all cases, involving 22 whites and a number of natives. His findings and recommendations should have dictated the entire direction and framing of the Courts Martial, namely that Morant, Handocck and Witton were following Captain Taylor's orders. According to Thomas, in defence of his clients, such orders were repeated by Captain Hunt of a policy to deal with Boer fighters.

What is unclear is that in naming Taylor as the source, why did St Clair's recommendations call for the prosecution of Morant, Handcock, Witton and Picton for murder? He says '*The two NCOs acted under orders but were not justified in obeying illegal commands*', whilst in the 6 Boers case he writes: '*Taking all the circumstances of the case into consideration the responsibility should rest with the officer Captain Taylor who gave the order to the NCOs through Sergeant Major Morrison'.* The conclusion appears to be a contradiction, attributing responsibility to Morant, Handcock, Witton, while identifying the culpability of Taylor.

The persuasive conclusion by St Clair of a "take no prisoners" order also corroborates John Dillon's accusation that senior military commander, Lord Kitchener and his subordinates Taylor and Hunt implemented the order, and this is reflected in St Clair's exacting analysis.

Conclusion — Major Thomas

While it could be argued that Thomas lacked the advocacy experience to capitalise on St Clair's conclusions about the "no prisoners" order, according to Witton he did attempt to 'run' a defence based on the culpability of British officers, including Hunt, Taylor and of course Lord Kitchener. However, to protect the reputations of senior British Command whatever Thomas did was in vain. Culpability for illegal orders was laid at the level of irregular Colonials, not professional British officers.

And What of Lord Kitchener?

Despite critics like Dillon and evidence of barbaric tactics implemented by Lord Kitchener, he remained silent as he continued to command a war against civilians in the interests of British economic and strategic power.

Weber's damning criticism of Lord Kitchener's *'scorched earth'* policy, in which some 28,000 Boers perished in the British concentration camps, nearly all of them women and children and *'take no prisoners'* summarised the brutality:[58]

> 'Even by the standards of the time (and certainly by those of today), British political and military leaders committed frightful war crimes and crimes against humanity against the Boers of South Africa — crimes for which no one was ever brought to account. General Kitchener, for one, was never punished for introducing measures that even a future prime minister called "methods of barbarism." To the contrary, after concluding his South African service he was named a viscount and a

field marshal, and then, at the outbreak of the First World War, was appointed Secretary of War. Upon his death in 1916, he was remembered not as a criminal, but rather idolized as a personification of British virtue and rectitude.'

Ultimately, Morant, Handcock and Witton paid the price of a brutal and illegal order, *'take no prisoners'*! During the Boer War, no British regulars were tried and convicted of shooting prisoners, just expendable colonials!

The question that has never been addressed since Lord Kitchener ordered the executions and successive British Governments have refused to investigate, why were these three volunteer Australian bushmen singled out for prosecution? The glaring injustice is that the British Government of 1902 approved the executions while ignoring summary executions carried out by British troops.

In searching for a motive, the public believed the two Australians were seen as expendable because they were "colonials" and could be sacrificed to appease the German Government over the death of the German missionary Daniel Heese.

A trial and execution could also have served as a deflection, to take attention away from the death of Boer civilians and destruction of Boer farms and property during Lord Kitchener's use of concentration camps and a scorched earth policy. The German Government had lodged a formal protest with the British Government about Heese's death and there was a possibility that Germany may side with the Boers and do more than just provide logistical support, guns, ammunition to fight Lord Kitchener's Army.

Good will eventually prevailed on both sides and a peace treaty with Britain, the Treaty of Vereeniging was signed on 31st May 1902.[59] It ended hostilities between the South African Republic, the Republic of the Orange Free State, and the United Kingdom.

It is fanciful to be satisfied that the lack of culpability for Heese's death posed a real threat that the negotiations to secure a peace treaty was at risk, more so because Morant and Handcock were found not guilty of his murder, it is arguable that the death of Heese without a conviction of his

Chapter 7: *War! What War? — 1880 — 1902*

assailants was a catalyst for the executions to proceed to demonstrate that British justice takes its course.

Lord Kitchener, the ruthless aristocrat appears to have had his way over Morant, the charismatic but undisciplined colonial. Lord Kitchener needed a scapegoat to appease protest over his brutal and illegal war fighting tactics and what better way to influence the peace negotiations than to proceed with the executions.

And so the war!

Australian volunteers like Morant, Thomas and others were deployed in sweeping the country side to isolate Boer guerrillas from support from farms and towns. It was in the midst of the guerrilla war that Thomas, Morant, Witton and Handcock were destined to meet.

The causes of all wars are complex and multifarious, but you can be assured that greed for land, power and resources are never far away. They were root causes of the fractious relationship which existed between the British and the Boers ever since both set foot in the Cape. The Dutch East India Company arrived first in 1652 and established a supply station for its trading ships before the British decided it was of vital strategic importance to its Far Eastern Empire and annexed the Cape. The Great Trek of 1835 saw the Boers leave to escape the rigidity of their laws and institutions and the abolition of slavery upon which they relied for cheap labour. One half trekked East to Natal, the other North to Transvaal. The British then annexed Natal before turning its attention to The Orange Free State where diamonds were discovered in 1867. Though they formally recognised The Orange Free State and The South African Republic (Transvaal) Britain then annexed both over the next decade. With Rhodesia also in British hands, the Boers had nowhere left to go and decided to stand and fight in 1881. The Empire suffered a bloodied nose and restored the Boer Republics. The peace was short-lived. Kenneth Griffiths, the noted Boer War antiquarian and historian re-enacted the moment when President Kruger and General Joubert were told in 1886 that gold had been discovered in the Transvaal in his 1999 BBC series *The Boer War*. Joubert smiled and Kruger admonished him saying that it was the worst news he had ever heard as the British Empire, with its voracious appetite for territory and resources, would soon come for it. How right he was.

The Bulletin, which was staunchly anti-war and remained so throughout, summed up Britain's shenanigans a commentary entitled, *"Border Movements"*.

> 'Consider Britain's luck. Gold was found on the borders of Venezuela, and Britain promptly discovered that the new field was really in its adjacent colony of Guiana. Diamonds were found in the Orange Free State and Britain found out almost immediately that the border was wrongly located., and shifted it so that the Diamond Fields were on her side. Gold was found in the Transvaal, and Britain has already ascertained to her own satisfaction that the Transvaal is properly British territory. The only rich foreign goldfields found in recent years which Britain hasn't suddenly discovered, to her own great surprise to be really on her territory were in Siberia. Russia is too large and fierce to stand any sudden discoveries of that sort.'

Alfred Milner and Prime Minister of the Cape, Cecil Rhodes, in league with the British Colonial Secretary, Joseph Chamberlain, whose shares in Rhodes' investment company proves that politicians with "conflicts of interest" were by no means a 20th century phenomenon, set about destabilising the Transvaal by means both fair(ish) and foul.

As the British, or *Uitlanders* as the Dutch called them, arrived by the shipload to seek their fortune in the Transvaal gold-fields they began to form a fair proportion of the previously sparsely populated Transvaal. The British Government demanded voting rights, which Kruger refused seeing it as a thinly veiled attempt at annexation through the back door. After "The Jamieson Raid", a coup d'etat cooked up by Rhodes, Milner and Chamberlain, failed to unseat President Kruger, Britain began issuing threats and ultimatums. It became apparent to Kruger that the issue could not be resolved by negotiation, so he put his trust in *"God and the Mauser"* and attacked British forces in Natal and the Cape on 11th October 1899.

Chapter 7:   War! What War? — 1880 — 1902

'The Republics are determined, if they must belong to England that a price will have to be paid which will stagger humanity.'[60]

Ironically, both sides went to war believing God was on their side. The Boers believed they had a "Covenant" with him, whilst the British had long invoked the name of God in its quest to rule the world claiming it was spreading enlightenment and civilisation. Despite the talismanic name of The Almighty being proclaimed, this unholy struggle would last two and half years with neither side showing much Christian charity.

The Boer attack caught the British totally unaware and it became quickly apparent that they were not going to be a push-over. If proof was needed, they soon found themselves under heavy siege in the key centres of Mafeking, Kimberley and Ladysmith. Regardless of the rights and wrongs of what Britain was up to in South Africa, the Empire was under attack and the call went out to defend her honour.

War today is not what it was one hundred years ago. Only in the latter third of the 20th century did we start questioning why we were going to war and if the sacrifice was necessary. The convergence of the Vietnam conflict and the "rock 'n' roll revolution" of the 1960s forever changed our perception of war. It was the first time that great certainties like laying down your life for Queen and country were openly questioned and the generation above me were about the first who could say it without being stoned and locked up for treason. It became obvious that despite all these wars, revolutions and coups, which were all fought in the name of freedom from something or other, that freedom was rarely, if ever, delivered to the man in the street.

Despite all the rhetoric about conflict, we kept having wars because there was one thing which overwhelms reason and that is tribal patriotism. It's guaranteed to unite a discontented nation in war. No matter how flimsy your pretext it quickly becomes the *raison d'etre* for the entire nation.

Chapter 8:

Australia Fights

Back in 1899, the Australians responded with more fervour than any other colony. In 1853, political maverick William Wentworth lamented;

> 'It has been the misfortune of all my countrymen, that we have not lived in troublous times, when it became necessary to subdue unrest at home or pour out our chivalry to seek glory and distinction in foreign climes. This has been a privilege that has been denied to us. It is a privilege which can only belong to our posterity.'

He didn't have long to wait before Victorian Government troops spilt blood on home soil at the Eureka stockade, but it was almost another half century, not counting the brief tribal skirmish in the Sudan, before Australia got to spill the blood of its young in that tribal rite of passage called the Boer War.

Recruitment bands marched round the country picking up men as they went. Country boys, their sense of adventure stifled by their small towns and finding work hard to come by in recession-torn Australia were eager to do their bit for what still was Queen and country. Australians they may have been geographically, but British they still were constitutionally and emotionally.

This was the chance that Australia and Wentworth had been waiting for, to prove their loyalty and to rid themselves of the stain of their origins. Like some pagan rite they sent forth their young to be sacrificed on the altar of war believing that once anointed with the sacrament of blood all past sins would be atoned and nationhood celebrated.

Thomas was the first to volunteer and Military Headquarters requested that he raise a contingent for South Africa. In less than three weeks on 3rd Nov. 1899, the first contingent known as the New South Wales Bushmen was dispatched composed of men from Toowoomba, Warwick, Stanthorpe, Glen Innes and ten men from Tenterfield.

War fever seized Tenterfield. *The Star* followed every step of the first Tenterfield boys who left with the First Contingent, produced blow by blow accounts of the battle and pull-out maps of South Africa to help the eager public follow reports which popped up from all manner of strange places. A satirical cartoon appeared in *The Bulletin* showing public interest in the war outstripping cricket in a country who had a test team before it ever had a Government!

The Australians would prove an invaluable addition to the British war effort. As an act of patriotism, a Victorian man of means called McLeod Cameron raised a regiment at his own expense. He colourfully summarised the virtues of the Australian horseman in the *Tenterfield Star*.

'As horseman, Mr Cameron rightly claims that they have no equals in the world, and their shooting abilities are of a high order. And he also insists on their natural instinct for learning the lay of the land and their ability to endure any hardships. They possess, indeed, the same qualities, which badly employed enabled the KELLY gang to defy the Victorian Government for years, and to traverse vast tracts of country with speed and a certainty which confounded all pursuit. It is hardly too much to say that men of this type should be a match or more than a match for the Boer and as scouts and raiders, they deserve to rank with those cowboys of the States who, under the leadership of Buffalo Bill and his companion, have again and again, under somewhat similar circumstances, rendered incalculable service to The United States war authorities'.

Hero

'Heroes are not giant statues framed against a red sky. They are people who say: This is my community, and it is my responsibility to make it better.'
Studs Terkel[61]

Many stories feature an unsung hero and a forgotten villain, two men whose lives would, in normal circumstances, never intersect. Of course it follows that the unsung hero remains un-sung and the appropriately named forgotten villain vanishes with them into obscurity. In contemporary society, the best example of heroes and villains is probably found in politics.

That is the pattern of this story. One man goes on to prosper whilst the other suffers a slow and painful destruction. In the case of 'Breaker' Morant, that unsung hero was an agapanthus grower and solicitor from the NSW country town of Tenterfield who would die a lonely death in a tin shed without a penny. The villain was a ruthless soldier of fortune and self-acknowledged killer from Dublin who became a respected landowner and died on his sprawling estate in southern Rhodesia surrounded by family and admirers. They were James Francis Thomas and Alfred "Bulala" "Killer" Taylor, a British Intelligence Officer who was responsible directly to Lord Kitchener and who was implicated in summary executions of Boer prisoners but never convicted. A sadist, as described by Davey who was never held to account and protected by Lord Kitchener to extract revenge against the Boers.[62]

Chapter 9:

Tenterfield and Beyond

In 1890, Thomas moved to Tenterfield, a town where in his own words lawyering *'was pretty straightforward, wills, conveyancing, bills of sale, nothing dramatic or outstanding'* and became not only a successful lawyer but also an outspoken advocate for all things Federal. His legal firm prospered and then in 1894 he purchased the local newspaper the *Tenterfield Star* which he would own until 1911. Thomas, the handsome bachelor, had become one of the most influential men in town. As editor of the paper, he published his own poetry and vigorously promoted his views on Federation even though at times they conflicted with those of the founding fathers:

> *'We are prepared to rely on the national growth of our sentiments and the beneficial influence of the great upheaval which is working for the welfare of the race; but let the leaders of Federation put a good workable scheme before the people and they will find them ready to accept it.'*

Thomas has been described as a man of gentle nature, a lover of simplicity who would give you the shirt off his back. He was an avid gardener who felt most comfortable in the bush, a man who during his mid war return from South Africa not only promoted the planting of the South African Agapanthus but is widely believed at the same time to have introduced the Gerbera to Australia. When he wasn't gardening, running his law firm or writing for his newspaper Thomas was also an active militiaman. He joined the local Upper Clarence Light Horse as a volunteer and was quickly commissioned into the New South Wales Mounted Infantry Regiment based in Tenterfield. In 1894, he completed his training at the Cavalry School of Instruction in Sydney, was promoted to First Lieutenant and took command of the Tenterfield Half Company. In 1895, he was further promoted to Captain and his leadership qualities came to the fore in 1895 when his local reservist troop, the Tenterfield Rifles won the Hutton Shield, a trophy contested annually by the elite of Australia's Light Horse contingents and awarded on the basis of excellence in dress, drill, cavalry attack, marksmanship, horsemanship, fire discipline and more importantly, command.

When the first contingent left for the Boer War in November, 1899, Thomas was aged thirty-eight, leaving for the Cape of Good Hope on the 28th of February, 1900 as the Officer Commanding A Squadron of the New South Wales Bushmen's Contingent.

Thomas reported regularly and very competently from South Africa to his newspaper the Tenterfield Star. For example, he wrote in May 1900:

'Such dreadful bungling there has been! Squadrons have been split up down here and dumped and there, with their horses also split up, and mostly separated from the men who owned them. But all of 'A' Squadron and about half the squadron horses were collected at Marandellas, and on the 3rd of May I started with 84 men of the squadron and 100 horses (mostly our own) EN ROUTE from Buluwayo as a sort of vanguard. We are rather proud to be the first to start, but shall be followed by the rest of the squadron and the other bushmen in detachments.'

Concluding his following letter thus:

'It is difficult to know what will happen, where we shall be next sent, or what we shall do. Fate alone can decide, and this country somehow seems to make one a fatalist. Let me live and die in Australia — I want no better country for my home: that is how the writer feels at present.'

His letter from Rustenberg, Transvaal, of the 14th of June 1900 about the relationships with the Boers is interesting in considering the events later in 1900 leading to the charging of Morant, Handcock and Witton for the murder of Boer prisoners:

Chapter 9:   *Tenterfield and Beyond*

'The Boer shooting, on the whole, has been very bad, and by no means equal to that of the British. At almost every farm which we have visited we have found the inmates wearing mourning, which is an indication that the Boers in this neighbourhood have lost heavily in the war. For the most part they seem to be heartily glad that the war is drawing to a close, and that they are back on their farms again. On their surrendering their arms and ammunition and agreeing not to fight further, they get a permit to remain on their farms. If cattle, ponies, forage, etc are required for the British troops, the owners are paid full value for them, and this almost mistaken generosity on the part of the victors is being taken advantage of in various ways.'

Thomas had a very poor opinion of the Boers, writing of them:

'They are for the most part dirty, hollow-chested, lank, often half-witted, lazy, cowardly, mean, unreliable.'

He concluded his letter of the 14th of June, 1900:

'All the Tenterfield boys are well, but Sergeant-Major Mitchell was left at Buluwayo. Our Tenterfield horses are also still all alive, but have more or less suffered from sickness of various kinds. Jim Struck has been promoted to Brigade butcher! I have had no news whatever from Tenterfield since I left, and only one Australian letter dated (12th March).'

Thomas provided a detailed report in August and September 1900 from Elands River. In 1992 Robert L. Wallace's Boer War study quotes from ten of Thomas' reports to the *Tenterfield Star*.[63]

Private S.J. Lawer of Tenterfield mentioned writing to the *Tenterfield Star* that Thomas had his horse shot from under him, yet Thomas failed to mention it or write about it:[64]

'One-day last week 40 of us on patrol were attacked by 80 of them. They were on top of a hill behind a rock and one thing and another. We were

on open ground on a flat. They sent the bullets in like hailstones, but only wounded one man. Captain Thomas' horse got shot from under him. We drove them back just as if you were firing at kangaroos and they were running away.'

In South Africa, Thomas commanded A Squadron, New South Wales Citizen's Bushmen with distinction. His squadron served at the relief of Mafeking with Colonel Plumer as part of General Baden Powell's column. A Squadron was also part of the famous Battle of Elands River where Thomas distinguished himself commanding night raids against the enemy. Thomas was a soldier of great merit, however in January, 1901 he was censured by his superiors for losing control over his men in a skirmish that led to the loss of a valuable convoy.[65] Thomas had spent valuable time at a crucial point in the attack helping wounded soldiers *'instead of providing leadership in defending the convoy from attacking Boers'*. In a hand-written note to the President of the Court of Inquiry on the 16th of January, Thomas stated:

'There were no field dressings with us, wounded men lying about without proper shelter from fire; I had a shelter made with sacks and, having some simple remedies and dressings on me and having 'done a good deal of doctoring', I tended the wounded, whose comrades had not offered to assist.'[66]

The charges affected Thomas deeply who, unlike many of his British counterparts, believed that the safety and wellbeing of his men was paramount.

After the loss of the convoy, he wrote on the 6th of February to Colonel Kenneth Mackay, Staff Officer, for Australasia and New Zealand at Naauwpoort:

'I observe that 1000 more troops are to be sent from N.S. Wales… If there is any chance of me getting command of a Regiment from N.S. Wales, I would accept… I have the substantive rank of Major & 2nd in command. I have had command of Detachments almost since we landed in

Chapter 9:   Tenterfield and Beyond

the country in April last… My private profession has suffered severely in N.S. Wales & I have scarcely the heart to go back. I arranged for its management for only 6 months and…like other officers I might have to sell out. This I would do if assured of a commission here for another 12 months…'[67]

Despite the reprimand, Thomas finished his first stint in South Africa highly decorated with three "Mentioned in Dispatches", the Queen's Medal with four clasps and was eventually promoted to the rank of Major after 12 months, service. Thomas and the NSW Bushmen's Contingent ended their tour of duty and returned to Australia disembarking on 11th June 1901.

Thomas returns

Thomas was not home for long. In 1901, Australia's unemployment rate was above 10% as it was to be during World War One and Two. Many of the men who had enlisted had gone to South Africa simply because it was a job, a chance to not only serve the Empire but to be employed, clothed and fed after years of hardship. However, when they returned after the first stint on the Veldt they found as their comrades from the Great Wars would, work was almost impossible to find. If they had had jobs before they left they found those jobs had gone to others, if they had been casual labourers they found that work was thin on the ground but they were also confronted by a change in the structure of the job market. Subtle though it was in those early days, within the short period they had been away increased mechanization had come to farms, women had entered the workforce and Australia was suffering from what has become known as the Federation Drought, a prolonged period of dry weather, an Al Nino that ran from mid-1890s until 1903, and it had the Australian agricultural community, and therefore the country as a whole, on its knees. Whilst the idea of a choice between soldiering in Africa or unemployment might seem strange to us now but back then it was a reality and Thomas as ever concerned for the welfare of his fellow combatants took up the cause. Within a month of his return to Australia he had begun to vigorously

55

lobby the Government to support a return to the war for unemployed servicemen.

'Do not want to act behind the back of the Government', Thomas declared in correspondence with reluctant high-ranking officials of the Defence Department:

> *'Lord Kitchener says he wants more men ... Large numbers of the men who returned with me have been utterly unable to find employment of any kind, and many are absolutely stranded ... great inducements were offered them to settle in South Africa, but our Government opposed [this] ... I have been asked by my men to try to get them back to South Africa where they will try their fortunes on the gold fields, and whilst the war continues they are willing to enlist again.*
>
> *'Personally, I have no special inducements for another period of hard service, but I like the men and I think they like me, and I am willing to go with them.'*

It was a fight that Thomas won, the Imperial Government subsequently providing free passage from Sydney on the steamer *Britannic*. He resigned from the NSW Bushmen's Corps, and having raised a force of some 200 men returned to South Africa, where he almost immediately found himself railroaded into the position of advocate before the Courts Martial of his friend and fellow lawyer, Major John Lenehan, an English Lieutenant Picton and Messers Morant, Handcock and Witton, an experience that would change him and ultimately, as we will discover, affected the rest of his life.

A country farewell

By now we have a fairly clear picture of Thomas before he left for the war. He was the farm boy who made good — fulfilling the potential his parents saw in him. Despite Bennett's allegations, for which this author can find no evidence in the pre- war period, about poor book- keeping and quality of the service he gave his clients, Thomas had built up a flourishing practice. To use one of those awful stock phrases he was a "pillar of the community" and the local Mayor, William Reid, said as much at the concert they held for him when he departed for the war having recently been offered a commission as Captain. If Thomas was the "hack" Bennett portrays him as, its unlikely Reid would have felt moved to deliver a eulogy such as the one he proudly delivered that night.[68]

> 'This... is the eve of your departure for South Africa... At first when we heard you were going to the war we felt we could not let you go without some act of courtesy and that were justified, and indeed in duty bound to offer you the attention we are showing you this evening. In addition to this concert it will be my duty to present you a purse of sovereigns in place of a gift. You will understand when we heard of your departure we felt anxious to tender you a gift of some sort so that whenever your eyes fell on it you might think of the many friends you are about to leave in this district. You have been here many years, and though not given to flattery I can conscientiously say no man in our midst would be more missed than you will be. We know duty calls you, and Tenterfield must think itself highly honoured in providing for the Empire a gentleman who has risen to the position of Captain in one of the finest armies going to South Africa. You will be accompanied by a number of the best young fellows we have, and it will be a grand advertisement for our district to supply such a gentleman as you to fight for The British Empire.'

With those fine words, the sound of the brass band and hearty cheers of the good- folk of the town ringing in his ears the train carrying Thomas pulled out of Tenterfield's picturesque little station and headed to Sydney to join his men. It was a scene repeated in country towns all over Australia.

Chapter 10:

And So Fate

Captain Thomas and the "A" Squadron of the New South Wales Citizens' Bushmen embarked in the transports *Atlantian* and *Maplemore* and sailed from Sydney on the 28th February, 1900. The contingent had been raised by public subscription. On leaving Sydney, its strength was 30 officers and 495 other ranks, 570 horses and 10 carts.

Amongst the first cinematic images ever recorded in Australia are grainy black and white images of men parading at barracks, marching through the streets and leaving on boats for war. Even without the ambient sound which was still some thirty years away, the crowded wharfs and waving hats and flags still manages to convey the sense of excitement and history in the making as Australians left *en masse* for the first time to fight in foreign lands.

The Contingent arrived in Cape Town on 2nd April, 1900, proceeded to Biera in Tanganika which they reached on 12th April, and then went on to Bulawayo in Rhodesia via Marandellas.

Thomas' leadership

Their first major action was a prestigious one serving under General Plummer at the relief of Mafeking which was greeted with euphoria and relief in Britain. Together with the breaking of sieges of Kimberley and Ladysmith, the British wrestled away the Boers early advantage. However, even Mafeking would be dwarfed by their next major action.

In the recesses of Sydney's Mitchell Library, this author discovered an unpublished, hand-written account of the numerous field actions in which Thomas and his Tenterfield boys were involved in during the two months between the relief of Mafeking and the Elands River siege. It is not signed, but appears to be written by a senior British officer with access to important documents copies of which are also included. It is simply

Chapter 10: *And So Fate*

entitled, *"Events Prior to Eland's River in August 1900 in which J.F. Thomas took part"* and from it come the following dispatches.

After Mafeking, Thomas and the "A" squadron then started a drive Eastwards to Rustenberg with General Baden Powell's column, under the command of Lt. Col. Hore. This unit was a mixture 110 Bushmen and 200 of Plummer's Rhodesian and some 120 Protectorate troops who were part of a column of 2,000 men. They got to Rustenberg with little incident on June 20th and took the town. Hore's unit, including Thomas, were left to guard the town but were advised to evacuate on July 3rd by Baden-Powell who had information that a Boer force of 2,000 with field guns planned to attack.

They decamped to Eland's River 40 miles away. On July 6th 1901 they received an urgent message from Major Hanbury- Tracey who had arrived in Rustenberg and were about to be attacked by the force which had menaced them whilst they occupied the town. Hore ordered Lt. Col. Airey and two squadrons of Bushmen to Rustenberg.

> *'... after marching 40 miles in 24 hours they arrived in the nick of time whilst the fight was going on and drove the Boers off the field in disorder... This Australian detachment is reported to have behaved with great dash and gallantry'.*

Thomas' Distinguished service

Thomas is mentioned on three occasions in the run up to the Elands River siege. The first:

> *'13th July*
>
> *'Captain Thomas, 1st Australian Bushmen, with 40 men was sent in the direction of Vlaksfontein to bring in some wagons said to belong to some loyalist Boers.*
>
> *'Captain Thomas, soon after finding the wagons, was vigorously attacked by some 40 or more Boers from surrounding hills and after a good fight lasting half an hour drove them off and returned to Eland Rivers camp.'*

Before his next mention, the Boers made clear their intention to attack after cutting the telegraph wires and forcing the British to go into laager. A few days before the seige began Thomas had the opportunity to distinguish himself once more.

> '1st August.
> 'Heard that Supt. Coutze, Bechuanaland Rifles who was scouting with a small detachment near Mabalstaadt had been attacked and had to retire, so Capt. Thomas with 60 men 1st Australian Bushmen was sent off at once (1.30 pm) to rescue this small party.'

> '2nd August,
> 'Capt. Thomas returned having successfully rescued Supt. Coutze's party. There were 2 wounded.'

These entries, plus the fact that Thomas was mentioned three times in dispatches shows he was a trusted leader and could handle himself, nothing like Denton's plodding,"... *good soldier... never spectacular, always efficient*". If he had been just that, he would never have taken on the might of the British Military in the Morant case and his life would have continued its upward spiral.[69]

On the 4th August the siege began. A Squadron, assisted by 50 other men defended Eland's River post against De La Rey with 1000 men and guns. For the first few days they were shelled from sunrise to sunset which brought home the brutality of the war.

The Eland's River battle

On the 29th July, the keeper of the Eland's River diary remarked that when ordered to entrench themselves:

> 'They were not very keen on it and did not realise the absolute necessity of cover, but this was down to a large number of them (mostly of the Australian Contingent) never having experienced shell- fire. However, in a few days their skill & capacity for work in entrenching improved in a most miraculous manner.'

Chapter 10: *And So Fate*

This point was illustrated starkly in a letter from Thomas, which first appeared in the *Tenterfield Star*, was re-produced in the *Glen Innes Examiner* on 26/10/00. It gives a fine firsthand account of what it was like inside the Elands River camp and describes the death of a Tenterfield man — Sgt.- Major James Mitchell on the 12th of August:

'The seige commenced unexpectedly on the morning of August 4th... The garrison (it was really only a camp) was commanded by kopjes all round — in fact it was so placed to almost invite and attack, a large store of valuable stores that we were in charge of, offering a tempting bait.

'I was in command of 110 NSW Bushmen, all told — with us being Sgt. Major Mitchell and troopers Struck, Grey, Lawler, Hurig and McDonald from the Tenterfield district. The Bushmen manned six small forts or sconces, made of stores and earth, biscuit boxes and flour bags, all on the eastern side of the main force guarding the water supply... Directly the attack began we rushed to our places, and none too soon, for the bombardment was terrible. During the morning a fine strong young fellow named Waddell was hit by the screw of a pom pom next to me, and in two or three minutes he was dead. almost at the same moment poor Jim Duff, another Bushman, was killed instantaneously by a pom pom shell in the sconce on my right. Next the shell struck the sconce that Sgt.- Major Mitchell was in — on my left — and he and several other men ran out and three of them were wounded, but Mitchell must have been wounded as he was running out, for he had a bullet hole through his leg. I said to Mitchell don't bring all those men into this sconce there are too many in it already, and there is plenty of room in the one on your left. I did not know that the men were hurt. He said, "I can't go I'm hit". he was then lying down under a wagon at the back of the sconce. I said, "Are you badly hurt?". He said, "I think my leg is broken". I said, "No, it can't be broken or you wouldn't have gone so far... I looked at his leg and found it was only a flesh wound, and bound it up with a handkerchief... and afterwards the doctor came and said he could remain. Poor Waddell lay dead close by and not far off poor Duff. My poor boys — I thought —

there will be a lot more of us join you before the day is over; but we only buried five that night, side by side in one grave, and only 14 altogether.'

As Thomas also noted, Mitchell's luck did not improve after being wounded:

'And now for the sad part of it. After our poor Sgt.-Major was taken to hospital a shrapnel shell fell into it and wounded him badly, also another of my men (Ralston). In the end the doctor advised amputation of Mitchell's leg above the knee. The latter sent for me and said he was satisfied to go under the operation. he was very plucky, and seemed quite cheerful, even after the operation was over. he told me that he felt very little pain, and that while he was under the chloroform he fancied he was in the midst of a great battle.'

On the 9th, General De La Rey commanding the Boer forces sent the following letter, addressed to Hore, offering them the chance to surrender and explaining why Mitchell was hit whilst in hospital:

'Whilst I express my regret at the fact that some of your sick and wounded have come under my gun-fire I am obliged to throw the blame of it upon you, since your hospital ambulance was placed by you inside a very small camp and in the vicinity of your guns, so that guns or gun-fire directed upon your camp had the possibility of hitting the hospital.

'Further I have the honour to inform you that reports, the accuracy of which is beyond doubt, have come into me that Rustenberg, Olifantsnek and Magatosnek have been evacuated by British troops and occupied by mine. I have received information that general Carrington's force which I myself drove across the Marico river and caused to be further pursued, has retreated through Zeerust. As you are persumably holding the camp at Elands river solely to protect that line of communication and since the communications is now totally non-existent I wish to submit to your very serious consideration that the time has come to avoid further bloodshed and to end your defence which you have carried on with so much courage. In the event of your handing over to me the camp with all that it contains without concealing or destroying anything in it then I am prepared and pledge myself to allow you and the troops under you to proceed to the nearest force of British troops wherever you may choose to go. The commanding officers will in that case keep their arms as a recognition of the brave defence of your camp. Kindly answer me as soon as possible. If necessary, I am prepared to have an interview with you in order to further discuss the matter and settle details.'

J.H. De La Rey

Commanding General.

Despite the terrific odds he faced, Hore's answer was short and sweet. Even as a veteran of Egypt, Sudan and the recently lifted siege of Mafeking, he perhaps preferred to face De La Rey's guns than Robert's wrath, had the supplies he was defending fallen into Boer hands.

To Ass. General De La Rey

'Sir,

'I beg to acknowledge the receipt of your letter 9/8/00 concerning your demand for the surrender of the British troops under my command at Elands River camp + in reply must inform you that as this post is held by Her Majesty's Forces I decline to surrender.'

C.O. Hore

Lt. Col.

Elands River 9/9/00.

Thomas' loss

An unpalatable but inescapable reality of war is that sometimes men are sacrificed for the "greater good". Whether a prompt surrender by Hore might have saved the lives of Mitchell and other wounded men is debatable, but Thomas remained at Mitchell's side during his final hours.

'... On the 11th he seemed very bad and he was wandering, and the next day was worse. The doctor told me he could not live, and the same evening (12th) he died quite quietly and we buried him by moonlight. Struck and Larver carried him to the grave. We placed grass at the bottom and wrapped him in a blanket. It was a sad duty for us — the saddest I have seen in South Africa. Sgt-Major Mitchell was always a keen soldier. He was for 15 years attached to the Tenterfield Corps and was, I think, for about 10 years (of) it Sgt.- Major. Now he has filled a soldier's grave — far better than to die, perhaps, from some lingering disease... This war is a sad cruel business — but it is an unavoidable evil. I think we all wish it was over — it is getting wearisome.'

It soon was. On the day that Hore defied De La Rey's offer of surrender, he had also ordered his men to conserve ammunition. They also suspected that the Boers were short after the fusillade of shells they had dispatched during the first few days. The last week of the siege was largely restricted to rifle fire, surprise attacks and cruder methods such as setting the veldt on fire. Shell-fire directed in other directions also suggested that other British troops were trying to reach them.

The siege was lifted on the 16th of August by Lord Kitchener's force supported by Lord Methuen's column which arrived from the North the next day. Again, in one of those strange historical coincidences, Thomas would have been overjoyed to see Lord Kitchener, little knowing that his saviour would soon become his nemesis.

As Gavin Souter in his 1975 book, *The Lion and the Kangaroo — The Initiation of Australia* put it:[70]

> '300 mixed Aussies, together with 200 Rhodesians covered themselves in glory at Elands River. They were pinned down by 1800 Boers with Pom Poms and heavy artillery. Although more shells were fired into their camp than Mafeking — they held out for 12 days until relief arrived. 75 Aussies died and that great chronicler of the Boer War — Sir Arthur Conan Doyle wrote;
>
> 'When the ballad-makers of Australia seek for a subject let them turn to Elands River, for there was no finer fighting in the war'.

Chapter 10:   *And So Fate*

But as Souter also observed Eland's River was more than just a military victory:

> 'It was exactly what Australia (and Wentworth) wanted — a chance to blood itself with honour next to seasoned Imperials with the mother country grateful for prompt assistance loyally given'.

R.L. Wallace also notes that during the siege Thomas had a narrow escape when his horse was shot from under him. God plainly had other designs for Thomas.[71] All of this tells us that by the time he came to defend Morant *et al*, Thomas was a seasoned officer who knew about the bloody nature of war. That phrase in his letter home, '... *This war is a sad, cruel business — but it is an unavoidable evil',* tells us he was a pragmatist and didn't take on the BVC cases out of some misguided sense of idealism, but rather out of the same compassion he shows for Mitchell. Tenterfield would lose another five men during the course of the war and though Thomas did not write eulogies for them all and on his return to Tenterfield he was instrumental in ensuring their sacrifice was fittingly recorded for Wentworth's *"posterity"*.

Going Home

Having served 12 months, the Contingent embarked at Cape Town for their return to Australia, on 9th May 1901. Of the 30 officers and 495 other ranks that went 1 officer and 29 men died; 6 officers and 8 others were transferred; 3 officers and 49 others were struck off strength in South Africa; 1 officer and 1 other were commissioned in the Imperial Army; 23 officers and 404 others returned to Sydney. The 4 additional officers in the total were appointed in South Africa.

The ship called at Fremantle, Adelaide and Melbourne en route to Sydney where Thomas landed on 11th June 1901 where he was promoted to Major the same day as well as being awarded the Queen's Medal with 4 clasps for action at Rhenoster Kop; Elands River; Relief of Defeating; and operations as stated from April 1900 to 31 May 1901.

Thomas' reflection

An understanding of his experiences in the war can be gleamed from the article that appeared in the Advertiser newspaper, (Adelaide) on 4 June 1901. The article included Thomas' quotes about his Squadron's performance in the field:

> 'The New South Wales men did an immense amount of work in the Eland's river district, mostly scouting. It was in this kind of service that the Australians mostly shine. "Although," says the Major, "they did good work all round." Many of the men suffered from enteric fever, but they pulled 'through in most instances wonderfully. In all the contingent lost ten men from the fever'.
> [72] (Annexure F)

Tenterfield's Recognition

More praise came Thomas' way four days later when he was presented with a plaque by Thomas M. Walker, the new Mayor of Tenterfield, on behalf of the townsfolk.

The Tenterfield Shire Council had prepared a tribute for Thomas, (the original of which is in a frame at Centenary Cottage, 136 Logan Street, Tenterfield), including these words being a reflection of Thomas' standing in the Tenterfield community.[73]

> 'July 20 1901.
>> To Major J.F. Thomas of the New South Wales Bushmen
>> 'Dear Sir;
>> 'Your fellow townsmen of Tenterfield feel it incumbent on them to present you with a lasting assurance of their sincere pleasure at your return unscathed from the perils of the South African War, and of their public pride and delight in the heroism with which you and your gallant comrades have maintained and promoted the honour and reputation of this State and District. The fame of Elands River and Rhenostet will henceforth shed reflected brightness on the pages of our uneventful local history.

Chapter 10: And So Fate

Your fellow towns men sincerely hope that the splendid efforts made on behalf of our Country and Empire will shortly prove to have secured for our fellow subjects every where a lasting and prosperous peace and that you may be long and happily spared to share therein is the earnest prayer of your fellow townsmen on whose behalf we have the honour to subscribe ourselves.
Thomas M Walker (Mayor)
Ron Stevenson (Clerk) Tenterfield
15th June 1901.'

During Thomas' next three months in Sydney, there was further evidence of his generosity of spirit and compassion. He was much quoted in the local papers and the subject of parliamentary questions in the NSW Legislature (see Appendix A). Thomas was appalled at the lack of employment opportunities for returned soldiers, gathered men to return to South Africa. He was doing this of his own volition rather than in an official capacity and with no Government assistance or funding.

The policy of the NSW Government, along with other states like Victoria, was to allow men who wanted to volunteer for service in South Africa to do so, but without any direct or indirect material or administrative assistance from the state Government. There was concern that the "cream" of NSW manhood was leaving the country and might never return.

In his 1988 article on the Morant affair, Barry Bridges mistakes this missionary zeal for *"Jingoism"*.[74] However, the correspondence from that period which appears in the Appendixes clearly shows, Thomas was not concerned with returning men to South Africa as cannon-fodder. Rather his intentions were far more public-spirited as can be seen from the series of letters in the Appendixes which clearly outlines his concerns for the men. Thomas made clear his own position in a 1916 publication entitled, *In Time Of War — The Recruiting Problem — Help Our Mates*. An Address to Fellow Australians by J.F. Thomas of the New England Recruiting Committee:

'... *The writer is a native born Australian, of strong democratic tendencies, a sympathiser with the best ideals of Labour, and of pronounced* anti-militarist views. From 1891 to 1903 he was a volunteer officer of the mounted forces, first of New South Wales, and after Federation, of the Commonwealth. In 1900 he volunteered for service in the late Boer War, believing at the time that the cause was right, and was accepted for a Captaincy in the New South Wales Citizens Bushmen (a regiment of 500 organised, equipped, and partly paid by the citizens of the State).

'He returned to this country in 1901 in command of the regiment (or what remained of it), which had been relieved (after twelve months' service, mark you).

'He returned to South Africa shortly thereafter in company with a number of men who volunteered for further service'.

It could be argued that as this biography was written after the Morant trial and includes the phrase, '... believing at the time that the cause was right', in reference to the Boer War, that Thomas had changed his tune retrospectively.

However, Thomas' letters to Government Ministers reveal that it was the lack of employment opportunities in Australia and the feeling that as a C.O it was his duty to be concerned, which motivated him to act. He warned the Ministers repeatedly about the numbers wishing to return to South Africa and proposed that the Government look into a land grant scheme to entice them to stay at home. His concern at young Australians deserting their homeland echoed his earlier concern — often expressed in the *Tenterfield Star* that they also left the country for the cities. It was only after his land scheme was rejected that he decided to go to South Africa and not because of his lust for war, but through a profound sense of duty. When his men could not find an officer above the rank of 1st Lieutenant willing to go, he agreed to return with them.

We are able to pin-point the day of his departure through a letter he wrote to *The Sydney Morning Herald* which appeared on 20th August, 1901 instructing men where to assemble for the departure of the *Britannic* the following day.

Chapter 10: *And So Fate*

Support for Australian veterans

Thanks to Thomas, the issue of employment for returning soldiers was raised in the NSW Parliament — albeit on September 3rd, two weeks after Thomas sailed. Mr E.M. Clark the member for Rylstone asked the NSW Premier, Mr See, about the numbers leaving for South Africa, the numbers returning, the numbers still there and the difficulty in them finding employment in Australia. Mr See produced the figures and admitted, '... *there is great difficulty in finding work for returning men*', but promised to look into it.

The Premier was further pressed on the same question by Mr Clark the following day after he met a returned soldier with a solitary shilling in his pocket and, '... *no idea where to go to find the necessities of life*'. Mr See's reply was an unsympathetic, '*I cannot help that*' and his answer to the crisis was to speak to the heads of the Police, Railways and Public service board with a request to give preference to returned soldiers. Before his departure Thomas acknowledged, '... *the Government has no moral obligation to find civil service billets for all returned soldiers*' but instead of looking more constructively at his land grant proposals, that was precisely what Premier did. Given the apparent indifference of home politicians who could blame Thomas for returning to South Africa with his men?

We were unable to find out about his activities on his return to South Africa — other than what he disclosed in that brief autobiographical passage in, *In Time Of War*:

> '... (I) *joined for a time, one of the "Irregular Corps" which were organised during the latter stage of the war. For reasons not necessary here to explain, he resigned from the Corps, but immediately afterwards found himself, by force of circumstances, in the position of advocate and still with the rank of Major, before the series of courts martials which sat at the town of Pietersberg in the Northern Transvaal, during many terrible days at the beginning of 1902 to try the officers of that notable irregular corps known as the "Bushveldt Carbineers" in which trials several Australian, and other officers were involved*'.

This gives a rough chronology of Thomas' movements between late September when he would have reached South Africa again and mid-January 1902 when he made his way to Pietersburg at the request of Major Lenehan. This author was unable to find out which "irregular" unit Thomas joined and why he left. Was he shocked at the less than chivalrous way this phase of the war was being conducted? Did it give him a personal insight to the issues that would later confront him in the Morant trial and was it the basis of his unshakable belief that Morant *et al* had a viable defence? Did he, as a Major, also receive orders to "take no prisoners"?

Chapter 11:

Brief to appear far from home

Thomas achieved lasting fame as the advocate for Morant, Handcock, Witton and Major Lenehan at British Courts Martial in January and February 1902. Morant and Handcock were executed and Witton was sentenced to death which was then commuted to life imprisonment, sent to England and after a lot of agitation by his supporters, released after three years and returned to Australia. Lenehan was cashiered and sent back to Australia. For convenience, the three trials are referred to as "the Morant trials". It is important to remember that Bruce Beresford's 1979 film *Breaker Morant* is inaccurate in many ways. The facts were "adapted" to heighten the dramatic effect. The film was based on the play *Breaker Morant* by Kenneth G. Ross (1978), which in turn took liberties with what actually took place.

The most accurate descriptions of the trials available are to be found in the *British Times*[75] (Appendix F) and in George Witton's *Scapegoats of the Empire*.[76] Thomas brought all his papers from the trial back with him to Tenterfield after he applied and paid for a copy of the transcripts.[77]

Denton also stated in his article, *Breaker Morant File — Bush Lawyer*:[78]

Back in 1921, Thomas wrote to the librarian at the Mitchell library and in a note at the end of that letter he said:
'It may be of some little interest to note also, that I have the whole of the proceedings of the Court Martial held at Pietersburg, correspondence and etc. The whole affair is a tragedy and might form a tragedy if written for one'.

George Witton also used his copy of the transcripts in his book which sets out verbatim and at length the submissions Thomas made at the Courts Martial. However, those papers have never come to light, even after extensive searching by Kit Denton.[79] Thomas wrote in the front of his copy of *Scapegoats of the Empire*:

> 'This book only gives a superficial statement of the facts; much that Lieutenant Witton probably did not know is not given. The true story of the Bushveldt Carbineers has never been written. These officers were truly 'scapegoats' — shot or imprisoned not so much for their own sins but for those of the system of militarism in which they were involved and which was responsible for the drastic instructions secretly issued from high places to irregular Corp against indomitable Boers. In the latter European War Regular Army Officers were not given the opportunity to season themselves victimising Colonial Officers, as was the case in the South African War.
> J. Francis Thomas
> (Advocate).'

It was whilst he was in-between commissions, that Major Lenehan contacted Thomas. Most likely, Lenehan, who was a lawyer in the Supreme Court of NSW, knew Thomas through the legal profession. Thomas' decision to represent him and the others in the Courts Martial proved to be the turning-point in his life.

According to Bleszynski, Thomas later commented on Lenehan's request:

> 'I did not like to refuse so I got a permit to defend them and proceeded to Pietersburg where I was engaged for about five weeks upon as difficult a task as I suppose ever fell to an advocate.'[80]

Thomas' claim of it being a difficult case was an insight as to his own ability and whether he was up to the task. In any event, he went to Pietersburg on 15 January 1902, the day before the Courts Martial were to begin. 'His original brief was to defend Major Lenehan, but on hearing the other accused had no legal representation, he agreed to defend them too.'[81]

'I have always found that mercy bears richer fruits than strict justice. Abraham Lincoln speech in Washington, D.C., 1865.'

Come to Attention — Courts Martial

The first Courts Martial of Morant and his co-accused began on **16th January 1902** before a President (LTCOL Denny) and six other Officers (Majors and Captains). The charge concerned the murder of the prisoner Visser.[82] Appendix C.

Morant, Handcock and Witton pleaded not guilty to the charge. In accordance with the provisions of Military trial procedure a Judge Advocate (Major Coplan) was appointed to decide questions of law. The hearing was adjourned to hear evidence from Hamilton.

A second Court Martial took place on **21st January 1902** to hear the case against Lenehan for failing to report the shooting of three Boers and the shooting of Trooper Van Buuren. Thomas represented Lenehan who was acquitted of the first charge and convicted of the second. The first trial resumed and Lenehan gave character evidence for the accused. The accused also submitted statements about their actions.

After this trial finished on 31st January, the prisoners were sent back to Pietersburg for trial concerning the shooting of eight Boer prisoners. It was during the train journey that the prisoners were called to arms when Boers were detected on the rail line. At the Court Martial that commenced on **3rd February 1902**, Morant made a detailed statement about his actions, including, *'I do not feel called upon, nor am I advised by my counsel that it is necessary for me to enter the witness box.'*[83] This statement infers that Thomas provided Morant with advice from which he could elect to either give evidence or tender a statement in evidence.

The next Court Martial involved allegations against Handcock and Morant of killing three Boers (2 men and a youth). The trial commenced on **5th February 1902**. Thomas again appeared as counsel. The accused pleaded not guilty, admitted the facts, but again argued superior orders as their defence.

The Court Martial of Captain Taylor was convened on **7th February 1902**. The charges concerned shooting Boers. Taylor conducted his own defence and was acquitted. The last of the Courts Martial was held in Pietersburg on **17th February 1902** and dealt with the shooting of the missionary Heese. Handcock and Morant pleaded not guilty to the charge and were eventually acquitted.

Role of Judge Advocate General (JA)

The JA's role at the time was expressed as follows:

> 'It was admitted that the Judge Advocate at the trial of a prisoner should preside as the legal Officer to watch the proceedings to see justice is done to the prisoner and to assist the court. The proceedings of all general courts martial of which the Sovereign is the confirming authority Officer are sent direct to the Judge Advocate General for his examination and approval. The duty of the Judge Advocate General is confined to an examination into the legality of the proceedings, the validity of the charges, the evidence of guilt and the sentences with reference to the Statute Law. The expediency of carrying out the sentence or of extending mercy does not come within his province.' In matters of the first importance the Judge Advocate General therefore advises upon the case and to prevent any possible miscarriage on mere legal or technical grounds frames the charges upon which the offender is arraigned. The facts being legally proved that is according to the law of evidence which rules in courts martial of which again the Judge Advocate General is the sole judge, the conviction is certain and the authority of the General is upheld.'[84]

This principle required the JA at the trial to preside over questions of law and procedure. The JA General's review of the proceedings must have confirmed the record, the conviction and sentence despite whatever submissions were made by Thomas.

Verdicts (Appendix C)

Following the Courts Martial, the court found:
- Morant, Handcock and Witton guilty of inciting the murder of eight Boer prisoners;

- Morant guilty of inciting the murder of Boer prisoner, Visser. Handcock, Picton and Witton were found guilty of the manslaughter of Visser;
- Morant and Handcock were acquitted of murdering the missionary Heese; and
- Morant and Handcock were convicted of inciting the murder of two men and a boy;
- Lenehan was reprimanded and Taylor was acquitted of all charges.

Sentences

- Morant and Handcock were sentenced to be executed;
- Witton's sentence of death was commuted to life imprisonment; and
- Picton was cashiered (dismissed from Army service).

Witton's case was reviewed by Sir Isaac Isaacs KC, MP in 1902 (destined to become Chief Justice and Governor General). This review led to a storm of protest from Australians and representations from the Australian, South African Governments and British politicians, including Winston Churchill for Witton's release. Finally, a petition signed by 100,000 Australians supported a petition for mercy sent to King Edward V11.[85] On 11th August 1904, Witton was released from prison and returned to Australia.

Recommendations for mercy[86]

The Courts Martial Officers, including the President cited mitigation in their recommendations for mercy for each conviction. The recommendations were significant and reflected the evidence and defence submission by Thomas that emerged during the trials. The recommendations:
- Morant acted under extreme provocation at the mutilation by Boers of his best friend Hunt;
- Morant's good service including his action in capturing Boer Commander Kelly;
- Handcock's good service record, his lack of previous military

experience and ignorance of military law, custom and procedures; and
- Witton's good service record and the fact that he and Handcock had acted under orders of Morant, their superior Officer.

Review of charges — prosecution evidence

The first charge of killing Josef Visser concerned his execution without arrest and lawful trial. According to the accused, when Visser was caught he was wearing British Khaki and had in his possession a pair of Hunt's trousers. The criminality of the accused was argued by the prosecution as illegal and contrary to the provisions of Military Law. Evidence was deposed from witnesses, including two soldiers who had been in the firing squad that executed Visser. Morant, Handcock and Picton testified that they had acted under the orders of Hunt to take no prisoners and to execute Boers wearing Khaki. Morant also testified that Hunt had told him that he had received his orders from Colonel Hamilton, the Secretary to Lord Kitchener. When called to give evidence, Hamilton denied such orders existed or that he had spoken with Hunt.

The second charge concerned the execution of eight Boer prisoners. The facts as alleged by the prosecution were not disputed by the accused. The prisoners had been captured and handed over to Morant, who stated he had orders to execute prisoners of war. The accused didn't testify, but handed prepared statements to the court as evidence. Morant stated he followed orders from Hunt and had the prisoners executed, as had been done by members of other irregular units. He also stated that he been reprimanded by Hunt for failing to execute prisoners in the past. He said he was justified in dealing with prisoners in a summary manner. He claimed that his state of mind was affected by Hunt's death and he had decided to summarily execute prisoners.

Handcock, Witton and Picton gave similar statements. A number of other witnesses stated in evidence that Hunt had given direct and unambiguous orders that no prisoners were to be taken and prisoners had been summarily dealt with in accordance with orders from Lord Kitchener.

Legal rulings

Defence and Prosecution submissions on both these charges were made. The JA made a number of rulings, including:
- A person is responsible for his actions and those of others at his instigation;[87]
- Military law dictates that an armed man could only be killed so long as he resists and once surrenders must be treated as a prisoner of war;
- Enemies rendered harmless by wounds must not only be spared, but receive medical attention;
- The wearing of Khaki of itself is not an offence, an intention to deceive must be proved;
- In law there is no place for revenge killings based on the settlement of personal grievances. Retaliation under military law has very specific application and does not shelter those who have personal reasons to settle issues or take matters into their own hands to extact revenge;
- Quarter must be given after a soldier surrenders and must be afforded proper trial before any sentence is imposed;
- Manslaughter can only apply in cases of extreme provocation resulting in momentary loss of control;
- Two wrongs don't make a right in law if it is pleaded that other cases had occurred when prisoners were summarily executed;
- The following of superior orders need not be obeyed if they are unlawful, it may however be relevant in mitigation; and
- An Officer is responsible for carrying out unlawful orders and is entitled to refuse to obey an unlawful order.

Errors by the Judge Advocate (JA)

This author's review of the evidence concluded that the JA did not perform his duty to a professional and requisite standard and the convictions were unsafe as the accused suffered prejudice as a result.

In particular, the members of the Courts Martial were not properly directed to a competent standard by the JA on issues including the lawful excuse of obedience to superior orders, evidence of provocation, evidence of the accused's limited military service, their status as volunteers and limited education and ignorance of military law could be used in determining criminal culpability, sentencing provisions and principles in accordance with the Manual of Military Law, admissibility and relevance of evidence of instances of the shooting of Boer prisoners and obedience to orders to shoot prisoners.

Manual of Military Law 1899 (MML)

The accused were not treated in accordance with MML procedures. Starting and ending with the premise that *'ignorance is no defence to a criminal charge'*,[88] the prosecution only needed to prove that prisoners were shot without military authorisation to secure conviction. The defence case on the other hand argued obedience to superior orders, justification due to the principle of reprisal and the accused were only accessories and not principals (who were never charged) as defences to charges of murder.

The MML stated that a right to kill only existed as long as an armed man resists, that quarter should never be refused to men who surrender and it is seldom justified for a man to take the law into his own hands against an unresisting enemy.[89] According to Bleszynski, the literal interpretation of the MML should have been balanced against the customs of law that existed at the time. He claimed that customary law permitted summary execution of enemy combatants in cases in which they were caught wearing British uniform. Bleszynski also argued that customary law permitted retaliation against enemy combatants who committed murder when displaying a white flag.[90]

However, reliance on customary law by defence counsel was problematic as chapter 14 of the MML created more uncertainty when it stated that customs of war are only principles that may be applied depending on the circumstances. The MML did not state that customs had to be applied in preference to the defined laws in the MML.[91]

In examining the performance of Thomas as defending Officer, it should be appreciated that:

- Thomas had the task of representing five accused that potentially exposed him to a conflict in interest, particularly as some

of the accused (Witton and Picton) claimed that they were following the orders of Morant in executing prisoners;
- Thomas was appearing as counsel without assistance from another advocate/instructing solicitor;
- Although Thomas' experience as an infantry Officer in the Boer War was an advantage, he had little experience as an advocate and certainly not before military courts; and
- Thomas only had one opportunity to make submissions regarding the law applicable to charges of murder and principles such as following superior orders. He was bound by rulings made by the JA. In the isolation of South Africa, without diplomatic support or opportunity to consult with Australian authorities or other legal counsel, he had no other avenues of appeal or assistance to petition the British authorities.

Notwithstanding that Thomas was inexperienced as an advocate and had not enjoyed a military legal career that would have put him in the same category as civilian counsel or the counsel who had been retained to prosecute the accused, he did come from a military background and had been a mounted infantry Officer. He had served in South Africa and had experienced firsthand the rigours of fighting an elusive enemy. His experience in an irregular unit would have prepared him for instructions from the accused that they had been fighting the Boers under orders to take no prisoners and to shoot Boer prisoners who wore Khaki.

What kind of Lawyer are you? Major Thomas' performance and rights of the accused

From his retention to defend Lenehan, Thomas faced a difficult brief. He was only afforded a day to prepare his case and was confronted with representing six personnel, a daunting task notwithstanding the principle that accused persons should be represented in a manner that avoided conflicts of interest.

According to Bleszynski, Thomas did a professional job as defence counsel:

'There can be no doubt however that Thomas gave a spirited defence which belied his experience' Despite his background he had little experience in criminal law and next to no experience in military law.'[92]

Denial of Rights — the Conspiracy

On the day of the first Courts Martial, Thomas only had a short time to converse with his clients yet according to the MML a failure to give a prisoner full opportunity of preparing his defence and free communication with others for the purpose, may invalidate the proceedings unless waived under Rules of Procedure 104[93]. This rule required the Court to balance the right of the accused to an adjournment and preparing a defence against the requirements to proceed with a Court Martial as soon as possible.

Did Thomas consider that his duty was to ensure that he was sufficiently prepared to represent the accused? Section 33 of the MML stated:

'The prisoner is to have proper opportunity to prepare his defence and liberty to communicate with his witnesses and legal adviser or other friend. The object of the rule is to give the prisoner full opportunity to prepare his defence but not to enable him to postpone his trial.'[94]

MML procedure rule No 13 further provided:

'A prisoner for whose trial by court martial has been ordered to assemble shall be afforded proper opportunity of preparing his defence and shall be allowed free communication with his witnesses and with any friend or legal adviser with whom he may wish to consult.'

Rule 13 also stated:

'A failure to give the prisoner full opportunity of preparing his defence and free communication with others for the purpose may invalidate the proceeding.'[95]

If Thomas considered this provision, it was not apparent as the Courts Martial proceeded. If he did make application for an adjournment for more time to prepare a defence and this had been refused, he had little choice but to proceed.

His only other option was to make direct application to Lord Kitchener to intervene as the convening authority. The lack of time for Thomas to prepare the defence case in accordance with provisions of the MML certainly prejudiced a fair trial, and should have invalidated the proceedings in accordance with Rule 13 of the MML. Had Thomas had time to seek instructions from the accused he may have used the opportunity to consider matters such as motions for separate trials and separate representation.

Gunter in *Outlines of Military Law* [96] explained the rights of an accused in preparation of his defence in reference to MML. Gunter stated that in the interests of justice an accused must be afforded a number of privileges, including:

- Be given as much or less time as is practicable before trial;
- An accused may make a statement in mitigation of punishment;
- May call witnesses and examine witnesses in defence; and
- May make a defence and ask for reasonable defence.[97]

It is extraordinary that the accused, who were arrested on 21st October 1901, (Morant about a week later), were placed in solitary confinement for three months while a court of inquiry was conducted and they were denied any contact with relatives in Australia and Government representatives. Even the military chaplain Brough was not permitted to visit them while the inquiry was conducted in such secrecy. The accused were given no information as to their possible fate and no opportunity to consult Thomas until the night before their trials commenced on 16th January 1902.

Despite the best efforts of Thomas and the persuasive evidence in favour of an adjournment to prepare for trials involving very serious charges, fairness did not prevail in accordance with the MML.

The Commander In Chief's Order — Shooting Prisoners

Lord Kitchener did not give evidence as a witness at the trials. Instead his secretary, Colonel Hamilton appeared. He denied the existence of orders that prisoners were to be summarily shot. With the luxury of post-trial research, many documents were discovered that suggest Lord Kitchener had issued orders about the treatment of prisoners, including execution for those caught wearing Khaki. Some of these documents included an order issued by Lord Kitchener on 3 November 1901 to British Commanders in South Africa, two months prior to the Courts Martial.

> *'In certain cases of Boers captured disguised in British uniform I have had them shot, but as the habit of so disguising themselves before an attack is becoming prevalent, I think I should give a general instruction to Commanders that Boers wearing British should be shot on capture.'*[98]

The shooting of prisoners was a controversial aspect and one that has attracted comment by historians. Considered in context of a war being fought by regular British soldiers, (who were versed in the intricacies of military law) and colonial volunteers, (who were ignorant of laws of war), it clearly provided Thomas with a significant hurdle to address in his defence of the accused.

Perhaps fearing that Lord Kitchener may be accused of conspiring to murder Boer prisoners, evidence (including the testimony of Hamilton that no such orders were in fact issued by Lord Kitchener), emerged that what Lord Kitchener did was approve the execution of prisoners only **after** they had been tried by Court Martial and had not condoned summary execution. This interpretation was favourable to Lord Kitchener and challenged his critics who claim that his order was a 'green light' to execute prisoners without trial. However, critics of Lord Kitchener claim that if Morant and Handcock were guilty of murder and that such orders did exist, then Lord Kitchener should have been charged with conspiracy to commit murder.

Had Thomas been successful in preparing the defence case, he may have located additional witnesses and documentary evidence that orders to summarily shoot prisoners had existed. Adequate time to prepare the defence may have ensured that Thomas could have arranged to serve Lord Kitchener with a subpoena to appear as a witness so he could be examined about the orders, including the one of 3rd November 1901. If this had occurred, Thomas could have secured acquittals on all the charges of murder or inciting to murder. In the case of conviction, proof of Lord Kitchener's orders could have provided Thomas with persuasive mitigation to argue that Morant and Handcock be shown mercy and not sentenced to death.

Constitution of the Court

Another issue that may have escaped the attention of Thomas (and the JA) was the procedural rule that stated that the court should include one Officer from an irregular unit like the BVC.[99] The court was comprised of six regular British Officers and this fact failed to ensure that at least one court member could account for the rigours that irregulars faced in fighting Boer commandos.[100]. This omission may have provided a ground of appeal or review by the Crown although it appears if the defect was discovered, it did not affect the confirmation of the convictions and penalties. Nevertheless, it was a technical point that could have delayed the trials and given Thomas more time to prepare the defence cases.

Jurisdiction

The principle of jurisdiction of Court Martial trial was recognised in British military law and expressed as follows:

> '*A prisoner moreover may validly object to the jurisdiction of the court if it appear that they have no proper authority for taking cognizance of the crime, as if a soldier were arraigned before a court martial for a crime cognizable only be the civil courts or arraigned before a regimental court martial upon a capital charge.*'[101]

There is no evidence that Thomas turned his mind to jurisdiction. The presence of the four accused in South Africa fighting the Boer as members of irregular units formed in Australia is fact. However, what is not clear is whether they were subject to the provisions of the British Army Act and the Manual of Military Law.

The MML provided:

> 'The court having ascertained the validity of their constitution will then consider whether the prisoner to be tried is amenable to their jurisdiction and whether the charge is properly framed, if not satisfied the court should adjourn and report to the convening authority.'[102]

Did Thomas consider the issue of jurisdiction? In the absence of a court transcript it is impossible to say. Witton's recollection in his book makes no mention of the jurisdictional issue. In addition, there is no record of such an application being made and recorded in the notes of the Judge Advocate. It is reasonable to expect that a competent advocate with sufficient preparation would have considered the issue, sought instructions from his client/s, have made an objection to the court and put the prosecution to the proof that the Australian accused were subject to the laws of war and British military law. Experienced counsel would have been aware that the accused were facing very serious charges for which the penalty was death and that any challenge to issues such as jurisdiction of the court should be scrutinised and argued before the court.

The MML states, '*None of these tribunals* (meaning Courts Martial), *has power to try any person unless he is subject to military law as provide by the Army Act.*'[103]. This provision was fundamental to the trials of the accused and one would expect that this issue would have been considered by the Officers of the court including Thomas. The issue of jurisdiction is a matter that would have required consideration of Part V of the *Army Act 1879*. Perhaps an experienced counsel would have reviewed the matter in the context of the recruitment of the accused in Australia and their service in the British military as volunteer Officers pursuant to section 175 of the Army Act. Section 177 of the Army Act also provided that volunteers raised in India or any other colonies were subject to British military law.[104]

Writ of Habeas Corpus — A Remedy Lost

If Thomas had raised doubts about the jurisdiction of the Courts Martial to try the accused, he could have sought an adjournment from the convening authority to consider the matter. In addition, he could have sought a writ of habeas corpus pursuant to Section 23 of the Army Act. This section provides:

> '... any person who is detained in what he conceives to be illegal custody by order of a court martial or other military authority can apply for a writ of habeas corpus. This writ is one of the 'corner stones' of British common law, being a remedy for a person wrongfully deprived of his liberty.'[105]

This writ had application to all civil and military jurisdictions at the time of the Boer War and could have been used by Thomas to gain the release of the accused pending a decision about jurisdiction.

Regardless of whether Thomas was "alive" to the jurisdictional issue, the members of the court, and at least the JA would have been aware that the MML stipulated criminal and civil liability for court Officers if a Court Martial 'assumes jurisdiction which the law does not sanction.'[106]

Separate Courts Martial

The principle of separate trials for accused persons charged with the same offence/s collectively, such as conspiracy has been a significant aspect of trial procedure enshrined in common and statue law. MML section 50 provided for separate trials in instances where several prisoners are charged with committing an offence collectively. The justification for such an application is that the evidence of one, some or more of the other prisoners will be material to his defence.[107]

There is no evidence in the JA's notes or Witton's book[108] that records if the accused made such an application at the instigation of Thomas. Should such an application have been made? While it is possible that Thomas considered the matter, it is probable that no such application was made. It is also possible that the matter was raised by Thomas but dismissed by the accused on his advice. Noting that the accused were charged collectively with the same offences of killing or conspiring to kill Boers and the defence issue of following orders was raised in the trial, an application for separate trials for each accused should have made in the interests of justice.

Major Thomas' conduct of the defence — What did he miss?

Thomas made a number of submissions to the Courts Martial about the criminal culpability of the accused. He also examined the accused and cross-examined prosecution witnesses. Reference to these submissions and examination of witnesses are included in Witton's book and the notes of the Reuter reporter who attended the trial.

Thomas took a pragmatic view of the prosecution evidence. While he didn't dispute the death of the missionary Heese, the prisoner Visser and other Boers, he argued that there was insufficient evidence to convict Morant and Handcock. The evidence led by Thomas focused on:

- orders received by Morant from his superior Officer, Captain Hunt;
- what the custom was in dealing with adversaries who used guerrilla tactics to fight the British; and
- the practices used by irregular units and in some cases regular British troops against an enemy who failed to fight in accordance with the laws of war and accepted custom.

Reporting of evidence was recorded in the *Daily Telegraph* newspaper on 17 April 1902. According to the newspaper, in response to the charge of killing Boer prisoners, Thomas called a number of witnesses who stated that Boers who wrecked trains, wore British uniform or articles of Khaki or murdered British soldiers (who were wounded and captured), were to be summarily executed. It was also reported that Thomas urged the court to accept that the actions of the accused had amounted to justified reprisal against a ruthless enemy.

The submissions were not accepted by the court. It was also reported that the Judge Advocate had ruled that prior actions of summary execution by other individuals or units did not excuse the actions of the accused.[109]

In response to the charge of killing two Boer men and a youth, the newspaper stated that Thomas submitted the accused had acted in accordance with the "take no prisoners order". He also submitted the accused were

Chapter 11: *Brief to appear far from home*

satisfied that the three Boers were at war with the British and were part of the group which had mutilated Captain Hunt. The court rejected this submission and agreed with the prosecution that the three Boers had surrendered, had not resisted and should have been tried by a military court. The court also rejected the reprisal argument put by Thomas.

With respect to the charge of murdering the missionary Heese, it appears Thomas successfully created doubt in the minds of the trying Officers. The Crown's case alleged that Handcock and Morant conspired to shoot Heese as he had been a witness to the detention of the eight Boers and may have alerted Boer commanders that the eight prisoners had been summarily executed. Handcock and Morant were acquitted of the charge. The Crown's case was weak and the charge relied on the prosecution to prove the charge beyond reasonable doubt. Thomas also led evidence from witnesses, including Handcock that amounted to an alibi, namely that he had been visiting two Boers when it was alleged that he had shot Heese under the order of Morant. However, to illustrate the difficulties that face counsel when representing accused persons is the expectation that counsel will get honest and frank instructions. This appears not to have been the case with respect to the charge of killing Heese.

In a letter in October 1929, Witton wrote to Thomas and discussed the circumstances about the charge of killing Heese. In short, Witton told Thomas that Handcock had admitted to him (Witton) that he had shot Heese on the order of Morant. *'I believe Morant got Handcock to deny the previous statement in which he made a clean breast of everything and they got to work to frame up an alibi which you know was successful and the means of their acquittal.'*[110] This assertion by Witton must have been devastating to Thomas as it confirmed that he had been misled by his clients and had unwittingly been a party to their deception. Witton's letter continued, *'Personally, I think the attitude you take with regard to Morant and Handcock and the Heese case is not the right one.'* This letter that was written so long after the trial demonstrates the effect that it must have had on Witton and Thomas. It demonstrates that Witton regarded Thomas as perhaps naive, inexperienced and too trusting of his clients. Would a more experienced counsel have been as trusting or able to get his clients to give honest instructions?

Mitigation

Witton's book does not contain any reference to pleas in mitigation made by Thomas, but implies that Thomas used his experience as a soldier to effect. The mitigating factors became apparent with the examination of witnesses and statements tendered by Thomas to the court. It should also be noted that the recommendations for mercy made by the court included reference to matters such as the accuseds' previous good character, ignorance of military law, that they had been profoundly affected by the mutilation and death of Hunt and good service during the war. It is reasonable to suggest that the recommendations made reflected the evidence tendered and submissions made by Thomas.

In Thomas' summing up in the case of the murder of eight Boer prisoners, he said of the Carbineers in the Spelonken:

> 'they had to work over a vast area of difficult country where in small patrols and parties they had literally to hunt down the shifting bands of enemy, in kloofs and almost inaccessible places, taking their lives in their hands. And sufficient evidence has come during these cases to show how excellently their work was done, even the prosecution admit that these Boers were of a bad class, and that this was the character of some if not all of the eight men alleged to have been murdered.'[111]

Thomas' submission was simple, reflected his own military experience and conditions that existed in conducting military operations. Although it didn't clear the accused of criminal responsibility, the plea must have had some influence as recommendations for mercy were made by the court in each trial.

Principle of Condonation

In his diligent defence of the accused, Thomas used every opportunity to represent the interest of his clients. However, he may have missed an opportunity to put a plea that may have secured pardons for his clients. During the trial, the fort at Pietersburg was attacked by Boers led by General Beyers on two occasions, once on 22 January and again the next day.

The first attack was successful for the Boers, however in the second attack the Boers were met with fierce resistance. Incredibly, Handcock, Witton and Morant were released from their cells and given firearms.

> 'These two Officers climbed on to a block house roof and from an exposed position poured a hot fire into the Boers as they closed in. They fought fearlessly until the Bores were driven off in a north easterly direction. Beyers second attack had been a complete failure and some of his men had fallen a mere few yards from the block house.'[112]

Renar noted that the officers were:

> '...brought out of their cells to help fight for the lives and freedom gaolers, Morant was in command at his own prison, and right gallantry he held himself fighting like the brave man that he was, and having probably in his hear more hope than fear of death since an evil fate threatened him just then so sorely. The other too, Lenehan, Picton, Handcock and Witton showed out as men of courage.'[113]

In addition to the actions of the accused, Handcock was credited by Witton with killing the Boer leader Beyers. During their confinement the accused were also involved in at least one other incident when they were called to bear arms. En route from Pretoria to Pietersburg on 31st January 1902 during their confinement for trial by Courts Martial their train halted near Warm Baths Station as Boers had been sighted on the rail line. This occurrence caused concern as Boers had been very successful in attacking, derailing trains, killing British soldiers and damaging rail property. Witton claimed:

> 'A member of the court came to our little sheep-truck and for the second time during our trial we were ordered to stand to arms.'[114]

Although no offensive action against the Boers occurred, the fact remains Morant, Handcock and Witton were ordered to bear arms and they did so even though they were in confinement.

Condonation is the excusing of an offence by virtue of mitigating circumstances such as an act of bravery after a military offence has been committed. '*The discharge of duty involves condonation, the performance of a duty of honour and trust after knowledge of a military offence ought to convey a pardon.*'[115] Further, Article 450 of the King's Military Regulations stated that an offender: 'is *not to be required while in arrest or confinement to perform duties except by order of the Commanding Officer or in an emergency or on the line of march.*'

The principle of condonation received judicial sanction in the 19th century:

'When any offence has been committed by Officer or soldier and that offence not punished or forgiven but advisedly overlooked, the person implicated being continued in his employment these circumstances are held to be a good plea of condonation and a bar to further proceedings.'[116]

In a despatch dated 11 April 1813, Lord Wellington stated:

'No soldier should be put on duty having hanging over him the sentence of a court martial.'[117]

Witton raised the plea of condonation, (through his counsel, Sir Issac Issacs, noted jurist, legislator and later Chief Justice and Governor General of Australia) in his petition to the King and this together with the other matters in the petition influenced the decision to grant his release. However, the question remains, why was condonation not raised by Thomas as a plea to the court?

The rules of procedure stated, '*if he offers a plea in bar the court shall record it as well as his general plea.*'[118] There is no record in the JA's notes or the court's decision transcript and recommendation for mercy. Witton makes no mention of a plea for condonation in his book. One may speculate why the plea was not made by Thomas and whether a more experienced military advocate may have raised the issue.

The absence of a plea of condonation by Thomas could have been due to his lack of military experience, insufficient time to discuss the issue with his clients or because he was not aware of its existence. An opinion of Helen Styles, lecturer in International Communication at Macquarie University and member of the Red Cross Committee on International Humanitarian law summarises the view of the legal proceedings and condonation and concluded the convictions were unsafe:

> 'I agree strongly with the argument that Morant, Handcock and Winton deserve to have the conviction quashed as unsound on technical grounds. They deserve to be pardoned on the basis of military practice and opinion juris, in accordance with Wellington's belief that the performance of a duty of honour and trust after knowledge of a military offence ought to convey a pardon.'[119]

It appears from the evidence that the trials were not conducted fairly, serious mistakes were made at every point from the arrest through to the executions. Regrettably, Thomas appears to have missed the opportunity to argue a significant point of law that may have saved his clients from death sentences!

Sentences — Denial of Right of Military Redress / Crown Appeal

Morant, Handcock and Witton were transported to Pretoria on 21st February 1902. On 26th February, the convicted Officers were informed by the Governor of Pretoria's gaol that they were to be executed the next day.

Witton's chilling description of the drama as Thomas desperately tried to save his clients. Witton stated:

> 'During the day Major Thomas visited us, the terrible news had almost driven him crazy, he rushed away to find Kitchener but was informed by Colonel Kelly that the Commander In Chief was away. He then begged

Colonel Kelly to have the execution stayed for a few days until he could appeal to the King, the reply was the sentences had already been referred to England and approved by the authorities there. There was not the slightest hope, Morant and Handcock must die.'[120]

Notwithstanding Thomas' attempt to have the sentences reviewed, the prisoners were removed to Pretoria without Thomas' knowledge. When Thomas discovered this, he was furious and rushed to Pretoria to try and intervene. His effort was also mirrored by Morant and Handcock. Morant petitioned Colonel Kelly, (who had been the Adjutant General responsible for ordering the Courts Martial). According to Witton, Kelly responded by rejecting the plea and told Morant: *'be prepared to bear it like a man.'* [121]

Conspiracy to pervert the course of justice

Handcock wrote to the Australian Government and begged for mercy on account of his family. Handcock's letter was returned to him. Witton also claimed that he sent two telegrams to Australia, but later learned they had been suppressed.[122] These actions by the British authorities (if true) were unfair and designed to frustrate any plea for mercy by Australian authorities and relatives of Handcock and Morant. The only other hope the accused had was for the confirming authority to direct that the sentences be referred back to the Courts Martial for revision. In such a case, a court could have substituted a lesser sentence. Given that the pleas for mercy of the court were rejected by Lord Kitchener and the sentences approved, it was unlikely that he would have returned the sentences for revision in accordance with the MML.[123]

Crown Appeal

An appeal could have succeeded if Thomas had raised evidence of a miscarriage of justice. According to Clode:

'The only appeal is by way of memorial to the Crown acting through the Secretary of State. It is the usual practice to refer the matter to the

Chapter 11: *Brief to appear far from home*

Judge Advocate General and if need be to the Law offices of the Crown for report that no man may suffer from error in the tribunal.'[124]

Assuming that Thomas was aware of the appeal and the revision process, perhaps communication with the Judge Advocate General and Crown offices was either not possible or delayed.

The fact that Lord Kitchener made himself unavailable immediately after the sentences were announced suggests that he contemptuously denied any opportunity to the accused or Thomas to seek his reconsideration. This action could be viewed as ignoring due process and the intent of the MML and affording the opportunity for these men to seek revision. The MML stated:

'The prisoners should have had the privilege of being able to petition the confirming authority (Kitchener) and /or the reviewing authorities using normal channels. An Officer should not have to be disposed to push to extremes his right his complaint before the Sovereign.'[125]

As a general rule, capital sentences were carried out quickly to minimise the anguish of the accused. However, it may have been done to frustrate any appeal by the accused and Thomas or to minimise interference by the Australian Government. Lord Kitchener either deliberately or carelessly omitted to advise the Australian Government of the outcomes of the trial and the pending executions. This failure by a senior British Officer has fuelled speculation that Lord Kitchener ensured that the court decisions would not be interfered with. This behaviour by Lord Kitchener gives rise to the allegation that he should have been investigated for conspiring to pervert the course of justice (an offence according to the law of 1902).

The circumstances that led to the execution of Morant, Handcock and the sentencing of Witton to penal servitude were characterised by indecent haste and a disregard for the rule of law. Although the MML did not prescribe a process to appeal convictions and sentences, it did contain some checks and balances against excesses in the conviction and sentencing of convicted persons.

This author's view is that Morant, Handcock and Witton were denied an appeal against their convictions and sentences and a plea to the King. They were also prevented from communicating with their relatives, the Australian Government and most importantly the sovereign King who could have examined their pleas for clemency. Had the executions been stayed for a few days, Morant, Handcock and Witton could have discussed their options with Thomas, and sought advice from the Australian Government.

The days prior to the officers being advised of their convictions and sentences were characterised by a shameful orchestration by military command to deny the convicted any hope of review. This was contrary to the principles of justice embodied in the theory and practice of military and common law.

Modern day Jurist and noted human rights lawyer, Geoffrey Robertson, AO, QC expressed his concern when he reviewed the evidence about the whole trial process and denial of appeal as follows:

> 'Part of the unfairness of the trial and I guess the final unfairness was denying any right of appeal these men were convicted in the afternoon and hung at dawn the next day and that was done deliberately to prevent them from using forms of appeal which existed to prevent the Australian Government even knowing of this. That was an outrageous insult to Australia which was of course federated the year before so it was a deeply offensive behaviour squalled and really a cover up because there was nothing other than a deal of guilt among the British army at the time'.

Executions — Ready, Aim, Fire!

The recommendations for mercy concerning Morant and Handcock were ignored by Lord Kitchener, but Witton's sentence was commuted to life imprisonment. Morant and Handcock were executed on **27th February 1902** in the grounds of the Pretoria gaol in the presence of about 30 people including Australian soldiers, including a number of BVC men.[126]

Chapter 12:

Protest Upon Protest

This author places great credibility on Thomas' writings. It must be appreciated that he sat through the trials, "sifted" through evidence, examined witnesses and had firsthand exposure to the evidence for and against his clients. His writings are one of the few 'eye' witness accounts that have survived to this day and as such are important.

The other credible source contemporaneous with the records of Thomas and Witton are from the Reuters correspondent who attended the trails and reported the experience for the *British Times* newspaper. (Appendix F)

This author's view is that the writings of Thomas and the Reuters correspondent rate highly alongside those of Witton, who survived to tell his story of what he witnessed during the investigation, trials and sentencing processes. The consistency in Thomas' writings from which he does not deviate, and immediately after the executions, protested to Major Lenehan:[127]

> 'I am full of bitterness. I cannot express my feelings. But when the time comes, if I am spared, I will. I know all that I expect ever will be known, and I am too true an Australian to shirk plain speaking if need be. And need there will be, I think. What I resented was dragging out a lot of details unless it was essential. I did not contemplate a sudden and unappealable death sentence. I thought the absolute acquittal in the Heese case would mean at most a term of penal servitude, which could be remitted later on.'

2nd May 1902, Thomas to The Hon. The Premier, Perth, West Australia.

Thomas wrote to the Premier of Western Australia on 2nd May 1902.[128] In the letter, Thomas attached a statement and asked the Premier to arrange for the statement to be published in a Perth newspaper. The Premier refused Thomas' request and instead sent it to the then Acting Prime Minister for consideration. In the statement, Thomas made comments including that his clients had followed orders not to take prisoners, their actions were sanctioned under reprisals against a ruthless enemy, the reprisals were legal and justifiable, the British press had attributed horrors and enormities to the BVC and his clients that had not occurred, the trial and sentencing of his clients had occurred without any reference by the British to the Australian Government. (Appendix E)

Thomas' comments were direct and borne by obvious grief about how his clients had been treated, particularly with the imposition of the death penalty.

> *'Personally, I think it almost an insult to our nationality, when the same is distinctly pointed out, to put one of our soldiers to death without any reference whatever (as appears to be the case with Lieutenant Handcock) to his Government.*
>
> *'As for Handcock the most that can be urged against him is that he had an exaggerated idea of patriotism and soldierly duty. He simply obeyed the orders of Morant, who alleged that the reprisals were legal and justifiable.'*

Thomas made a heart-wrenching plea for the plight of Handcock's family:

> *'I shall never cease to grieve for him and I feel his death very, very bitterly. Pending fullest particulars, I would ask the public, especially those of his own State, to believe what I say about him; and as he left three young children unprovided for, I pray my fellow countrymen or their kindheartedness, not to forget these poor little ones thus INS by a hard misfortune left fatherless. I pledged myself to poor Handcock that Australia would not forget the children of a brave soldier torn from them by severely (too severely) hard luck.'*

The response from the Western Australia Premier's office dated 6th June 1902 addressed to Thomas gives a telling clue that the issues Thomas raised in his correspondence caused concern and embarrassment. It stated in part:

> 'The Premier is, however, unable to comply with your request as he cannot be in any way associated with the publication of a statement which might be considered a reflection upon the Military Authorities in South Africa.'

Thomas concluded his statement by declaring his intention to advocate the case on his return to Australia and bring his concerns to the attention of the public.

17th May 1902, Thomas to Hon. John See, Premier of New South Wales.

> 'I say, and always will say, that Handcock's life should have been spared — for he was a splendid stamp of man, and with a young family. I also consider that Lt Morant should not have been put to death; but your Govt of course is specially concerned with Handcock. He was a man for whom I had the very greatest regard. Whatever he did (and it was very little) was in conscientious obedience to orders received.'

6th June 1921, Thomas wrote of his pain and anguish

> 'I was present at the burial and helped to carry them and placed the Australian flag on their grave. I have a photograph of this somewhere. It is not true as stated in Bushman and Buccaneer that the burial was not fully and properly conducted, for it was. All that I wrote in that letter is true and much more might have been written and may yet be written for the full facts have never been made known, also I have the whole proceedings of the courts martial held at Pietersburg, correspondence etc. The whole affair is a tragedy and might form a tragedy if written for one.'[129]

On 14 June 1923, Thomas to the Editor of the Sydney Morning Herald, Sydney:

> 'the detachment with which Morant served was taken out of the command of Major Lenehan and placed under that of a certain "Captain" Taylor, under special order of Lord Kitchener........ Taylor was in supreme command of this special detachment, both before and after the arrival of Hunt and Morant, and though a charge was preferred against him in connection with these previous shootings, there was no conviction. The true story of the Bush Veld Carabineers has never been told, but perhaps someday it will be.'

Despite his protest and failure to convince any authority to convene an inquiry into the circumstances surrounding the trial of his clients, Thomas appears to have resigned to the fact that he would remain unheard.

In Australia, he did not resume his solicitor's practice immediately. Shields & Carnegie revealed that Thomas begged the Australian Government to grant Handcock's last wish, to help his wife and kids, but ended up helping them himself.[130] He made it clear in a letter to NSW Premier John See that Handcock and Morant shouldn't have been shot. Thomas asked him to start an inquiry — but none came. His advertisement in the *Star* which had informed clients that another solicitor was handling his business in his absence only reverted back to Thomas on 13th August.

Thomas resumed his civilian life, but things would never be the same again. Having established the tone of Dr Bennett's article, this author agrees with Bennett that, *'Thomas went home emotionally crippled by his war experience. His pride and self-esteem were crushed. He never recovered'*. However, the reasons we shall have to agree to differ on as neither of us can claim to be psychologists.

Whereas Bennett puts it down to *'deflated vanity'*, this author thinks that the experience destroyed his value system, *'the paths of truth, honour, manliness'* which were instilled in him as a young man came crashing down about him during that fateful month of the Courts Martial. The great pity is that he never published the *'facts based on private information by courts martial officers'* he claimed to have, as it would have given us a greater insight into what traumatised his mind. Perhaps it was the constant "re-playing" of the Courts Martial in his mind and the lack of a cathartic outlet which caused things to become distorted. Whilst this author does not claim that this excuses Thomas of every wrong he may have committed, it is worth bearing this preface in mind as we chart Thomas' slow, sad *denouement.*

The first in a long series of clashes with officialdom came when Thomas resigned his commission voluntarily over the issue of writing a book about the affair and was not dismissed as Davey wrongly alleges in his book, *Breaker Morant and The Bushveldt Carbineers.*[131] Davey doesn't state why Thomas had been dismissed and what logic he applied to suggest that this tainted his defence in the Morant case.

Thomas resigned his commission because the question of his military status arose when he decided to write his account of the Courts Martial. The attitude of the Army was that if he intended to publish material impugning decision of a Court Martial — then he had better resign! Thomas replied that he didn't intend to 'impugn' but to publish the plain facts of the matter. He made it clear that he tried the case 'NOT AS AN ARMY MAN BUT AS A PRIVATE PRACTITIONER OF LAW' — but was resigning anyway out of honour.[132] Despite the inscription on his gravestone put there by the Commonwealth Graves Commission, he never used the title "Major" after this incident.

In any event, the book did not appear. Bennett seized upon this and asks why he did not use his newspaper *'to publish the facts'* as he claimed he wanted to do. This author's thinks that Thomas decided to defer to Witton when he was released in 1903 Thomas' probable rationale was that Witton served with Morant in the BVC, was there during the now infamous shootings, had served time in prison and all these factors would give the story more impact than if Thomas had written it.

> *'I'm a lawyer. I go for due process; I go for fairness and equity — these values mean a lot to me.'*[133]

Thomas' Performance

Thomas' overall performance was compelling given the difficult circumstances that confronted him. He represented several accused, (in hindsight trying to represent so many was a mistake) and was afforded insufficient time to prepare himself to defend Lenehan let alone other accused. Against all of this Thomas' reputation has been recognised by many, including Denton who stated:

> 'No matter the outcome of the courts martial there is no way in which James Francis Thomas could have been accused of failure as an advocate.'[134]

Denton asserted that by the time the trial commenced:
- the accused had been through a difficult Inquiry;
- had endured twelve weeks of solitary confinement without legal or other advice;
- had no time to brief Thomas who had been appointed as defence counsel the day prior to the commencement of the trial;
- Thomas had no knowledge of the accused, the circumstances that led to their arrest or the military law that they had been accused of breaching; and
- Thomas had no court experience that could have prepared him for the rigour of a military trial.[135]

Thomas' application got Lenehan acquitted of one charge and only a reprimand for the offence for which he was convicted (for which the maximum sentence was death).

He also got Morant and Handcock acquitted of one offence of inciting and instigating the murder of Heese and constructed a plea Morant, Handcock and Witton that resulted in the court making recommendations for mercy to Lord Kitchener.

The Reuters Correspondent's Account

The report about the trial proceedings appeared in the British *Times* newspaper on 17 April 1902.[136] (Appendix F)

The opportunity for a media representative to write about the trials was extraordinary given Lord Kitchener's efforts to keep the arrest, investigation and trial of the accused a secret to the point of not appointing a defending officer until a day prior to the first trial commencing on 17 January 1902. Lord Kitchener must have been infuriated to discover the *Times* article had been published, but relieved it had not been made public in an edition during the trials proceedings in January and February 1902.

The reporter's account of the proceedings is accurate in the sense that it corroborates the version recorded by Lieutenant Witton in his book, *Scapegoats of the Empire*. While the correspondent did not provide editorial opinion about the style and effectiveness of Thomas' advocacy as a trial lawyer, the recorded detail of the evidence was meticulous. It explained what Thomas did to represent his clients on their instructions that they had followed orders to take no prisoners and believed they were justified in doing so.

Woolmore's opinion was:

> 'The trials and executions had a deep and lasting impact on Thomas and affected the rest of his life in many ways. He believed the BVC officers had been badly and unfairly dealt with. In a letter dated 27 February 1902, the day Morant and Handcock faced the firing squad Thomas wrote, "I know all that I expect ever will be known, and I am too true an Australian to shirk plain speaking if need be. And need there will be I think, I did not contemplate a sudden and unappealable death sentence".'[137]

The opinions of Senior Legal Counsel & a Moot Court hearing, 2013

> 'Justice knows no time frame, were these men fairly treated? Were they given a fair trial? Even today those issues are important as a matter of law, as a matter of history, as a matter of respect for their families. Congruent with these values is Australia's tradition of trial according to due process, the presumption of innocence and that an accused is entitled to a fair and unbiased hearing. With the passing of time, this case has been singled out for particular attention to our commitment to such principles and values.'[138]

This author put his research to the test and had it examined by senior legal counsel in 2013, when he participated in the filming of a documentary for Foxtel, *Breaker Morant — The Retrial*. The success of the documentary was due in part to this author's production of a 'moot trial in the Supreme Court of Victoria on 20th July 2013.

Until this author researched the case, no-one had objectively looked at the legality of the trials and the sentences. The Moot Court hearing was an opportunity to expose this author's research to exacting critique.

At the Moot appeal, a group of Australia's most prominent jurists, including barristers, Gerard Nash QC, Alexander Street SC, Andrew Kirkham QC, Gary Hevey and others heard the appeal against the convictions and sentences and found that the men had not received fair trials according to British Military and Common law of the period. The Court ruled that the executions were unlawful. The appeal did not acquit the men of the murders, but rather it determined they had been denied fair trials and executed before Major Thomas could lodge appeals against their convictions and sentences. Morant and Handcock were both shot within eighteen hours of being sentenced having been denied their common law and statutory right of appeal. The moot court also focused on Thomas' plea that the men had followed Lord Kitchener's order — under the principle of exacting reprisal against Boer insurgents. Obedience to superior orders was a legitimate defence in 1902, a defence that eluded Thomas' attempt to succeed as legal counsel.

While the Moot Court is not legally binding, it created a legal joust between the British Crown and counsel for Morant, Handcock and Witton. The event was staged as an historic aspect of Australian military and judicial history and centred on the denial of fair trials and a right of appeal for Morant, Handcock and Witton according to military law of 1902. The appeal and arguments for and against were heard by respected Judges for the event, barristers, Andrew Kirkham, QC and Gary Hevey. Counsel for the Crown was led by noted barrister Gerry Nash, QC and Alexander Street, SC (now a Federal Court Judge) and this author, as counsel for Morant, Handcock and Witton.

Alexander Street's submission to the Court was noteworthy and focused on significant evidence that the men were not given fair trials according to the law of 1902. The following is one aspect that he highlighted concerning Thomas' ability to represent his clients and get them fair trials:[139]

> 'J F Thomas, arrived the day before the trial commenced with the limited experience of being a solicitor from Tenterfield. Thomas was a solicitor experienced in probate, conveyancing and petty sessions matters. He had no experience as a criminal advocate and had not served in the Boer War as a legal officer. His ability to defend 5 officers on serious charges without any assistance, including from Australia put him a serious disadvantage. His request for an adjournment was denied. The incarceration of Breaker Morant in the three months leading up to his trial and overlapping the Court of Inquiry, completely deprived him and the other accused of the opportunity of properly preparing his defence or the benefit of any input from the Australian Government.
>
> 'These failures were not mere irregularities but a fundamental denial of the requirements for a fair trial and, as such, the appellants contend give rise to a material miscarriage of justice of sufficient arguability to warrant the continuation of the stay by this court. Those grounds of fundamental irregularity and denial of procedural fairness extend to the role played by Lord Kitchener.'

The Court's Decision

Judges Andrew Kirkham and Gary Hevey recognised that Morant, Handcock and Witton had suffered a fatal denial of justice and a substantial miscarriage of justice in the trials due in part to the inexperience of their counsel, Major Thomas:[140]

> 'It is submitted by counsel for the Crown that the case against the three applicants was, and is, so strong that absent any procedural unfairness as described, their respective convictions were inevitable. However, this is not to the point. We consider that in cases where there has been a significant denial of natural justice and procedural fairness at trial, it would be wrong to uphold a conviction merely because an Appeal Court

is of the opinion that on a proper trial the appellant would inevitably have been convicted. Suggestions to the contrary have no application where an irregularity has occurred which is such a departure from the essential requirements of the law that it goes to the root of the proceedings. If that has occurred then it can be said without considering the effect of the irregularity upon the Court's Martial verdict, that the Applicants have not had a proper trial and there has been a substantial miscarriage of justice.'

The forensic examination of the materials before the court and its decision was strengthened by the very detailed legal opinion of Jerry Nash, QC in late 2013:[141]

'Clearly, in my opinion, the executions were unlawful and motivated otherwise than by a concern for justice. The descendants and relatives of the executed men have legitimate grounds for seeking a review of the circumstances in which those men were killed (unlawfully in my view) by a British firing squad. The failure of natural justice was not a minor failure. It involves a total failure to accord procedural fairness or to comply with the requirements of the Manual of Military Law.'

Respected and Compelling Opinions

A modern-day perspective of Thomas' almost impossible task of getting fair trials for the accused or at least a review and a reduced penalty for Handcock and Morant can be gleamed from modern day legal opinion. The opinions of such eminent jurists, including, Geoffrey Robertson, QC, Gerry Nash, QC, David Denton, QC Alexander Street, SC, Sir Laurence Street, AC, KCMG, KStJ, QC, Dr Howard Zelling, AO, CBE and Charles Francis, QC, is a tribute to the effort of Thomas to address what he argued was an injustice.

Appendix B also contains opinions of community leaders whose views are persuasive in recognizing the injustice done to Morant, Handcock and Witton and the need for resolution.

The opinions not only recognise the injustice, but also corroborate this author's view that Thomas achieved what he could under very oppressive circumstances and the manner in which he was treated by the British Military, as previously discussed.

For example, the legal opinion of noted barrister, human rights advocate and author, Geoffrey Robertson, QC stated:

'Examples abound in military courts of wrongful convictions — from Dreyfus to General Yamashita — and of wrongful acquittals (eg of Col Medina over the My Lai massacre). "Breaker" Morant's trial was a particularly pernicious example of using legal proceedings against lower ranks as a means of covering up the guilt of senior officers and of Kitchener himself, who gave or approved their unlawful 'shoot to kill' order. Morant may have been all too happy to obey it, of course, in which case he deserved some punishment. But it was wrong to use him as a scapegoat for an unlawful policy. I regard the convictions of Morant and Handcock as unsafe.'[142]

In an interview conducted by this author with Robertson in 2013 during the filming of a FOXTEL History Channel documentary, *Breaker Morant, The Retrial*, Geoffrey Roberston stated: [143]

'They were treated monstrously. The case of Morant and Handcock, the two men who were executed, is a disgrace. Certainly by today's standards they were not given any of the human rights that international treaties require men facing the death penalty to be given. But even by the standards of 1902 they were treated improperly, unlawfully and I can make that good by just listing a few of the errors of their courts martial. They were kept in solitary confinement for three months without any legal access, without even telling the Australian Government, their Government, that they were in peril. Whilst the prosecution of course got its witnesses in order but they weren't allowed to approach anyone. They didn't have a lawyer. They got a country solicitor who happened to be serving in the force to defend them at the last moment one day before the trial started. They had no chance, their graves were dug even before. They were convicted at the trial itself. The injustice was outrageous, they weren't allowed to call evidence, they weren't allowed to cross examine, on the vital issue and this was the political aspect of the trial, namely the fact that the higher-ups in the British army all the way up its suggested to Lord Kitchener had given a take no prisoners order.'

The view of current and former politicians about the case are noteworthy and strengthen this author's view that the opinions expressed support Thomas' opinion that his clients were denied fair trials and sentences according to the law of 1902.

Another view that supports Geoffrey Robertson's opinion should be noted. Mr Greg Hunt, Australian MP and Minister of Health, made a statement which is compelling. In an interview with this author for the documentary, *Breaker Morant — The Retrial*, Mr Hunt stated:[144]

'Well I actually agree with Geoffrey Robertson. Not only is he probably the most esteemed international jurist in the Human Rights space that Australia has produced in the last half century, but I think he's right.

'What he is saying is the underlying act was unforgivable, and so we must never try to gloss over that, and we must acknowledge responsibility as a country. However, the response was equally reprehensible where there were many people involved, only Australians were selected out, the third member of the Australian team that was convicted was subsequently subject to a commutation as a result of actions by Sir Isaac Isaacs, and was in fact released from prison. So, of the three members, two were executed, one was... the third one was released, and the Australian Government of the time responded in 1903 by changing the law so as no Australian serving under the British military authorities could ever again be subject to execution. So it's clear that this is not just a historical rewriting, but the fact that in... at the time there was no chance to prepare a defence, there was no chance to call defence witnesses, there was no chance to plead the primary case of acting under express clear orders and indeed British policy, and there was no chance for the Australian Government to be notified, and finally there wasn't even a chance for appeal, there was a conviction in the evening and an execution in

the morning. These things say that the process, the procedure, the trial context were clearly those of a show trial no matter how unforgivable the subject of that trial was.

'Well my view is that any Australian Government at any time should seek final resolution, and if we are elected then I will continue to work within the parliament to see that outcome. Well I think the concern is that two Australians were executed in a summary fashion without justice. Now none of this excuses what was clearly a heinous act in relation to the prisoners under care, but it is time, in my judgment, for a proper independent inquiry. That may not change the decision of the court, it may reverse the decision, or it may say that there were mitigating circumstances that these were actions taken under orders. But there was no justice, there was a summary execution after a sham trial and there deserves to be a full trial. This will not ever excuse their actions, but similarly it is clear that the actions of the colonial administration of those who were running the Boer conflict were equally reprehensible. And if there is a stain on the historic record we need to address it.'[145]

Greg Hunt's insightful analysis and support for a review of the case to achieve a Parliamentary resolution must be respected. However, the refusal of Government in 2018 to act continues to deny the descendants of these men a just outcome and resolution of this controversial case.

In concluding the case for review and addressing the injustice that Thomas tried to address, the following quote aptly identifies what Australia's political leaders should achieve:[146]

'But should our politicians and institutions ever have an attack of conscience, or find the courage to do what New Zealand did in a similar situation and hold an independent judicial review, there are compelling legal grounds for doing so.'

Solitude in Grief

Thomas was deeply affected by the experience of trying to save his clients from the firing squad. The body language in the photograph is confronting. In a letter Thomas wrote home, he stated, *'I feel quite broken up. It is too painful to write about.'*[147]

JF Thomas standing over the grave of the men he couldn't save (photo courtesy of N.Bleszynski)

The Flag — Coincidence or Fate?

Thomas' forlorn and despondent look over the grave and Australian flag has endured to this day. An extraordinary find at the municipal tip at Tenterfield, New South Wales, in 2016, has again focused the attention on Morant, Handcock and Witton.[148]

> *'Items were found in an old hessian bag discarded with other rubbish destined to be buried as land fill! Perhaps the most valuable item is a red ensign Australian flag that bears the handwriting of Major J.F. Thomas. Thomas' comments on the flag bears witness to his claim that*

the men were indeed scapegoats for the crimes of their British superiors for orders to take no prisoners.

'Breaker artefacts include the inscribed Australian flag that draped the grave of Lieutenants Morant and Handcock, some other items have emerged. The following images of the flag bear the handwriting of Major Thomas, inscriptions include: **utter scapegoats of the empire, Lt Henry. H Morant Dec 9th 1864 Feb 27th 1902 RIP, Peter. J Handcock Feb 17th 1868 Feb 27th 1902 RIP**, *a bayonet scabbard with initials HM, silver cigarette case initials, H.M, British penny, used for identification, inscribed* **EDWIN HENRY MORANT** *damaged by what may be a bullet ricochet, a British penny 1900, Queen Victoria, inscribed, good luck to Australian Bushmen Corps 1900. This penny is of great significance since it appears it was minted specifically to honour Australian volunteers.*'[149]

The story of the trial has now been told in many different ways, including the play and film referred to above and the books by Kit Denton (which was fictionalised), and Closed File, 1983,[150] Some matters however are worthy of emphasis:

(1) Firstly, the Australian Government was never notified that Morant, Handcock and Witton had been arrested, held in remand and eventually tried. Witton stated in his book that he wrote home to Australia about his predicament, but none of those letters were delivered, so it seems unlikely that any message from Thomas to the authorities in Australia would have been sent on by the British authorities.

(2) Secondly, Thomas himself wrote in his letter to the *Tenterfield Star*:

'I am determined to have nothing more to do with the South African Irregulars — if I could not serve as an Australian and with Australians, I did not want to serve at all. So I got ... a free passage back to Australia to leave for Cape Town early in January 1902.

'But the Bushveldt Carbineer officers were in trouble, and, on 7th, 8th and 9th of the last mentioned month I received urgent telegrams from Major Lenehan (an Australian) asking me to go to Pietersburg and assist at the court martial.... where I was engaged for about five weeks upon as difficult a task as I suppose ever fell to an advocate... but the true story of the Bushveldt Carbineers has never yet been told. I may yet tell it; but for the present it will be sufficient to say that the task (a self-imposed one) did not end with the tragic end of Lieutenants Morant and Handcock. Lieutenants Witton's relatives cabled to me to assist their efforts. I wrote to Sir Edmund Barton whilst he was in London; wrote to the Royal Commissioner on military law sentences when at Pretoria; attempted (unsuccessfully) to see Mr. Chamberlain on his arrival in the Transvaal; and co-operated with the Australian at Cape Town when they tried (also unsuccessfully) to interview Mr. Chamberlain.'

(3) Thirdly, The Morant trials were probably the only ones in which an Australian was Court Martialed by British Officers. Thomas, a strong supporter of Australian Federation, submitted to the Court Martial that it did not have jurisdiction to hear the trial. Although Morant was born in England and came to Australia, it seems in his late teens and Handcock was a farrier from Bathurst.

(4) Fourthly, George Witton had obviously thought that Thomas had done his best to represent their interests under very difficult circumstances, writing of the events on 25 February, two days before the execution:

'During the day Major Thomas visited us; the terrible news had almost driven him crazy. He rushed away to find Lord Kitchener, but was also informed by Colonel Kelly that the Commander-in-Chief was away, and not expected to return for several days. He then begged Colonel Kelly to

Chapter 12: Protest Upon Protest

have the execution stayed for a few days until he could appeal to the King; the reply was that the sentences already had been referred to England, and approved by the authorities there. There was not the slightest hope. Morant and Handcock must die.'[151]

Witton also wrote:

'Those courts-martial were the greatest farces ever enacted outside of the theatre, and were held purely to conform to the rules of military law. The sentences were decided upon the evidence taken at the court of inquiry, at which no one was given an opportunity of making a defence, or even of denying the slanderous and lying statements made by prejudiced and unprincipled men.'[152]

Morant had written in his statement to the court:

'Captain Hunt had been my most intimate friend in South Africa. We were engaged to two sisters in England....The Boers had left my friend's body, the body of an Englishman and officer, lying stripped, disfigured, and not buried — thrown into a drain like a pariah dog... I have been told that I was never myself after the death of Captain Hunt, and I admit that his death preyed upon my mind when I thought of the brutal treatment he had received.'[153]

Thomas himself submitted to the court that the killing of Visser was legitimate retaliation, and quoted from the manual of military law: -

'Retaliation is military vengeance; it takes place when an outrage committed on one side is avenged by a similar act on the other';[154]

But the British prosecutor, Captain Burns-Begg, saw the killing of Visser in a different way...

'As to Major Thomas' argument, based on the state of the country, could *anything be more preposterous than to say that minor officers are entitled to make war on principles of barbarity, approved only by themselves? If they do so they must abide by the consequences.'*[155]

Andrew Barton "Banjo" Paterson, Australian poet, war correspondent, journalist, lawyer and author

"Banjo" Paterson knew Thomas well. He was a fellow lawyer, frequent visitor to Tenterfield, and a very close contemporary. Paterson was born in 1864, three years after Thomas, and died in 1941, one year before Thomas. Paterson actually married in the Presbyterian Church in Tenterfield on the 8th of April, 1903. Thomas wasn't at Paterson's wedding, as he returned from South Africa about five months later in August 1903. He wrote in a letter to the *Sydney Morning Herald*:

> *'I happened to know all that there was to know about Morant's trial and execution, for the lawyer that defended him, one J.F. Thomas, of Tenterfield, asked me to publish all the papers — evidence, cablegrams, decision, appeal, etc. — a bulky bundle which he carried about with him, grieving over the matter till it seriously affected his mind. He blamed himself, in a measure, for the death of Morant, but I could not see that he had failed to do the best he could with a very unpleasant business.*

"'Morant was sentenced to death," Thomas said, *"but I never believed the execution would be carried out. When I found that the thing was serious I pulled every string I could; got permission to wire Australia, and asked for the case to be reopened so that I might put in a proper defence. It was of no use. Morant had to go. He died game. But I wake up in the night now, feeling that Morant must have believed that he had some authority for what he did and I ought to have been able to convince the Court of it"'*.[156]

This assessment of Thomas' handling of the case for the accused in the Morant trial, written as it is by another lawyer who also reported the Boer War, is probably the most accurate one available. It is an assessment confirmed by Colin Roderick, renowned for his meticulous care with facts. Roderick wrote:

> 'The only legal profession in this and the other courts martial, Major J.F. Thomas, acted for the defence. He performed well in a hopeless case, made more difficult because Morant and Handcock did not tell him the truth.'[157]

A revealing letter

Thomas continued his efforts to expose what had befallen Morant and Handcock. In revealing newspaper articles in March and April 1902, the *Bathurst Free Press* and *Mining Journal* published a letter that was written by Thomas, to Witton's father.[158] (Appendix F).

The letter contains insight into the outrage expressed by Thomas about the manner in which his clients had been treated and the grief he suffered as a result. The letter also explains some of the mitigation surrounding the case and is suggested that Thomas' interpretation may explain the rationale behind the recommendations for mercy made by the Courts Martial. The letter stated in part:[159]

> 'Your son has been sent a prisoner to England and I think it will be wise to defer any active steps concerning him till the Australian Government is in possession of the facts. The defence maintained was that under the customs of war the shooting of these Boers was allowable as they were merely running bandits or marauders. It was proved that in other cases exactly the same procedure was adopted and approved of by other officers. Consequently, you will see that from a soldiers' point of view at any rate the crime was not so dreadful as might appear. I only regret that poor Morant and Handcock did not receive a sentence of penal servitude, but poor fellows they were shot at 18 hours' notice. As counsel for your son and the other officers I should like to see that all the facts from the prisoners' point of view are fairly brought forward. When everything is known you will not think the disgrace amounts to much of anything. War is war and rough things have to be done.'[160]

Perhaps this letter revealed Thomas' realisation that "*by the book*" his clients were guilty of murdering Boer prisoners, but the penalty did not "fit" the crime. He had been denied the opportunity to have mitigating circumstances put by way of a plea to the King for mercy, particularly in light of the mercy recommendations made by the members of the Courts Martial.

The pain and the sense of injustice remained with Thomas. Many years later, in a letter dated 6th June 1921, Thomas wrote:

> 'I was present at the burial and helped to carry them and placed the Australian flag on their grave. I have a photograph of this somewhere. It is not true as stated in Bushman and Buccaneer that the burial was not fully and properly conducted, for it was. All that I wrote in that letter is true and much more might have been written and may yet be written for the full facts have never been made known, also I have the whole proceedings of the courts martial held at Pietersburg, correspondence etc. The whole affair is a tragedy and might form a tragedy if written for one.'[161]

Thomas' opinion and protest received support from Mr J. Heath, an ex trooper who served with the Bushveldt Carbinbeers. In a newspaper report dated 8 May 1902, Heath gave a firsthand account of the actions of Captain Taylor in the execution of 6 Boer prisoners. Heath claimed to be one of the troopers in the firing party and he acted under orders relayed to him by his Sergeant, to shoot the prisoners. He also gave details of the charges against Morant, Handcock and Witton and their defence of obedience to orders to take no prisoners.

Heath also discussed Hunt's direction to Morant about not taking prisoners and Hunt's subsequent murder by Boers.[162] (Appendix F)

Chapter 13:
Reflection

Notwithstanding the efforts of Thomas, there was little he could have done to have secured an acquittal on the murder charges or persuade the convening authority to remit the sentences back to the court for revision. Without prejudice to the British Government, there is a compelling argument for a review of the trials and quashing the convictions. Without agreeing to a process of review of the convictions, Morant, Handcock and Witton will remain "martyrs".

Ironically, it is the view of Lord Kitchener on the subject of the law that recognised Handcock and Morant and the injustice of unfair and politically motivated trials. Lord Kitchener stated:

> *'It does no good to act without the fullest inquiry and strictly on legal lines. A hasty judgement creates a martyr and unless military law is strictly followed, a sense of injustice having been done is the result.'*[163]

Outcome

Thomas did not overcome all odds; he was only partially successful in the defence of his clients and suffered the agonising realisation that two of them were executed. However, it appears he behaved with the utmost integrity and did not refuse to represent the accused at a time when he was disenchanted with the British military and was on his way back to Australia. Although he failed to appreciate the ethics of representing many accused and a possible a conflict of interest, he pressed on with the job without the benefit of an adjournment to prepare the cases. His only reward was his belief that he did his best and acted professionally. Perhaps this was his greatest achievement.

Thomas was a gentleman of impeccable values and was highly regarded in the Tenterfield community. His care for the citizens of Tenterfield was an aspect that he cherished as revealed in an open letter he wrote in the *Tenterfield Star* prior to his second tour of duty to South Africa:

'Having whilst in South Africa arranged for the efficient conduct of my private business and which arrangement will not expire until the early part of next year, I have decided to return to Capetown where certain duties await me.'[164]

Thomas' challenge

Thomas arrived at Pietersburg on the 15th January 1902, the day before the trial was due to start. It was only then that Thomas found out about the other accused and agreed to defend them, though he was not obliged to. Having said that, it would have been un-Australian and not in keeping with Thomas' character to abandon them to fate. It also appears that Thomas' intervention had to be agreed to by the, '...*Gods in Pretoria*' which further suggests that Thomas was only originally scheduled to defend Lenehan.

One can only speculate what was said at Army HQ in Pretoria when they heard that an Australian country solicitor with little civilian and military advocacy experience was to defend the accused on capital charges. It would give an air of legitimacy to the whole affair and satisfy any critics that they had been properly represented and fairly tried — a point Lord Kitchener was at pains to make to Australian Prime Minister Barton after the executions.

It is perhaps on the point of representation that this author is at odds with Dr Bennett. He transposes a reference to Thomas being, '... *impetuous, headstrong and self- opinionated'*, which was made by a passing acquaintance much later in his life when his mind had clearly become unhinged, back to 1902 and has Thomas thrusting '... *his services upon them at a time when, in their bewilderment, the devil they knew seemed better than the one they knew not. It is not hard to imagine that Thomas (in his own perception), having, through his newspaper, guided the paths of statesmen, and held Federal Australia's future in the palm of his hand, was an influential person to be reckoned with, who would soon set this court-martial to rights'.*

Thomas was the proprietor of a small country town newspaper, not the *Sydney Morning Herald*. Again, there is nothing in the pages of the *Star* during the long Federation debate to support the impression that Thomas saw himself in such self-aggrandising terms. It is noticeable that

Chapter 13: Reflection

excerpts from the *Tenterfield Star* are not used to back his argument and nor are they listed as a principal research source.

Bennett makes a big call when he says Lenehan would have known that Thomas was a lawyer of little stature and experience and '... *almost the last person to be entrusted with the careers and lives of his fellows*'. As a lawyer, Bennett fails to address a number of key issues in his discourse, not least the issue of why Lenehan did not defend himself and his fellow compatriots? After all, as a lawyer in the Supreme court of NSW and the Commanding Officer of the BVC in the field, Lenehan was better qualified and better placed to mount an effective defence. Did Lenehan fear that as he was only being held on a minor charge his intervention on behalf of the others might prejudice the outcome of his case and damage his career prospects? Not having been present in that dingy Pietersburg gaol in 1902, this author wouldn't presume to know, but it is an intriguing question. Also, what were the alternatives with the trial a day away? It is a far more likely proposition that Thomas found himself in the position of being the *only* one they could turn to for help. The account that Lenehan gave to NSW MP J.C.L. Fitzpatrick on his return suggests that the Australians were being pressurised and did not feel they could trust Imperial officers.

It is not intended to deal with Thomas' performance as a lawyer or the *ins and outs* of the trial itself at this point, as the legal review section covers that part in full, except to say that Thomas did everything in his power to win every legal point and or, at worst, make a case for mitigation. However, this author agrees with Bennett's observation that Thomas' lack of experience was evident and he did make errors during the proceedings.

If it pleases the Court

The first sign that Thomas knew little of the British Military Law came when he asked for a day's grace to prepare his case. This is something that even the critics of Morant acknowledge — the lack of time to prepare a capital case. Thomas, had no experience of Military Law and was unaware of the rudimentary justice dispensed at British Courts Martial.

In this important respect the film did the story a disservice. It looked like a civilian court, sounded like a civilian court and even used the same legal language, but British Military Courts Martial were not about truth and justice, but crime and punishment. Julian Putkowski, the man who did much to uncover the injustices of British Courts Martials during World War 1, stated:*' first thing you must do is disengage your audience from their cosy, pre-conceived ideas.'*[165] The truth is that a day was all you got to prepare your defence. Many trials took as little as 20 minutes and amounted to little more than a testimony from an officer with the transcript taking up less than half a page.[166] The Courts Martial was not going to be the 'level playing-field' Thomas imagined.

Citing an article by Professor Colin Roderick on "Banjo" Paterson, Bennett confidently brushes aside the allegations that the proceedings were tainted or subject to a cover up by the British authorities. He makes no comment on the many inconsistencies the trial threw up or any new evidence to support his views. More surprisingly for a legal historian, Bennett does not commit himself to what defence Thomas should have employed, other than to admonish his conduct and defence strategy, and offers no further insight into the Courts Martial. Maybe he did not wish to provide additional ammunition for the dreaded "Morant industry", or like Lenehan, he did not wish to risk his reputation.

Returning to Bennett's assertion that during the trial Thomas, *'... adopted the role of lecturer, expatiating on subjects as if to an audience bound in ignorance'*, he *was* talking to an *'... audience bound in ignorance'*. None of the Courts Martial panel including the Advocate General had any legal training and even the replacement advocate, Major Bolton, did not feel he had sufficient legal expertise to try the Heese case.

Thomas failed to win the cases partly due to the tactics he employed and mistakes he made, but in larger measure because of the selective nature of the evidence the prosecution presented and the rigid way the Judge Advocate chose to interpret some points of Law and ignore others. A cover-up began long before the Courts Martial and the key issue was not, as most historians believe, the Heese case.

However, Thomas' defence elicited a great degree of sympathy from the men supposedly prosecuting them. Witton mentions that he more

Chapter 13: Reflection

than once saw a tear in the eye of one of the panel during the case and by the end even the prosecutor, Major Bolton had been won over. The only explanation could be that they were trying men for actions that they themselves had either ordered or witnessed themselves. Yet, those who support Lord Kitchener's actions insist that Lord Kitchener was livid about such breaches of discipline and determined to punish the perpetrators and that the Army and the British Government were in full agreement. As we shall see, were that true they would have ended up shooting more of their own men than the Boers.

The Courts Martial ended on 9th February 1902 and because, unlike Taylor, they had not been acquitted in court they knew they had been found guilty. The sentence was all that remained. However, it never occurred to any of the accused that they might actually be shot for killing Boers. In a letter to his brother, written whilst he awaited his trial, George Witton said confidently;

> '... I shall come out of this all right, they can't surely crucify me. I reckon it will be rough if I'm cashiered'.

Even the cynical Morant felt no need to take up any of the many offers he had to help him escape.

> '... But it is damned rough this treatment from our own British (?) side! However, I put my faith in the Lord and Headquarters, in Pretoria, and hope to see a fox killed and kiss a Devon girl, again'.

As we now know Morant remained incarcerated and met his fate and Witton wasn't cashiered or faced a firing squad.

Hope — A reprieve from execution?

On the eve of the 20th of February 1902, the accused were given more reason for optimism. Despite Bennett's claim of Thomas' incompetent defence, the Courts Martial officers found them not guilty of the Heese killing, which was regarded as the principal case. Despite finding them guilty on the charges of inciting the shooting of Boer combatants, the Courts Martial cited seven separate points of mitigation in their Recommendation to Mercy. Thomas won one of the two key points in the case — that Morant et al killed the Boers to avenge their senior officer, Captain Hunt. The delivery of a case of champagne to the prisoners' cells confirmed their opinion that they had escaped death. One can only imagine their feelings when Lord Kitchener ordered the death sentence and ignored their pleas in his telegrams to Roberts and Barton (post the executions) where he stated that there were, '... *no grounds for mitigation.*'[167]

What the trying officers didn't know was that in practical terms a recommendation to mercy was meaningless. It carried little weight and effectively passed the responsibility further up the chain of command where the ultimate decision was made. For reasons that will become clear, only a "not guilty" verdict on all counts was the decision that would have spared them and that would have been a tall order for a lawyer of greater ability than Thomas... or Lenehan.

It took three weeks for the death sentences to be confirmed. Such was Lord Kitchener's desperation to '... *swiftly apply military justice forthwith*' that he ordered the prisoners be brought to Pretoria on 21st February for sentencing on the 26th without informing Thomas. Major Bolton must have had a terrible foreboding when he wrote, "... *and I watched with a sick feeling in my stomach as the train pull out of Pietersburg with poor Tony Morant aboard her.*'

Desperation at the 11th hour

Thomas arrived on the next train to discover when he got there that they had been sentenced to death by firing squad the next morning, the 27th. He rushed off to Army HQ. at Montrose House to plead for their lives, not, according to Bennett, out of any sense of duty or compassion for his clients and fellow countrymen, but only because he felt '*stulified by personal failure*'. In any event, Lord Kitchener was not there and it was left to Major-General William Kelly to break it to Thomas that The Sirdar was uncontactable, the sentences had been confirmed by London and nothing could be done as the case had stirred up, '... *grave political trouble*'.

Chapter 13: *Reflection*

This was a huge blow for Thomas as he was convinced based on previous evidence, that the King would spare them. King Edward VII had already shown himself to have a compassionate soul having already exercised clemency for the "Williamsrust three" and also intervened on behalf of a young English soldier accused of deserting his post. Indeed, it would have been interesting to see what would have happened if word of the trials had leaked out to Australia and the King was petitioned by the Australian Government.

Witton and Lenehan both tell in compelling detail how they were prevented from contacting Australian representatives. In Lenehan's case, given the minor charges laid against him, it amounted to false imprisonment. In any event, the Australian Government did not find out until too late and to this day have never been fully appraised as to what took place in the Spelonken.

Deceit and cover up

This incident gave rise to two important myths which have lingered for more than a century:
- Lord Kitchener, consumed with guilt, left Pretoria for four days so that he wouldn't have to face Thomas.
- Morant and Handcock were shot at the behest of the German Government to atone for the death of the Rev. Heese.

The second myth is part of a later debate in which we will overturn a century of assumptions by introducing dramatic new evidence which proves that the Heese murder was in fact, peripheral to the real issue at the heart of this controversy — the "cover- up" of Lord Kitchener's orders to shoot Boer prisoners. However, the first myth we can dismiss.

During the course of this book many charges have been levelled at Lord Kitchener, but those can be substantiated, whereas the disappearance of Lord Kitchener as part of some international conspiracy cannot.

Given the widely-held belief that Germany was involved in an international conspiracy to have the accused executed; the myth that Lord Kitchener fled is perhaps a natural extension of that logic. Davey even suggests that perhaps Lord Kitchener did not even leave HQ at all. Both these stories are incorrect.

The truth can be found in Sir Ian Hamilton's revealing papers in which he confides more to his wife than his biographer. This day-by-day account of life under Lord Kitchener is both interesting and illuminating as it not only gives us a record of Lord Kitchener's movements around the period in question, but an insight into the operational workings of Lord Kitchener's staff and the man himself. His letters record that Lord Kitchener quite often went on field operations.

On the actual day of the execution Hamilton notes, *'Lord K. away at Harrismith'* and he received the following cable from him:

'... Harrismith Feb 27th 4.30 pm
'Majuba Day so far produces 400 stop Hope for many more as I have received few reports stop Country seen from Platberg is black with cattle being driven in'.

By the time Hamilton had received this cable, Morant and Handcock were dead almost twelve hours and had been buried. As it was one of the largest successes that the British had enjoyed for some time, there was every reason for Lord Kitchener to be present. Hamilton adds:

'... I have heard nothing from Lord K. since, but I hear from Intelligence that there are over 600 prisoners there are also, intelligence say, 18,000 cattle and 10,000 sheep. Altogether this is the biggest thing we have done for a long time'.

Hamilton's account is backed up by the diary entries of Pt. Will Saxon of the Manchester Volunteers. He was manning a blockhouse near Harrismith and confirms that it was part of a longer-term plan to trap the elusive De Wet who had run rings round Lord Kitchener and single-handedly mocked his elaborate blockhouse and barbed wire system since the guerrilla war began. Three times in less than two months he defied him by slipping through British lines. Saxon recalls:

Chapter 13:   Reflection

'... By the time this letter reaches home you will have heard of Kitchener's Drive. We the Manchester Vols. held an active and responsible position holding the part of the blockhouse line from which the Boers recoiled. Over 1,100 Boers were captured. Innumerable cattle &c have been driven through our lines during the last few days. From the 24th to the 27th Feb. we have stood all night in trenches waiting for the Boers (nice warm nights). Several commandants have been taken but the slippery De Wet escaped once more'.

Therefore, whilst we can explode the myth that Lord Kitchener had gone into hiding, we can also say that he was contactable. The idea of the Commander-in-Chief, especially one as "hands-on" as Lord Kitchener, being out of touch with HQ is unthinkable. Saxon's diary entry also suggests that Lord Kitchener had left Pretoria even before Morant and Handcock were brought down from Pietersburg to be sentenced. It would appear that once he received confirmation from London on 22nd February, he issued orders and left it to his men to do the deed.

Whatever the legitimacy of Lord Kitchener's mission, this author still believes given the great care Lord Kitchener took to ensure that as little as possible about the affair became public knowledge, he would not have wanted to be in the vicinity should the unthinkable have happened and an 11th hour reprieve arrived. Wilmansrust and many other smaller incidents during the war had proved that Australians would not be as easy to punish as the British.

Whilst Lord Kitchener busied himself in Harrismith counting livestock, the executions went ahead as scheduled.

We all know from the "Breaker" Morant film that the men died bravely. On many late nights this author has pictured them waiting, sleepless in their cell, dreading every footfall. As they emerge from their cell, you can feel the night air cooling the perspiration on their skins and the thumping of their hearts keeping time as they are marched across the hard, sun-baked veldt. Ahead they see the eerie figures of the Cameron Highlanders waiting for them in the half-light, their kilts flapping in the breeze like the wings of predators. How strange and melancholy it must have been to see the birth of a new day — feel the first rays of sun on your back then to die with a bitter taste of betrayal in your mouth... yet still have the presence of mind to hurl that final iconoclasm out into the ether like a message in a bottle hoping that someone will find out why they really shot you;

'Shoot Straight You Bastards! Don't make a mess of it.'

The film has been criticised for taking artistic licence with certain parts of the story, but this statement in the Melbourne Argus from Harry Morrow, who was Morant's gaoler in Pretoria, confirms that the film did not take any historical liberties with Morant's final scene.

> '... Morant asked them to take off the blindfold, crossed his arms over his chest and looked them in the face. He said if they didn't fire he would look down the barrels of their rifles for the bullets! They fired and Morant got it all in the left side and died at once with his arms folded and his eyes open. You would have thought he was alive.'

Though Thomas makes no mention of attending the execution, it is hard to imagine that he would not have been there to lend what little moral support he could in the circumstances. His last painful duty was to attend their funerals. Morrow ended his above letter by saying that they were buried properly with a hearse and a mourning coach and 30 Australian officers were present at the funeral. Another says it was the Australians who re-claimed their bodies and took them on a carriage with 12-20 mourners (including Thomas) to the Pretoria cemetery. Though the numbers attending vary from account to account, Morant and Handcock were lucky as their comrades spared them the usual fate of the disgraced soldier — a pint of quicklime and an unmarked grave. Renar quotes one of the mourners who attended the funeral. He says there were;

> '... about a dozen persons altogether. I followed the horse to the cemetery and saw the funeral. The parson from the Cathedral here met the coffins at the gate and led the party to a detached portion of the ground, where a service took place after the bodies were lowered. The parson recited a preamble to the burial service which included the words, "... For as much

Chapter 13:   *Reflection*

as this is unconsecrated ground", letting his hearers plainly know the difference between "consecrated ground" and a "dedicated grave". Some of the service was omitted too. It was a woeful sight.'

Anguish and grief

It was here, in the Pretoria cemetery that the image of Thomas standing over the grave was taken. He had helped carry their bodies to their final resting place and spread the Australian flag over their coffin.

The brown, scarred earth has sunk and is covered with grass and the sweeping avenues of trees which leads you past neat rows of gravestones have an air of tranquillity and the neatly clipped hedges, respectability. But the sanitary scent of Scots pine cannot disguise the whiff of disgust you feel when you see that the grave of Morant and Handcock is well away from the other 1,100 servicemen who are also interred there. Executed soldiers were not thought to be fit company for those who have fallen in battle.

It is a bitter-sweet irony that Morant, who always aspired to be amongst the great and the good, now lies in their midst, though it is Boers and not Englishmen who keep him company. However, given the ambiguous riddle of his epitaph, perhaps he would have preferred them anyway. It is a biblical line from Matthew 10:

'He that shall lose life, shall findeth it.'

The real thrust of it is found a little way back in the verse:

'A man's foes shall be they of his own household.'

Given the tangled web of Morant's origins, this could be a reference to his real father or the Morants' failure to acknowledge him as kin, or the British Empire which had used him to fight their tawdry war, given him orders and then shot him for carrying them out — or both!

Were it a reference to the latter, then Thomas would have been in hearty agreement when he said of the case:

'... But though not guilty, Morant and Handcock would have not died over that case because our own (no not our own altogether) people would have them convicted before a trial.'

The *Bathurst National Advertiser* also printed a letter Thomas wrote to Witton's father from Pretoria, dated March 1902 warning:

'.. Your son has been sent a prisoner to England and I think it will be wise to defer any active steps concerning him 'till the Australian Government is in possession of the facts.'

This author wonders if Thomas ever thought back to Henry Parkes' historic Tenterfield speech and realised that this was exactly the type of scenario he was alluding to. Australian soldiers under Imperial command being tried by their flawed system of justice with no recourse to appeal to their own Government that were powerless to act in any case.

In this post-execution analysis, the signs are already there of Thomas' distress, fuelled, this author suspects by his knowledge that they were a victim of a cover up. If we were able to somehow transport ourselves back to the aftermath of the executions in South Africa 1902 — it would have seemed incomprehensible that Morant and Handcock were executed for shooting Boers. In the same abovementioned letter Thomas makes this very point to Witton's father:

'... The defence maintained was that under the customs of war the shooting of these Boers was allowable as they were merely running bandits or marauders. It was proved that in other cases exactly the same procedure was adopted and approved of by other officers. Consequently, you will see that from a soldier's point of view — at any rate — the crime was not so dreadful as might appear — though technically it was a crime. I only regret that poor Morant and Handcock did not receive a sentence of penal servitude, but poor fellows they were shot at 18 hours' notice... As counsel for your son and other officers I should like to see that all the facts from the prisoners' point of view are fairly brought forward. When *everything is known you will not think the disgrace amounts to much, or anything. War is war and rough things have to be done. Only yesterday news came in of horrible barbarities on the part of the Boers towards some of our colonials. I say — they deserve what they get and with less nonsense and sentiment the war would be over.'*

Thomas remained in South Africa for another year after the trial, as a "legal-military authority". This author's belief is that he was compiling evidence on the circumstances leading up to the trial in preparation for the book he twice claimed he was going to write.

Thomas' return

He returned to Australia in '... *the early part of 1903*', yet the *Tenterfield Star* makes no mention of it. Even allowing for the fact that by the end of the war the big welcomes had fizzled out and the public and the men had become disillusioned by both the cause and their treatment by the British, it seems odd that such a public figure would arrive home unheralded. On the other hand, perhaps it was not surprising if one looks at the fate of the other accused, as they too failed to re-integrate back into their communities.

Handcock's wife was not informed of his death and was given no financial help; his parents left Bathurst to escape the tittle-tattle and shame. Handcock's name was left off the local War Memorial and on the day Lord Kitchener arrived to unveil it, his wife was warned by police to stay away and not to cause any trouble.

Major Lenehan was discredited and hounded by General Hutton who defied the wishes of the Australian Government to reinstate him in the Army. He was not allowed to fight in The Great War.

Witton, it seems, was the only one to have achieved any degree of normality, maybe because he was widely seen as being wrongly implicated and had been released from prison.

Though Thomas was not implicated in any of the crimes, his vigorous defence of the accused both during and after the trial would have not made him popular with those who felt Morant and Handcock brought disgrace on Australia and those against the war who would have interpreted his comment to Witton's father that, '... *rough things have to be done in war... I say — they deserve what they get and with less nonsense and sentiment the war would be over*' as Jingoism. How large a part these perceptions played in his downfall is hard to say, but officialdom gave him little quarter during the next 40 years.

Upon his return, Thomas strongly supported Federation through editorials in The Tenterfield Star. He had bought the Tenterfield Star in 1894 and he was to write later in Early and Later Tenterfield in 1921, that there were no proper records kept of earlier issues of the Tenterfield Star until he assumed ownership of it.

Running a law office and a newspaper at the same time was obviously very challenging, so Thomas had a building designed to house both the newspaper and his law office and erected in 1913, which still stands, and the plans for it are sometimes on display in the newspaper office. In due course it became apparent, even to Thomas that he could not successfully attend to all his clients, as well as to all the tasks involved in producing a newspaper twice a week, so in July, 1915 he sold the newspaper and remained in practice until he sold his law practice in 1919.

When the Great War started in August 1914, Thomas, aged fifty-three was too old to enlist, but very concerned and involved, and on the 29th of October, 1917, he wrote a pamphlet *In Time Of War — The Recruiting Problem — An Address to Fellow Australians*. In this address Thomas quotes sections from the *Commonwealth Defence Act 1903-1915*, as any good lawyer would, and urged the Commonwealth Government to act under Sections 59, 60 and 61, to conscript young men for Military Service in Australia but not overseas, seeing conscription for service overseas as being "Militarism in disguise".

The whole of Thomas' 15-page address is interesting. He wrote in vigorous but plain prose, with appropriate quotations from the Hon. Alfred Deakin in 1907 and Mr Lloyd George, the British Prime Minister. It is however more informative for the way Thomas tells his own story:

> *'May the writer briefly explain his own position and views... The object of this little, hastily-compiled pamphlet (is that) all patriotic fellow Aus-*

tralians, all fellow residents of the New England district (which sent the — Battalion of Volunteers to the front, and probably sufficient for another battalion independently) will agree to help to send more volunteers to relieve and reinforce those volunteers who have led the way to the front. That is the immediate objective. The writer is a native born Australian, of strong democratic tendencies, a sympathiser with the best ideals of Labor from 1891 to 1903 he was a volunteer officer of the mounted forces, first New South Wales, and after Federation, of the Commonwealth. In 1900 he volunteered for service in the late Boer War, believing at the time that the cause was right, and was accepted for captaincy in the New South Wales Citizens Bushmen (a Regiment of 500 organised, equipped, and partly paid by the Citizens of this State).'

When the Great war broke out Thomas had no Australian commission and had passed military age. He nevertheless, offered his services in any capacity — and, in default of any other, as voluntary drill instructor of Citizen Soldiers in his own district. The offer was declined. Nothing, therefore, was left to be done except to assist in recruiting under the present system (as such it may be called), and other war work, as an ordinary civilian. (May the writer further say that, rightly or wrongly, he has been a consistent conscriptionist as regards obligatory home-training "in time of war", and a consistent anti-conscriptionist as regard compulsory service abroad)

Chapter 14:
Social and Political Reformer

Back from his trip to Western Australia in 1920 and self-exiled in Sydney from his home town Tenterfield, Thomas soon discovered that he had left his heart in the highlands and needed only a little prompting from the Town Clerk of the municipality of Tenterfield to embark on writing of his *Early and Later Tenterfield — Historical Sketch from the First Days of Settlement,* the first attempt anyone had made to record Tenterfield's origins. He received a letter from the Town Clerk dated 19th October, 1921 asking him 'has progress been made' in the preparation of a history for the town's jubilee. He replied on 21 October:

> 'The difficulty about Tenterfield is that practically all the records of the town in the shape of early newspapers and Minute Books of Public Institutions have been destroyed or lost (there was a newspaper as far back as 1860-1861 — but only a portion of one copy remains to 1894).
>
> 'In 1894 when I had The Tenterfield Star, I started to keep the files of that newspaper and have them in tact up to the present date… I suppose that I have during the past 25 years collected as much material relative to the history of the district as anyone.'[168]

Thomas mentions in his Historical Sketch, the manuscript of William Gardner (Mitchell Library) written in 1884 and subsequent years and he was also intrigued with the Aboriginal name for the Clifton Station area "Moombilleen", and wrote;

> '… so let Tenterfield to the poet be 'Moombilleen' if he will…'

He also tells some of the early history of the School of the Arts:

Chapter 14: *Social and Political Reformer*

'In March, 1871, the enrolment at the Public School was 135. In April a public meeting decided to establish a School of Arts, and at a later period a sum was provided for a library... In November 1876 the local Pastoral Agricultural and Horticultural Society was formed. The first show was held at the School of Arts on the 5th of April, 1877, and by steady progression it has reached its current position with its fine pavilion, of which the foundation stone was laid in September 1914 (a month after the declaration of war), and its memorials and improvements. The School of Arts, from a small reading room, has developed into a fine and popular institution (a sort of Town Club) at the corner of Rouse and Manners Streets.'

He also sketched in the history of the present War Memorial Hall, which he had played a part in improving;

'The Gymnasium and Drill Hall built in 1893, and several time enlarged since, with its Boer War Memorial, will, it is hoped, as a result of the present Jubilee celebrations, and after over quarter of a century of usefulness, be replaced by a larger and more presentable structure, which will serve the purpose both of a lasting memorial to District Citizen Soldiers who lost their lives in military service, and also of a gathering place for the coming generations of Tenterfield and for recreation purposes.'

He concluded his Historical Sketch with this observation:

'And with the advent of a Northern State, the town and district of Tenterfield may face the coming half century — indeed quarter century, with confidence...'

Thomas also maintained his interest in Tenterfield's history for the rest of his life.

Having been brought up on a dairy farm it was natural that he should buy a farm out of Tenterfield, named "Haddington" on the road to Mount Mackenzie after a town in Southern Scotland. After the Boer War he was to build a house like the ones he had seen during his three years in South Africa. He also had a property at Boonoo Boonoo where there had been some mining activity, and at both properties he had presentable gardens. He called his house in Tenterfield "Bivouac".

The evidence which Thomas gave to the Cohen Royal Commission on the 26th of August 1924 reveals some of his best qualities.

He knew the law about the formation of new states, and he also saw the insuperable hurdle of persuading a majority of people in Newcastle, Sydney and Wollongong to vote for a subdivision of the State, which would mean the establishment of a rival state capital city. He also saw the value of existing Sydney facilities, the Mitchell Library, Art Gallery and so on, to people of NSW.

In short, he showed his soundness in reconciling principles with practicality by suggesting the formation of Provincial Councils with power to develop public works, education, lands, public health and local Government. It was no fault of Thomas' that the New State Movement pressed, following the Third Armidale Convention at the Armidale Town Hall in April, 1929, for a New State Referendum.

Chapter 15:
The Tragic Final Years

Thomas' post-Boer War years were painful after he returned to Australia in early 1903. Thomas resigned his commission after pressure from the Army over his intention to publish material critical of the Courts Martial decisions and Lord Kitchener. He unsuccessfully lobbied the NSW's Government to inquire into the trials and for financial assistance for Peter Handcock's children. He returned to Tenterfield and gradually isolated himself from the community that once hailed him a hero and community leader. In 1915, he sold the newspaper he owned and in 1919 he sold his legal practice. Reflecting on his newspaper ownership of 16 years, he stated that he had purchased the paper for the purpose of advocating the cause of Australian Federation and the formation of the Country Party.[169]

Thomas' life deteriorated virtually from the day he sold his law practice in 1919 to P.H. Monkley, with whom he had been briefly in partnership. He bought a farm near Tenterfield, but sold it after about two years. Having a long-standing interest in Aboriginal languages and Australian natural history, he went by rail on a trip to Western Australia in 1920. He wrote to George Mackaness on the 31st of May 1932 to give permission for his verse *Miril Yiril Yiri* in a proposed *Anthology of Australian Verse for Children*. He comments in that letter that he got this Aboriginal name '*in vocabulary of words kindly sent to me, about 1927, by Mrs Daisy M. Bates, the well known Aborigines' philanthropist.*'[170]

In 1920, he went to live in Sydney in Wentworth Court, 19 Elizabeth Street, and while he was there he wrote the first short history of Tenterfield, Early and Later Tenterfield, for the Jubilee celebrations in 1921. He didn't like living in Sydney as it was crowded and costly. He wrote from Sydney on the 22nd of February, 1923 to Justin MacCartie, Publicity Centralization. On the 26th of August, 1924, he told the New State Royal Commission:

'It has been suggested that 'country councils' in the north and south of this State might be formed by combinations of shires and municipalities, which means an extension of local Government. Why not go a step further (it might be a step towards ultimate formation of a new States) and advocate self-governing provinces with the State?

'This would at least mean a move in the direction desired by ardent new Staters. It would enable the provincial nestlings to settle down in their nests on separate boughs of their State tree until their wings were strong enough to enable them to fly away (if they so desired) and build nests in their own trees.'[171]

In 1923, he was taken down by a client he trusted, James Thomas Jones, who was later sentenced to 18 months hard labour in Goulburn gaol. The report of this in the Tenterfield Star[172] is headed "*Confidence Tricksters — Mr. J.F. Thomas Victimised — Retired Manager Also Duped*". The reports states that:

'J.T. Jones obtained the transfer of 'Brooklyne' in consideration of a promissory note at four months for 550 pounds ostensibly signed by Captain Warren.'

Doubtless this loss would have contributed to Thomas' insolvency and bankruptcy three years later. While in Sydney he conducted lively correspondence gathering information for his publication Early and Later Tenterfield.[173]

After returning to Tenterfield late in 1925, he reopened a law office in Tenterfield and promptly became involved in litigation. He stated in his Bankruptcy Affidavit of the 27th of October, 1932:

'For over twenty years I have never needed to see a doctor, but towards the end of 1925 I had to do so, as I was nearing a break-down and in December 1926 I was advised I was suffering from blood pressure.'

However, in December, 1926, he was sent to Long Bay Penitentiary for contempt of court, in not responding to a series of questions put to him by the Supreme Court. He was, however, far from penitent, maintaining that he had been so wrongly treated in the litigation that a judicial inquiry was warranted. The Crown made Thomas bankrupt on the 20th of August, 1928 after discharging him from prison. He was discharged from bankruptcy in November, 1932.

Just before he left gaol and before he was made bankrupt, the Incorporated Law Institute applied to the Supreme Court to strike him off the Solicitors Roll, and that order was made on the 9th of March, 1928 on the ground that he has misappropriated the proceeds of the sale of land in a deceased estate of Mills, that he held in trust for infant beneficiaries, since turned adults, but not paid to them. Thomas did make restitution before his name was struck off, but his conduct was considered reprehensible. He did not agree and appealed to the High Court which re-determined the matter on the 18th of April, 1929 in the same way as the Supreme Court had.[174] Thomas' spirit must have been shattered. His own low spirits coincided with the economic depression. On the 8th of October, 1932 he made an affidavit in bankruptcy describing himself as "commission agent" in which he stated that:

> *'My means of livelihood is a very small commission agency which brings in not more than about one pound a week and I have to live with the most rigid economy and with scarcely the necessities of life, let alone small luxuries which one might expect at seventy years of age.'*

Thomas' two Bankruptcy Affidavits contain his comments on all his debts totalling £5,869, 4 shillings and 1 penny, assets of £2,631, 10 shillings. The stories he tells in these affidavits of 8th and 27th October 1932 leave the impression that he was foolishly generous and trusting. These Affidavits may not attract spontaneous compassion, but they tell a series of sad stories of unfaithfulness by others, probably similarly brought low by the economic depression. It was during the period in 1929 that he received the revealing advice from George Witton about Morant and Handcock, who had not returned his trust either.

'The most terrible poverty is loneliness, and the feeling of being unloved.'[175]

After his kidney operation he had to wear a rubber drainage bag, which made him walk oddly.[176] The discomfort and indignity of this made him even more unsociable. He was poor and disgraced. He had no close friends. It seems his brothers ignored him. It is little wonder he shunned company and became a recluse. In a newspaper article in the *Lismore Northern Star*,[177] John Stubbs wrote:

> *'Thomas was given brown bread and barley soup by people worried about his starved condition soon before his death… a deserted Boer style cottage, its glowing rosewood and silky oak panelling infested with white ants, standing next to a goat paddock outside Tenterfield, is a neglected and little known memorial to the strange life of a man who defended Breaker Morant and who, it appears, was broken by Morant's execution…*
>
> *'After the war his behaviour became increasingly strange. It is said he slept on a saddle in his office, and sometimes in the Tenterfield Cemetery and that he lived on raw onion… room in Tenterfield to "Boonoo Boonoo", and he died there that night.'*[178]

N.H. Edgar Jennings, a solicitor in Tenterfield wrote to Messrs Stephen, Jaques and Stephens, Solicitors in Sydney on the 30th of March, 1939 in response to a request to *'convey some impression of J.F. Thomas.'* Thomas was of course still alive at that time. Jennings' letter includes the following impressions:

> *'Thomas was once a solicitor. Despite that fact he is a man of ability and probably because he is eccentric…*
>
> *'There is no doubt as to the public spiritedness of his early days. He was a moving spirit in most public affairs in Tenterfield and very liberal in supporting them both with money and energy.*
>
> *'The old hands have often told me how they would go into his office and find him surrounded with heaps of documents and papers in every*

Chapter 15:   *The Tragic Final Years*

conceivable part of the room which would support a document or paper. It appears that one had only to mention a matter possibly years old when Thomas had the uncanny faculty of being able to put his hands straightaway on the file.

'I have often been told that he would work night after night until well after midnight and would be seen leaving his office to walk to his farm some three or four miles from Tenterfield. He used to take a short cut through the local cemetery and when exhaustion overtook him would rest his head on a tombstone, snatch a sleep and afterwards continue his journey to arrive at his farm about daylight, when, more often than not he would hack a piece of bread from a loaf, seize an onion or anything else which may have been handy for his breakfast and set about the return walk to his office.

'I have been told that clients have often walked in to find him asleep in the office chair with his head resting on a bundle of papers or perhaps stretched out on an old couch with a saddle as a pillow.

'He is knowledgeable on Australian History, Flora, Fauna and has contributed articles to journals specialising in these departments, in fact he is a brilliant conversationalist along those lines, although he is evasive to the direct question and discursive in conversation.

'After his bankruptcy and when he was struck off the Rolls, Thomas returned to Tenterfield. How he exists is a little puzzling. I understand that he collects the rents from a few old estates in the case of absent Trustees or beneficiaries and also has an Insurance Agency. I do not think the commissions from these collections would maintain him.

'His mode of living is certainly eccentric. I do not think he eats with the regularity of the average individual, but when hungry he possibly pulls a carrot out of a small vegetable garden he has and chews that.

'Although at one time it possibly could be said that he was the leading citizen of the town with the respect and esteem of all classes, nowadays he makes very little contact with his fellow men.

'... I think he is a member of the Historical Society. Thomas is a bachelor.

'The above certainly reads like gossip, but I have endeavoured to give you some impression by creating an atmosphere of Thomas' personality and trust that what I have written may assist you.

'Yours truly....'

Miss Winifred Percival, who had a bookshop in Tenterfield for many years, described Thomas as she knew him as an old man *'He was big, loose-limbed, rangy style of man with good big hefty feet.'*[179]

His obituary in the Tenterfield Star[180] must have been quickly compiled as he died on the 11th of November, 1942:

'One of the best known citizens of Tenterfield, passed over the Great Divide yesterday morning, at a property in which he was interested, at "Boonoo Boonoo". The late James Francis Thomas was a personality who played a big part in the activities of the town and district for many years, particularly in his early manhood.

'In early life he was associated with the Upper Clarence Light Horse, and was an officer of the Tenterfield Troop, which afterwards became the Tenterfield Mounted Rifle Club, of which he was a life member. He served in the South African War, and rose to the rank of Major. On his return he led a proposal to establish a memorial to the veterans of the South African War, and the Gymnasium was erected to their memory. After the 1914-18 War, he took an active part in organising the erection of the memorial to the soldiers who fell in the Great War, and the brick façade was added to the hall, which then became known as the Soldier's Memorial Hall. Mr Thomas was a trustee of the Memorial Hall at the time of his death.

'He has said that among his papers are many valuable documents which should prove invaluable to the district and country. Some years ago he was made a member of the Royal Historical Society of New South Wales.

'The late Mr. Thomas had served on the committee of the Tenterfield P.A. and M. Society, and was a venerated member of the R.S.S.A.L.L.A. From the time of its formation, he took a keen interest in the local T.M.

Chapter 15: The Tragic Final Years

and S.C.M.W. and Patriotic Fund, until declining health prevented him from attending meetings and functions.

'It would be difficult to name all the various organisations with which he was connected over the years; but it is common knowledge that he lent all possible aid to any good cause designed to further the progress of the town in which he lived, or to benefit individual citizens. His unobtrusive acts of kindness were legion, and it may be said that he would give his last shilling to a needy person.

'About six months ago, the deceased became ill, and his decline caused his friend grave concern; but his extremely independent nature made it difficult for them to do anything for him.

'He was a great lover of Nature. Many of the town's stately trees were planted by his hands, and until recent months he tended his several gardens.

'He is survived by two brothers, Mr. W.B. Thomas (Concord) and Mr. H.E. Thomas (Sydney). Another brother, well known to Tenterfield, Rev. L.D. Thomas, predeceased him a few years ago in England.'

Thomas died intestate on Armistice Day 1942, and on the 6th of May, 1948 Letters of Administration were granted to his brother William Beach Thomas of 29 Gipps Street Concord. Thomas' death Certificate provided by Dr. J.V. Guinane gave two causes of death — 1. (a) Uraemia (b) Chronic Nephritis (c) Hypertrophied Prostrate 2. Malnutrition.[181]

Thomas' life can be seen as tragic. As a young man he was very public spirited, a poet, a recruiter of soldiers, effective, if not heroic, in the Boer War, a laudable citizen of Tenterfield, editor of the Tenterfield Star, an early supporter of Federation, and local historian. His career deteriorated after the Great War and through the Depression years. He went to gaol, was bankrupted, was deregistered as a Solicitor, and became increasingly reclusive until he died aged 81. The very characteristics which made him so successful were eventually to play a part in his downfall; his independent self-reliance which was so common and appreciated in the 1890s and his generosity and trust which eventually were not reciprocated.

The first signs of his emotional distress came with his increasingly physical isolation from the community of which he had become such an integral part. This is evident through the series of properties he owned which diminished in size and quality as his fortunes declined.

In 1900, Thomas bought a property, known as Westfield, from the Sommerlad family. It comprised some five acres had a commercial orchard, a nursery and a brick cottage which Thomas re-named "Bivouac".

Thomas sold that and bought a piece of farm land outside Tenterfield in 1907 where he built the Arcadian dream which he mused upon in his early poetry. *"Haddington"* — the house he had built was supposedly based on the Dutch/Boer style that he had seen whilst in South Africa.

Though it now resembles a lonely farm shack in a distant paddock and parts of the original outhouses have been demolished, closer inspection reveals that it was once a quite exquisite house. Its internal features include intricate oak and rosewood panelling, split level floors, stained glass door panels, large open fire places, one with mantel and surrounds of marble and tiles and ornate wrought iron work. What is more astounding is the fact that the one man responsible for this workmanship was blind!

In a 1989 interview with researcher Ted Robel, Fred W. Bailey then aged 86 recalled:

'J.F. Thomas and I were almost neighbours when he lived at Haddington. He had a very nice house. He dressed well. We often picked him up and bought him into town. He used to ride into town. He did have a horse. I don't not think that he drank at any of the hotels in town. The gardens at Haddington were beautiful.

'There was a cheese factory at Haddington. J.F. started it. J.F. owned a property in George Street; Number 40... two men came out from England to build Haddington. A stone mason by the name of Smedley did all the stonework around the gardens and may have built the chimneys. Thomas never had a dog. The Ricksons were share farmers that Thomas hired. Another share farmer was the Wrestons from New Zealand. The Wrestons lived in the main house and Thomas lived on another part of the property or in the kitchen. The property ran cows. The stones used at Haddington came from a quarry at the back of the property.'

Chapter 15: *The Tragic Final Years*

Thomas was a nature lover. He kept pigs, turkeys, ducks, fowls, peacocks and koala bears. His peacock run was called Peacock Avenue, and was covered with vines for shade. In the fowl yard he planted fruit and nut trees. On the western side of the property, known as the Cohens, there was an orchard; pears, plums, apricots, figs and English chestnuts. It has also been generally accepted that Thomas brought back to Australia the Gerbera, a flower native to South Africa which is also known as the African Daisy.

Despite his unsavoury experiences in The Boer War, Thomas retained an interest in the Tenterfield Rifles which underwent a series of name changes after the Boer War. As the Tenterfield half squadron of the 6th Australian Light Horse he was appointed Trustee and Patron of their Rifle Club and helped fund-raise to enable a team to compete in the 1910 and 1912 Prince of Wales Cup which replaced the Hutton Shield. Tenterfield won in 1910.

More significantly, he became involved in a campaign to pay tribute to the local dead of the Boer War and WW1. The four were originally commemorated on a rough hand-hewn stone which due to the sterling efforts of historian Bob Wallace now resides in Canberra. Thomas headed the effort to build the war memorial which carries the names of the Tenterfield men who died in South Africa and a memorial front to the drill hall. It is said a large portion of it came out of his own pocket.

On the surface though things seemed to be carrying on as normal. The *Star* was 43 years of age, and in 1913 moved into present premises on The High St. Joan Starr, was in her second spell as editor of the *Tenterfield Star*. Her father was a great friend of Thomas who spent hours sitting on the verandah of the skinners' hut which was next door to the *Star*. However, he never brought up the subject of South Africa. Thomas had a room in there for many years from where he ran his solicitor's and accounting business. Although hardly the most respectable place to run such a business, its proximity to the *Star* allowed him to run between both places trying to keep up with his many commitments.

She recalls her father telling her that Thomas was gaining a reputation for being increasingly eccentric. After a particularly arduous day he would often fall asleep on the floor of the editor's office with his head resting on a saddle. There were other stories that he would take a nap on a gravestone whilst walking back to Haddington at night. Many a person recalls seeing Thomas walking from "Haddington" across the fields to his office in Tenterfield, a distance of some 4 miles. Usually, he was eating his breakfast which consisted of a large piece of cheese and a hunk of bread. Joan was in no doubt what caused this change in character and tallied with what others told us. The 'events in South Africa', she said, troubled him to the end of his days.

In April 1915, came the first of his asset disposals. Thomas sold the *Star* newspaper to G. C. Stevenson, who also bought the opposition paper of the time, the *Intercolonial Courier*. In an interview in the *Star* Thomas said, an agreement had been reached whereby both the *Star* and the *Courier* will have a new proprietor, forecasting the sale of both these papers to Mr G.W. Stevenson, who took over in July of that year.

From the *Tenterfield Star* 1870-1970 centenary supplement issued on 5th November 1970 came the following explanation as to why he was selling:

'... Mr. Thomas said that he had been at the helm for 16 and a half years, and was relinquishing it with regret. He had purchased it for the purpose of advocating the cause of Australian Federation, which had then become a question of practical politics. In spite of the cold — not to say hostile — reception which Federation at first received in the electorate, this journal had the satisfaction of seeing the question carried in it by a majority of two to one.

'Several considerations decided the proprietor to retire from local journalism but the principal one was the constant tax which it meant on all his time outside his profession as a solicitor. The supervision of the newspaper therefore entailed long hours of night work, and that year after year. He said the 'Star' had in no way gone back as far as support was concerned, but on the contrary had progressed more in the past twelve months than ever before, and it never had a better staff that it had now.

'Mr Thomas wrote that he believed the 'Star' to be the first country

Chapter 15: *The Tragic Final Years*

newspaper to advocate the formation of a Country Party — a movement which is slowly growing.'

However, despite throwing all his energies into his law practice his financial position worsened and he was forced into a further disposal of assets. In 1919, he sold the Law practice he had in Tenterfield to P.H. Monkley with an agreement that Thomas could not practice law in Tenterfield until the last day of 1925.

In 1920 he went to Sydney, *'... and did my best to carry on some old matters'* and installed himself in an office in Wentworth Court, Elizabeth St. It appears that his increasingly erratic nature caused him to become embroiled in a number of legal tussles which drained his personal resources and later contributed to his bankruptcy.

In 1922, he sold his last major asset, Haddington, to a Captain Horatio King D.S.O. Like Thomas he was born in Sydney and educated at the Kings School in Parramatta.

Thomas returned to Tenterfield in 1925 and began practising again when his five years were up, but financial problems continued to plague him.

His financial problems led to bankruptcy and 12 months' imprisonment at Long Bay gaol for contempt of court orders.

His time in Long Bay was described by a fellow solicitor as;

'He continued to conduct his practice in jail and work seemed to continue to arrive from Tenterfield and he seemed to also to be the jail solicitor, representing some other prisoners.'[182]

Chapter 16:

Decline into professional disrepute

Thomas' denouement falls into three parts.

Firstly, Thomas fell out with a long-standing and prominent Tenterfield family called Power. In 1926, litigation was started by Mrs Elizabeth Jane Power and in January 1927 he was imprisoned at Long Bay gaol after having been made bankrupt by means of a Chamber Summons for costs outstanding relating to the E.J. Power Litigation case. An article which appeared in the *Smiths Weekly* on 7th May 1927 put Thomas' case as follows:

> '... Thomas prefers to remain in Long Bay as a confinee in contempt rather than pay £77 8/- 8d, legal costs, which the Supreme Court of New South Wales ordered him to pay. He is in Long Bay on principle and considers himself a victim of injustice. For over 30 years, Thomas in a legal capacity acted for a Tenterfield family named Power. A few years ago there was a break. He had a dispute with one Elizabeth Jane Power. She was dissatisfied, or at least professed to be, with Thomas' management of her affairs...'

It appears that Thomas was duped by a solicitor named Linton who, related to E.J. Power, acted on her behalf in order to "stitch" Thomas up. Power knew nothing of the litigation.

This perhaps gives credence to the perception of some that Thomas was a marked man.

How do you plead?

His imprisonment at Long Bay penitentiary for contempt of court in not responding to a series of questions put to him by the Supreme Court demonstrated a stubborn attitude and lack of remorse. He maintained

Chapter 16:   *Decline into professional disrepute*

that he had been so wrongly treated in the litigation that a judicial inquiry was warranted. The Crown made Thomas bankrupt on the 20th of August, 1928 after discharging him from prison. He was discharged from bankruptcy in November, 1932.

In a letter dated 15th October 1980, WP Walters wrote to this author Kit Denton. As a young law clerk he had dealt with Thomas in Long Bay on some small legal matters. He agreed that Thomas was in Long Bay on a point of principle.

> *'He was a stubborn man who had gone to jail on a point of principle over a debt that he would not acknowledge or pay.'*[183]

In prison it is said he helped other prisoners with their appeals for free — a prototype of the Legal Aid system. This is supported by Walters who got the impression that he was carrying on as a lawyer as he had his own office in the prison and there were files everywhere, *'... work in progress'*. He said:

> *'He was eccentric, even then. He could have got out of jail even then. He could have got out at any time by either paying the debt or voluntarily declaring himself bankrupt. He refused to do either. Perhaps he never had it so good. He had his meals served to him. He was waited on by people in uniform.'*

Secondly, if prison did not interfere with his legal practice — then the Law Institute did. In the first of two body blows Thomas was disbarred whilst he was in Long Bay. Walters believed,

> *'... Thomas was not disbarred for "malpractice" but for being a bankrupt. Thomas was in Long Bay in 1927/ 28 for 12 months for refusing to allow examination of his property and means, or declare himself bankrupt, or pay. The NSW Attorney General had Thomas declared bankrupt (without a hearing).'*

He added that The Supreme Court doesn't favour bankrupt solicitors and thought that was the only reason he was struck off.

In 1928, Thomas was "struck off the roll" of legal practitioners in NSW for professional misconduct. In March 1928, his appeal to the High Court of Australia was not successful. Coincidentally, the Chief Justice of the court who dismissed Thomas' appeal was Sir Isaac Isaacs who in 1902 crafted Witton's petition to the Crown for his early release from gaol.

However, his disbarment was neither related to his bankruptcy or his refusal to co-operate with the tax office. The *Tenterfield Star* in 1928 says he was struck off the roll of New South Wales solicitors for professional misconduct relating to his dealings with a deceased estate. The charge was that:

> '...Thomas was acting for the estate of Thomas Mills, deceased, and held certain monies from the administration of the estate on trust for two sons William and Thomas Mills, then under the age of 21 years. From 1922 the sons made application for the money. Thomas contended that he was always ready and willing to pay the money, but being very busy he could not find it convenient to visit Wallanga nee, where he said he would pay it. Thomas paid £40 and £27 into the court. Thomas was admitted to practice on May 28th 1887. Mr Loxton KC submitted that the entire facts of the case substantiated innocence and bona fides of Mr Thomas. Having reviewed all the facts of the case relating to Mr Thomas, the Chief Justice said the court had come to the conclusion that Mr Thomas advanced no justifiable excuse for having acted as he did. The court was also of the opinion that he was guilty of conduct that showed that he was not a fit and proper person to be allowed to continue as a solicitor of an honourable profession.'

The *Australian Law Journal* of 15th May 1929 records that Thomas unsuccessfully appealed against the decision at the High Court in Sydney on 18th April 1929.

Chapter 16: *Decline into professional disrepute*

Thomas v. The Incorporated Law Institute of New South Wales[184]

'The Full Court of the Supreme Court of New South Wales ordered the name of T. (Thomas) to be struck off the roll of solicitors of the Court on the ground that he had been guilty of mis-appropriating the money from a client. From this decision T. appealed to the High Court, and filed an affidavit wherein it was stated that the appeal was in respect of a final judgement pronounced with regard to a matter at issue amounting to or of the value of £300, and involved directly or indirectly a civil right equal in value to that amount. At the hearing a preliminary objection was taken on behalf of the Law Institute, that the question at issue was T's right to practice as a solicitor, and that such a right was not a civil right, nor did it involve a sum of £300, therefore, the appeal was not competent. It was contended that the civil right intended by s.35 of the Judiciary Act must be a civil right with regard to property: Amos v Fraser (1907 4 C.L.R. 78, at pg. 87). The Court (Issacs, Gavan, Duffy and Starke JJ.) held that the appeal was in respect of a civil right, and that there was sufficient evidence to show it was worth more than £300. Having overruled the objection the court dealt with the matter on the facts and dismissed the appeal.'

On the 9th of March 1928 Thomas' name was removed at the instigation of the Law Institute of New South Wales.

Worn and Bankrupt

Finally, on the 20th of August 1928, just before he was released, a sequestration order made Thomas bankrupt. According to Kit Denton this stemmed from his stubborn and persistent refusal to allow his accounts to be inspected by the tax department.[185]

Walters also said that Thomas had almost had to be ejected from Long Bay gaol.[186] Who could blame him? He had lost all his assets, he had been stripped of his livelihood and he was not adjudged to be financially competent. Life would get no easier for the hapless Thomas following his release.

Despite the disgrace, Thomas returned to Tenterfield where he scratched a living giving quasi-legal advice[187] and accounting. Ellie Cowan was 86 in 1989 when she recalled that J.F Thomas used to do the tax papers for her and her late husband;

'He was a lovely man...

His office was always cold. I used to freeze while waiting for him to finish with other people, waiting to do the taxes... When my husband and I used to go to his office to get the tax paper done — he used to sit at his desk.

Papers were all around him on the floor, but he used to know where everything was. The arthritis was in his hands and in his legs. He could hold a pen with difficulty — he was a beautiful writer.

He was a nice man to do business with. I liked him a lot. Some lady used to bring him a cup of tea when I was there on tax business. I don't think that it was his wife.'

Joan Starr also said that Thomas managed her parents' books for many years without any problems. She also recalls that papers were strewn all over the place, but that he had the uncanny knack of putting his hand on anything he needed. She was suspicious of claims that he was corrupt. The evidence we have presented and anecdotal evidence we gathered from various towns' people attest to his honesty and integrity and his kind and generous nature and contradicts Kit Denton's suggestion that he was lining his own pockets with client's money[188]. Perhaps his increasing eccentricity made him less methodical and his stubbornness against officialdom was the unwillingness of a proud, independent and once prosperous man to admit his perilous financial state.

At his lowest ebb, Thomas appears to have revived his interest in writing a book about the Morant affair and wrote to Witton about it. The inference is that Thomas believed that Witton had not published all the available facts. Witton wrote the book with typical Victorian reserve — leaving out some of the more colourful cameos and comments that later came to light.

On 22nd October 1929, he received an earth-shattering reply from Witton. He told Thomas that Morant and Handcock had not taken him fully into their confidence.

> '... But you must not forget Kitchener held Handcock's "confession" in which he implicated me as an accessory no doubt unwittingly done while in a high shivery nervous state — but that accounts for the reason why only Morant, Handcock and myself were punished and the War Office so adamant in my case. Had there been no Heese case the shooting of prisoners would not have worried them much. But the shooting of Heese was a premeditated and most cold-blooded affair. Handcock with his own lips described it to me. I consider that I am the one and only one that suffered unjustly (apart from yourself). Morant and Handcock being acquitted my lips were sealed.'

In the Preface to his 1974 book, *The Australians at the Boer War*, historian Bob Wallace tells of the shock he felt at the moment he discovered the letter, '... *I felt so stunned that I as I looked across the room it seemed hard to realise that nothing else round me had changed in those few minutes.*'[189]

He was also in no doubt about the effect it would have had on Thomas when he read it;

> '... the effect on Major J.F. Thomas would have been shattering.'

Those words would have destroyed Thomas' last vestige of pride and self-belief which would have been at a low enough ebb already. Thomas' single comment on the matter conveys his sense of resignation and defeat;

> 'I think its best if we just forget the whole thing.'

Not surprisingly, the book never appeared and we were denied vital information which may have finally laid this controversy to rest.

Though he lived another thirteen years that was the last significant event in the life of Thomas. In what must have felt like a biblical retribution, he had been denuded of everything he held dear and was entitled to ask, *'Why me God?'* when those more deserving of such a fate continued to prosper and their reputations grow.

He spent his time between his little room in town and a property 30 kms from town at *"Boonoo Boonoo"*. It comprised of a hut, fruit trees and a vegetable garden. The hut had an old tin-style chimney, *"... a proper house with ornamental trees around it"*. The structure no longer exists and only the ornamental trees mark its location... long gone and forgotten, just like its owner.

Thomas' twilight years saw him become the figure of ridicule described by Kit Denton. His kidney trouble meant he needed a colostomy bag which he had to wear inside his trousers which caused him to walk with a strange gait.[190] Local kids imitated and mocked him in the street and called him, *'Old Man Thomas'*, but like all his other misfortunes he bore it stoically.[191] Various local accounts confirmed that he lived very frugally, but despite being down on his luck there was still a lot of respect and affection. J.F. Ellie Cowan said;

'I think that he lived very rough. Some said that he was an alcoholic — I wouldn't agree with that. He was living at the bottom of the old convent at Sextons Green (now demolished). I never saw him on a horse. Some of the things that he did got him the label of being eccentric. The last time I remember seeing him, he was crossing the road. I saw him on my way to the cemetery... I remember seeing J.F. sleeping in a tent in the cemetery — Well there was a tent there and he was near it. He was a proud and independent man.'

Another resident recalled how her mother would send her out with a bowl of soup for Thomas which he always refused, except on a few rare occasions. Given such instances it is hard to believe that a man who would not accept a bowl of soup, would knowingly embezzle money.

A lonely death

It was not long before Thomas was residing permanently in the town cemetery. On November the 10th 1942, he was taken ill in his room in town. Sensing the end of his long journey was nigh he asked to be taken out to *"Bonoo Bonoo"* where he was found dead the next day — Armistice Day 1942 (aged 81). Ironically, there had been no respite from Thomas in the 40 years since the Boer War — he was still fighting it. The saddest part is that his death certificate records Uraemia, Chronic Nephritis, Hypertrophied Prostate and malnutrition as the causes of death. As Kit Denton acknowledges:

> '... It was a sad way to end a life of action and passion, broken in body by neglect and hunger and in mind by the stresses set up during a few miserable weeks in South Africa forty years earlier.'[192]

Thomas' obituary, which appeared in the *Tenterfield Star* the following day, should lay to rest Bennett's proposition that *'Citizens of Tenterfield may be dismayed to find one of their heroes threatened by this paper's iconoclasm'* and that, *'... Thomas must be stood down from his pedestal'*. If Dr Bennett had read the obituary, he would have realised that Thomas was too modest a character to regard himself as a hero or require a pedestal. For all his faults and eccentricities, the *Star* summed up the collective feeling about Thomas that our research and conversations with the old-timers who knew him personally confirmed;

> '... His unobtrusive acts of kindness were legion and it may well be said that he would give his last shilling to a needy person.'

Thomas' resting place

Thomas lay unrecognised until Jack Thompson revived interest in him. At first, no one could find Thomas' burial plot and it was thought he had been buried elsewhere. Eventually, his modest plot was discovered and has now become a feature of the Tenterfield heritage trail.

The cemetery is built on a hill on the edge of town and when you stand by his grave which is on the upper rise you can see, framed by greenery, the railway station from which he left for war. Had Thomas stayed where he was and been content to live out his life in quiet obscurity and left the Empire to fight its own battles he would have been a lot better off — unless fate had some other cruel designs for him. The inscription on his stone was provided by the Commonwealth Graves Commission and simply reads,

> 'Major James Francis Thomas
> Major, Australian Bushmen's Contingent
> South Africa 1900'

That is incorrect, because as detailed Thomas served in South Africa 1900 and 1901, but so many details of Thomas' tragic life have been misconstrued or simply forgotten and not acknowledged. That basic inscription tells nothing of the story of the man who lies beneath it — nothing of the pride and passion he carried to war and nothing of the pain and disillusionment he returned with, but war memorials never do and as long as we continue to romanticise their senseless sacrifice we'll keep on building them.

However, in a belated recognition of Thomas' portrayal of him by Jack Thompson in the movie *Breaker Morant*, the cemetery's website has the following inscription:[193]

> 'Country Lawyer. Attorney appointed to defend Lt. Harry H. "Breaker" Morant, Lt. Peter Handcock, and Lt. George Ramsdale Witton, during the Boer War. Portrayed by Jack Thompson in the movie "Breaker Morant". Thompson won the 1980 Australian Film Institute Award for

Chapter 16: *Decline into professional disrepute*

Best Actor and the 1980 Cannes Film Festival Best Actor Award for his portrayal of Maj. Thomas.'

A further plaque that accompanies the head stone recognises Thomas' service to the Tenterfield community, as Commanding Officer of "A" Squadron New South Wales Citizens Bushmen, country lawyer, his distinguished and decorated service in the Boer War, and his defence of Lieutenants Morant, Handcock and Witton.

It also stated:

'In civilian life, apart from his law practice, Thomas for a period owned the Tenterfield Star newspaper. He retained a lively interest in researching and writing the history of Tenterfield and supported many causes to further the progress of his community.'

Vale

In a gratifying tribute, the inscription includes the words, '**friend to the death.**'

Despite this story, Australia has yet to recognise Thomas as a hero, preferring instead men with more "agricultural" qualities like cricketers and footballers. We can only wonder at what conspiracy of fates combined to deny Thomas the recognition he deserved. It was as though the Courts Martial was a poisoned chalice which sapped his will, confidence and good fortune he and everyone else involved in the case, had enjoyed before the war.

Perhaps his association with Morant, Handcock and Witton has forever sullied his reputation, but whatever your opinion of the men he defended, Thomas should not be tarred with the same brush. He simply did what any good lawyer would do — defended his clients to the best of his ability — which was considerable. If he made errors, he can be forgiven as he had not appeared in a military court before, unlike the military lawyers who prosecuted. Thomas had a best a rudimentary understanding of British Military Law, little time to prepare a defence and he was not starting on the "level playing-field" he imagined British justice would afford him. He was up against a formidable prosecution team that had three months to prepare a case with unlimited resources! The defence had no such opportunity. Thomas should have been engaged to provide legal assistance, when the men were arrested, investigated and incarcerated until the first trial commenced in January 1902. The failure to do this was an indictment on the Military authorities and contrary to the provisions of the MML.

This author agrees with Dr Bennett that Thomas was a bad lawyer, but only in the sense that in that he broke the "golden rule" so beloved of today's rapacious lawyers, *"don't get personally involved"*. Thomas cared too much for the plight of his fellow Australians and that may have made him a bad lawyer, but he was a decent human being.

Perhaps, as Witton suggests, Thomas was not privy to everything that went on in the Spelonken, but the same can be said of Witton himself and even Morant who did not realise the real issue behind the Courts Martial. This author doubts that Thomas' conviction was based on just the testimonies of his clients. He may have been trusting, but he was not naive. The fact that he built a case so quickly around customs of war and superior orders suggests that as a senior officer he may well also have received such orders and witnessed similar actions. Morant and Handcock were economical with the truth, but so was Lord Kitchener, the British Military Legal system and ultimately the British Government. His certain knowledge that a double standard had been applied and that they were unjustifiably executed shattered his whole value system which was based on the values of *"honour, manliness, and truth"* instilled in him as a youth at Kings.

It's taken us a century to recognise it, but Thomas followed those paths to the end, it's just that those around him did not aspire to the same high standards.

Chapter 17:
The Thomas Family Speaks

The Thomas family tree reflects a rich history of British ancestry. In this author's research of James Francis Thomas, he encountered William Beach Thomas, a solicitor living and practicing in Sydney, Australia. His parents were Owen James Thomas (a nephew of JF Thomas) and Sylvia May Thomas (nee Reid of Tenterfield) who were married in Tenterfield NSW on 5 May 1921.

J.F. Thomas was the first-born child of Beach Thomas' great-grandparents.

This author's research of Morant case and the struggles of Thomas not only led this author to form a close relationship with the descendants of Morant, Handcock and Witton, but also with Beach Thomas.

Beach Thomas has become immersed in the life of his great uncle and frequently commented to this author that the mental anguish that Thomas endured and the fatal end of his life in poverty and abandonment was a matter that had always troubled the Thomas family and something that he wanted to address. Unfortunately, with the demands of life and a busy legal practice, Beach Thomas could not devote the energy required to seek justice for J.F. Thomas.

It has been this author's privilege and pleasure to have formed a bond with the Thomas family and Beach in particular to bring comfort to them in knowing that Thomas' suffering and extraordinary life in Tenterfield in service to the community and the men he served in the Boer War is being recognized.

In his involvement, Beach had the honor of attending the moot court hearing the author had organised in the Supreme Court of Victoria during Melbourne Law Week in July 2013.

At a function that followed the hearing, Beach delivered an eloquent family portrayal of the burden carried by his family regarding Thomas' fate:[194] This author has included excerpts of Beach's address as they demonstrate the respect that he had for his great-uncle:

'After the findings of the courts martial were handed down and when all the circumstances of the events and the recommendations for clemency were taken into account, JF had reasonably believed that the death sentences, which automatically followed the convictions for murder, would not be confirmed by the Commander-in-Chief of the British forces in South Africa, Lord Kitchener. When only Witton's death sentence was commuted to life imprisonment with the death sentences for Morant and Handcock being confirmed by Lord Kitchener, JF made strenuous endeavours to have the sentences of death by firing squad for Morant and Handcock stayed by Lord Kitchener until representations for clemency could be made to the King and the Australian Government advised of the position. However JF was informed that Lord Kitchener was "uncontactable" and that nothing more could be done. Morant and Handcock were executed the next morning.

'JF died a lonely and broken man on Armistice Day in 1942 — he was 81 years old. He died in a shack on a small piece of farmland at Boonoo Boonoo near Tenterfield, a piece of land which is now registered in my name as administrator of his interstate estate.

'JF was devastated by the executions of Morant and Handcock and the sentence of life imprisonment given to Lieutenant Witton, and spent many years afterwards trying to have Witton released from prison in England and the record set straight for the families of Morant and Handcock.

'In 1902, JF was 41 years old, a country solicitor from Tenterfield NSW who was on his second tour of duty in South Africa as a general field officer (not a legal officer). Notwithstanding that he lacked any experience as a military or criminal trial lawyer, he was asked in desperation by Major Lenehan (a legal colleague from Sydney) to represent him as defence counsel in his court martial in South Africa.'

Chapter 17: The Thomas Family Speaks

Beach concluded his address by highlighting the desperate position that Thomas found himself in trying to represent the accused on serious offences which carried the death penalty:

'JF was summoned to Pietersburg, South Africa, arriving on 15 January 1902 (the day before the court martial was to commence) and met Major Lenehan who briefed him on the charges against him. JF was then asked by Lieutenants Morant, Handcock, Witton and Picton to also represent them in their courts martial as they had no one to represent them. Major Lenehan had no objections.

'With grave reservations and aware of the complexities of representing five accused with probably differing defences, JF nonetheless agreed to do so. With little time to prepare defence cases for the five accused, JF requested a delay in the start of the courts martial, but his request was refused. As a result the first of the courts martial commenced the next day, 16 January 1902 with less than a day's preparation.'

Beach proudly mentioned his visit to the Tenterfield cemetery when he spoke at the unveiling of a new plaque on JF's grave on 31 May 2002 (to mark the 100th anniversary of the end of the Boer War). He concluded his address by noting what he saw as JF's qualities:

(a) 'A well-educated, sensitive and compassionate man — a writer of occasional poetry, A good horseman and an excellent shot,

(b) A man amongst men — he raised and maintained a contingent of volunteers in the Tenterfield Arm of the Upper Clarence Lighthorse for some ten years and lead those men in combat in South Africa with distinction

(c) A supporter of Federation who promoted that vision through the Tenterfield Star newspaper

(d) A competent country solicitor who, when unexpectedly called upon to defend five officers accused of murder in South Africa in January 1902, acquitted himself well before the Courts Martial notwithstanding having no experience in military trials or in trials for capital offences.

(e) He was overcome by the outcome of the trials and during the rest of his life appears to have been unable to come to terms with it. He died a lonely and somewhat embittered man on Armistice Day (11 November) 1942.

(f) He was, however, when all is said and done, a "gentleman" — may he rest in peace.'

Beach continued his appeal for justice that had eluded J.F. As this author continued his research and lobbying for an enquiry into the Breaker case and ultimately posthumous pardons for Morant, Handcock and Witton, the descendants of these men and Beach kept agitating in writing letters to politicians.

In an article for *The Australian* newspaper in 2011, Beach appealed for intervention by the Australian Government to hold a formal enquiry into the case. He also used the article to highlight the plight of Thomas. The article stated:[195]

'He said his uncle was devastated by the events and fought to have the record set straight for the families of the three men. He said it would allow him to rest in peace if a judicial inquiry were held.

'Mr Thomas junior said he decided to write to Mr McClelland for the first time last month, 109 years after the trial of Morant, Handcock and Witton, to support calls for a judicial inquiry. 'This is an application for a judicial inquiry that will hopefully look at the legalities of what went on," he said. "I thought that being a solicitor and a relative of the lawyer who defended them, if I wrote to the Attorney-General it might put before him an aspect of the matter he may not have thought of".'

As this case matures to a just outcome and conclusion for the descendants and the Thomas family, the tabling of a motion in the Australian Parliament on 12th February 2018 was an event that was celebrated by them.

The Australian Parliament Speaks — 2018

Beach Thomas, accompanied by other descendants of Morant, Handcock

Chapter 17: The Thomas Family Speaks

and Witton attended Parliament and witnessed a motion and outcome that had eluded J.F. Thomas since the sentences were carried out on 27th February 1902.

In the House of Representatives, the motion was supported by three MPs from the two major parties. The motion expressed:[196] **Appendix D**

> *(a) sincere regret that Lieutenants Morant, Handcock and Witton were denied procedural fairness contrary to law and acknowledges that this had cruel and unjust consequences; and*
>
> *(b) sympathy to the descendants of these men as they were not tried and sentenced in accordance with the law of 1902.'*

Descendants of Morant, Handcock, Witton and Thomas pictured with James Unkles,(far right front row) Scott Buchholz,MP and Mike Kelly, MP at Parliament House with the flag that draped Breaker's & Handcock's grave

In light of this motion, Thomas can rest knowing that his advocacy for his clients was professional, that he did all that he could to achieve a just appeal, and he and his clients had been scapegoats for a brutal British policy to prosecute a war against the Boers and had been used to appease the Boer Command to achieve a peace treaty.[197]

Although the Australian election in 2022 produced a change of Government, this author's work will continue to achieve etc

This author's work continues to achieve a legislative outcome through an Act of Parliament granting posthumous pardons for Morant, Handcock and Witton, not as a denial of the crimes for which they were convicted, but for the cruel and unjust manner in which they were tried and sentenced be recognised. Their descendants seek resolution that Thomas had sought and this author's work is to make resolution a reality.

George Christensen MP – Support for Independent Review

Mr George Christensen, a former Member of Parliament is supportive of an independent inquiry. He addressed the Parliament's Federation Chamber on 2 December 2021.

His address reflected the sentiments of other community leaders and senior legal counsel who have urged an independent inquiry.[198]

His advocacy to Parliament is compelling:[199]

> 'We can still afford Breaker Morant, Peter Handcock and George Witton the legal processes they deserved at that time. That's why I'm calling on the government to initiate an independent review into those allegations, the evidence, the trial and the legal processes to determine whether justice was properly served and whether those three Australian soldiers really were just scapegoats. I know many people have spoken about a pardon, and descendants of these men would be extremely happy to have their ancestors exonerated. At the very least we should give them the courtesy of proper due process and properly investigate the circumstances that led to the execution of Morant and Handcock. If an independent review finds grounds for an exoneration, then a pardon from the Australia then a pardon from the Australian government for those men who served their country in the Boer War would be the appropriate course of action'.

In May 2021, Mr Christensen also urged Darren Chester MP, the then Minister for Veteran Affairs, to convene an inquiry:[200]

> 'I write to support the call of the descendants of these men for an independent inquiry and assessment noting the work of Mr James Unkles who has requested "an independent inquiry ... to bring a conclusion on the facts and matters in dispute and provide reassurance to Commonwealth countries that democratic traditions and the rule of law are paramount in reviewing cases in which there is credible evidence of a miscarriage of justice. This is not a case of seeking pardons, but merely an assessment of the evidence, in the manner similar to that carried out by the New Zealand Government in 2000 in relation to the execution of five WWI soldiers'.
>
> I write to support the call of the descendants of these men for an independent inquiry and assessment noting the work of Mr James Unkles who has requested "an independent inquiry ... to bring a conclusion on the facts and matters in dispute and provide reassurance to Commonwealth countries that democratic traditions and the rule of law are paramount in reviewing cases in which there is credible evidence of a miscarriage of justice."

Chapter 18:
A final salute

Thomas' life was an intriguing example of the reciprocal action of character and events. In the Boer War, things started to go wrong for him when he was censured for caring for wounded soldiers instead of leading his men to protect a convoy from attacking Boers. Back in Tenterfield, as a solicitor, he cared more for helping disadvantaged clients than for his own financial welfare and so ended up bankrupt. He never regained his former idealism after those two hot hectic months in January and February 1902 he spent unsuccessfully trying to save Morant and Handcock from the firing squad. Neither did he ever walk tall again after his twenty months in Long Bay gaol followed by his being struck off as a solicitor and his ignominious bankruptcy. It is the destiny of trusting people to be betrayed, and of idealist to be disillusioned. There is little doubt that Thomas was brought low by events which he had a hand in creating himself.

This author's opinion concerning the British Military's failure to provide Thomas' clients with fair trials according to the law of 1902 has not only been tested by his own research but has been shared by some of Australia's finest contemporary legal minds. While it could be argued that Thomas failed in his professional duty to achieve an acquittal of all the charges or at least the implementation of the recommendations of mercy for all three accused, it is satisfying that the legal opinions of the modern era validate what Thomas always knew, that his clients' fate was sealed before they were tried, taken hostage to political interference greater than events on the battlefield.

However, did Thomas betray himself? Was he true to his own values and character as reflected in his poetry?

Perhaps the Morant trials and his experience of British "injustice" had a profound effect on his mental health. Bleszynski summed it up as follows:

Chapter 18: A final salute

'Thomas cared too much, he made the cardinal mistake in legal practice of getting personally involved, he was a bloody decent human being, a man Australia has yet to recognise as a figure of national importance.'[201]

Thomas' life and aspirations came to lonely end. By any assessment he contributed to Australia's emergence into nationhood through his service to his community and his leadership and service in the military:

Thomas' Epitaph

In his despair, perhaps he sought solace through his own words:
'And here we learnt to love the paths of honour, manliness, and truth.'[202]

At Ease

Thomas did not overcome all odds; he was only partially successful in the defence of his clients and he suffered the agonising realisation that two of them were executed. However, it appears he behaved with the utmost integrity and did not refuse to represent the accused at a time when he was disenchanted with the British military and was on his way back to Australia. Although he failed to appreciate the ethics of representing many accused and how to avoid a conflict of interest, he pressed on with the job without the benefit of an adjournment to prepare the cases or the knowledge and support of the Australian Government. His only reward was his belief that he did his best, and was professional to standards of advocacy. Perhaps this was his greatest achievement.

Thomas' Legacy

Thomas' defence of his clients and support to Witton in his plea to the British Crown was professional. He also ensured one outcome was achieved. Following the news of the executions, the Australian Government expressed its concerns to the British Government about the Courts Martial and execution of Australian citizens. As a result, the Australian Government denied the British military the right to execute members of the Australian forces under British command (for example in World War

1). Since the executions of Morant and Handcock, no Australian has been sentenced to death for a military offence.[203]

Australian MP, Alex Hawke, recognised this when he stated in the House of Representatives in 2010 during his address about the case and his call for resolution:[204] (Appendix B)

> 'So since this incident there has not been a case of an Australian military service person being executed. The 1903 Defence Act was very important in preventing the deaths of many Australian service personnel in World War I, unlike the many soldiers from other countries, such as Ireland, Canada and indeed the United Kingdom, who were shot and executed for desertion and other matters that have subsequently been the subject of pardons from the British Government in recent years.'

Conclusion

The consistent theme in Australian history regarding this case has been the concern surrounding the circumstances that led to the trial of these veterans and the execution of Morant and Handcock. As a result of persistent and professional research, the suspicion of cover up and injustice has matured into credible evidence and certainty that these men were not tried according to law, were denied a fair process and suffered fatal sentence without respect for their right of military redress and appeal.

The fact that the men were dealt with in utmost secrecy and the Australian Government and the public were denied any knowledge that three of their volunteer soldiers had been arrested and tried has remained a permanent stain on the reputation of British justice. The smell of being scapegoated continues to this day as the chorus of injustice grows and resolution is advocated.

The case that Thomas championed was not resolved in his life time. In his letter to the *Sydney Morning Herald* in 1923 he expressed his anguish, but also his insistence the case was deserving of review, '*The true story of the Bush Veld Carabineers has never been told, but perhaps someday it will be.*'[205]

The *someday* remains this author's focus.

Chapter 18:   *A final salute*

A final question

While Thomas' service was recognised with the award of the Queen's South Africa Medal (QSA) with four clasps for his service during the Boer War, the intriguing question remains. Did he receive the medals?

This author researched this question with Thomas' descendants and discovered that the medals did not exist and had not been issued to him. On behalf of the family, this author made an application to the British Department of Defence. In June 2018, he received the following response:

> 'I can confirm that the MOD Medal Office do not issue any medals from this era of service. If you wanted to obtain replicas of medals you believe your relative was awarded, you would have to approach a medal production company and purchase them.'[206]

The response from the Australian Department of Defence — Medal section was equally disappointing and stated:

> 'As the British realm issued these imperial awards we have no authority or capacity to issue or reissue Boer War medals. We can only recommend that once you have ascertained what awards he qualified for you purchase replicas from a medals dealer.'[207]

Even in death and recognition of Thomas' service, his descendants have been denied the pride and peace that would come from the receipt of his medals. Instead, they have been left to secure medals from a commercial supplier. These responses from the respective Defence authorities is a sad reflection in failing to recognise Thomas' service to the Crown.

And so it is!

> 'And Thomas was victim too, Fourth of that tragic crew
> The court martials left him grieving for things he could not do
> Sad despair filled up his soul and struck deep in his heart
> James Francis Thomas citizen, began to fall apart.'[208]
> Copyright © James Unkles 2018

Epilogue

The Legal Industry pays tribute to Major Thomas

The outstanding features of Major Thomas' life, included his contributions to Tenterfield, his contribution to Australia's commitment to the Boer War and as a solicitor. Admitted to legal practice in May 1887, to being struck off (*'not a fit and proper person'*) the practitioner's roll in New South Wales as a solicitor in March 1928, Thomas remained devoted to the industry that had been the focus of his life.

Major Thomas' decline in his mental and physical health took a terrible toll on his career as a lawyer, his life in Tenterfield and ultimately resulted in his extreme isolation and destitution.

A Celebration

On 30 September 2019, the New South Wales Law Society, launched this book and celebrated Major Thomas' membership of the Law Society.

This was a joyous event for the descendants of Major Thomas as they joined guests, descendants of Morant, Handcock and Witton, members of the legal profession and the Law Society to recognise Major Thomas' contributions to the profession and community. Appendix G, page 224.

The Law Society's recognition was an appropriate salute to recognising Major Thomas.

This was reflected in a feature article in the Society's Journal[215].

The article included an extract from this book and an introduction:

> *'James Francis Thomas achieved notoriety as the lawyer who represented Harry "Breaker" Morant in his controversial trial for murder during the Second Boer War. Lawyer JAMES UNKLES has spent a decade investigating the case and hopes to secure posthumous pardons for Morant and his co-accused. As the 118th anniversary of Morant's arrest falls*

this month, Unkles shares an exclusive extract from his new book, Ready, Aim, Fire'.

Senator Jim Molan, AO, DSC officially launched the book and delivered a tribute to Major Thomas. His address was reflected in his Facebook post:[216]

'I had the pleasure of recently launching the book, Ready Aim Fire by James Unkles. The book tells the story of Major James Francis Thomas, defence lawyer in the 1902 Breaker Morant trial. Himself a military lawyer, James Unkles wrote it to acknowledge Thomas' sacrifice in taking on the case, which detrimentally affected his life and reputation for years afterwards. A great read for anyone with in an interest in the Military law and this remarkable period in Australia's history'.[217]

David Unkles with Marie Unkles, James Unkles and Jim Molan

Judge Sandy Street, QC, RANR, Nick Blesnynski and James Unkles

Jim Molan and James Unkles

Guests, including Beach Thomas, great nephew of Major Thomas, Peter Petty Mayor of Tenterfield James Unkles and Jim Molan

Thomas' Community speaks

In November 2019, an extraordinary vote of confidence was expressed by the Tenterfield Council on behalf of its citizens.

Mayor Peter Petty and his nine fellow councillors voted unanimously to move a Mayoral Minute to the Australian Government.

The Minute entitled: *Request For Review Into The Execution of Lieutenants Harry Breaker Morant, Peter Handcock and life sentence of George Witton – Boer War 1902*, included the following extract (see also Appendix H on page 229):

> 'I, Councillor Peter Petty hereby move the following Mayoral Minute at the Ordinary Council Meeting held on Wednesday, 27 November 2019.
>
> That Council supports Mr Unkles' submission to the Prime Minster, The Honourable Scott Morrison MP as follows':
>
> 'The Tenterfield Council supports the proposal that the Australian Government appoints a suitably qualified person, such as a former Judge, to review the evidence and submission that three (3) Australian veterans,

Lieutenants Harry 'Breaker' Morant, Peter Handcock and George Witton were not tried and sentenced by Courts Marital according to the law of 1902 and suffered a terrible injustice as a consequence.

The descendants of these men seek redress to mitigate the adverse effects the trials and executions have had and continue to have on the families of these men. Aggravating aspects include:

- *The veterans, individually and through Major Thomas, were denied the right of appeal and petition to the King for clemency;*

- *They were held in isolation during the trials and were denied the opportunity to contact their families in Australia;*

- *Major Thomas had one day to prepare complex trials on charges, which carried the death penalty. The prosecution had 3 months and unlimited resources to assist in preparing the cases. Major Thomas had no such support and was denied the opportunity to contact the Australian Government;*

- *The British Military's decision not to consult the Australian Government about the arrest and trials was an appalling tactic to ensure these men were tried and sentenced without Australia's intervention;*

- *The execution of Morant and Handcock was carried out with indecent haste, within a few hours of the sentences being proclaimed. This was a cruel decision and one that prevented any judicial or Australian Government intervention*

The granting of statutory pardons, will remove the stigma associated with the military service of these veterans and the dishonour to Australia's history.

Pardons will also acknowledge that the executions of Morant and Handcock and imprisonment for life of Witton were penalties they did not deserve noting the significant mitigating circumstances and recommendations for mercy that were made by the trial officers but not implemented by the British authorities"[218]

Comment

The support of Council was a significant step in recognising Major Thomas' sacrifice to secure fair trials and sentences for his clients.

Peter Petty affirmed his community's support for the case for independent review and posthumous pardons, to achieve an outcome that had eluded Major Thomas.

Peter Petty also highlighted Tenterfield's support for the resolution in his letter to the Australian Prime Minister, Scott Morrison, MP[219] The letter quoted from the Mayoral Minute and asked the PM to take appropriate action. (Appendix I).

Conclusion

It remains to be seen if Scott Morrison acts on the recommendation of Council and take action to review the case that has remained unresolved for 118 years. The case put to Scott Morrison highlights the injustice and identifies strong compassionate grounds to provide pardons that acknowledge Morant, Handcock and Witton did not deserve the sentences they received.

The descendants of these men and Major Thomas are right in seeking an outcome that provides relief for the decades of shame and guilt they have endured. They are not seeking monetary compensation, but an acknowledgement that the circumstances that prevailed during the arrest, trial and sentencing of these men were oppressive and the right to Major Thomas to prepare for the trials was denied and was contrary to law. Their denial of appeal and to seek the assistance of the Australian Government and their families was cruel and unfair.

A final sentiment

One of the descendants of Peter Handcock, Richard Williams expressed his thanks to the Council on behalf of his family and his sentiment reflects the respect that other descendants have for Major Thomas:

Dear Mr. Petty,

'As a great-grandson of Lieutenant Peter Handcock I am writing to thank you for your interest in this matter and your recent motion to write to the Prime Minister letting him know of you and your council's support for pardons for Lieuts. Morant, Handcock and Witton. Over the years I have developed a great deal of respect, regard and sympathy for Major Thomas and I believe he is someone that your community can be very justifiably proud of'.[220]

Chronology & Summary of Major James Francis Thomas

Date	Event
25/7/1861	J.F. Thomas born at Bayley Park near St Mary's, New South Wales.
	Parents: James Henry Thomas Sarah Eve Dawson They were married on 17th September 1859. **J.F. Thomas had the following siblings:** Henry Percival Thomas Ann Thomas Hugh Ernest Thomas William Beach Thomas Gilbert Stephen Thomas Leslie Dawson Thomas
1876 — 1877	J.F. Thomas attended The Kings School, Parramatta for the years 1876 & 1877.
1883-1887	J.F. Thomas signed Articles of Clerkship with an unknown Sydney Solicitor
28/5/1887	J.F. Thomas signed the roll as a Solicitor of the Supreme Court of New South Wales
1888	J.F. Thomas settled in Emmaville, NSW, and established a legal practice in the town.
1890	J.F. Thomas moved to Tenterfield and transferred his legal practice. He hears Henry Parkes give his Federation speech in Tenterfield.
10/2/1891	J.F. Thomas commissioned Second Lieutenant in the Tenterfield Arm of the Upper Clarence Lighthorse, a volunteer defence force.

Date	Event
1892	J.F. Thomas graduates from the Second Cavalry School of Instruction and promoted First Lieutenant. Appointed OC of the Tenterfield Mounted Rifles.
1895	Promoted to Captain
1898	J. F Thomas purchases the *Tenterfield Star*. He uses it to campaign for Federation and is a founding member of The Country Party.
1899	Commencement of the Boer War
28/2/1900	Departed Tenterfield for Sydney to embark for the Boer War in South Africa in command of a squadron. Listed as OC A Squadron of the NSW Bushmen's Contingent. Sailed for South Africa the same day.
March 1900 — May 1901	Served with distinction in South Africa seeing action at Rhenoster Kop & Elands River. Awarded the Queen's South Africa Medal with Four Bars
11/6/1901	Disembarks in Sydney at conclusion of his first tour of duty in South Africa. Promoted to Major
15/6/1901	J.F. Thomas presented with a plaque by Tenterfield Council.
June-August 1901	Active in recruiting men to return to South Africa.
21/8/1901	Embarks at Sydney on the Brittanic for return to South Africa for second tour of duty
15/1/1902	Arrives in Pietersberg, South Africa, at the request of Major Lenehan to represent him before a Court Martial in respect of the following charges: (i) The murder of Boer prisoners; (ii) The murder of a German missionary — Heese On arriving in Pietersburg, he ascertained that there were four other defendants charged with capital crimes namely: Lieutenants Morant, Handcock, Witton and Picton. They were unrepresented and at their request, he agreed to represent them.

Date	Event

15/1/1902 (continued)	Despite a request by Major Thomas for a day's grace to prepare his case for the defence, the Court Martial commenced the following day without regard to his request.
	The substance of Major Thomas' defence presented on behalf of the defendants was as follows:
	1. All defendants denied the killing of missionary Heese.
	2. As to the charge of killing Boer prisoners -
	   (a) Picton denied he was involved in the killings and it was not denied that Morant, Handcock and Witton were involved in the killings.
	   (b) The defence was raised that the accused were following superior orders which effectively meant that "no prisoners were to be taken".
	   (c) That the three accused did not personally carry out the killings although they did not deny that the killings were carried out with their authority.
	   (d) The killings of the Boer prisoners were justifiable acts of retaliation or revenge. In this regard it was submitted that acts which would otherwise be regarded as crimes in peacetime might be justifiable in times of war and in particular in the case of guerilla activities in South Africa.
	   (e) Lenehan, Morant, Handcock and Witton were entitled to a pardon due to their courageous defence of a fort whilst in custody. This pardon was based on the convention established by Lord Wellington.

20/2/1902	**Courts Martial** Verdict announced acquitting Lenehan and Picton of the killing of Boer prisoners. Morant, Handcock and Witton were convicted resulting in an automatic sentence of death, but the Courts Martial recommended clemency on a number of grounds. Lord Kitchener, the Commander in Chief of the Armed Forces in South Africa, after consulting with the UK, commuted the death penalty in respect of Witton to imprisonment for life, but confirmed the death penalty in respect of Morant, and Handcock.

Date	Event
Early 1903	Major Thomas returned to Sydney from South Africa.
1903	Returns to Tenterfield and resumes law practice.
1904	Lieutenant Witton released from prison in the UK after two years of his life sentence following a petition to the British Government.
1914-1918	Active in trying to promote a proper recruitment programme for WWI in Australia.
1915	Sold the *Tenterfield Star* Newspaper and purchased the Border Record in Killarney, Queensland.
1919	Sold his legal practice to P H Monckley with a covenant by him not to practise in Tenterfield until after 31/12/1925.
1919	Purchased farm near Tenterfield.
1920	Came to Sydney and established his solicitor's office at Wentworth Court in Elizabeth Street, Sydney
1921	Wrote *Early & Later Tenterfield* historical sketch.
1922	Sold "Haddington" the home which he had built near Mount McKenzie
1925	Involved in costs dispute with former client — Mrs E J Power — lost the dispute and ordered to pay the costs of the dispute which he refused to do.
1926	Re-opened his legal practice in Tenterfield. In December 1926 he was, on the application of a former client, attached for contempt of court for filing to pay the costs as ordered and was committed to Long Bay gaol in January 1927.
9 March 1928	Struck off the roll as a Solicitor of the Supreme Court of New South Wales on the application of the Law Institute on the grounds he had misappropriated or failed to account for the proceeds of sale of land in a deceased estate of which he was the trustee. He was so struck off notwithstanding that restitution was made at the last minute. The Supreme Court found that in the circumstances he was not a fit and proper person to remain on the roll

Date	Event
August 1928	Released from Long Bay gaol on the direction of the Attorney-General notwithstanding that he had still not purged his contempt.
1929	April — Appeals against the decision striking him off, but fails to have it overturned. October — Lieutenant Witton wrote a letter to Major Thomas informing him that Handcock and Morant had confessed to Witton in 1902 prior to the trial, that they had killed or murdered missionary Heese. This came as a shock to Major Thomas in that his instructions at the time were that Morant and Handcock were not involved in the murder and the Court Martial had acquitted both men of that charge.
1932	Major Thomas was carrying on business as an "Agent" in Tenterfield and living at Boonoo Boonoo a small holding in Thunderbolt bush ranging country near Tenterfield
11/11/1942	Major Thomas died in Tenterfield aged 81 years.

J.F. Thomas — what were his qualities?

(a) A well-educated, sensitive and compassionate man — a writer of occasional poetry.
(b) A good horseman and an excellent shot.
(c) He raised and maintained a contingent of volunteers in the Tenterfield Arm of the Upper Clarence Lighthorse for some ten years and led those men in combat in South Africa with distinction.
(d) A supporter of Federation who promoted that vision through the *Tenterfield Star* newspaper.
(e) A competent country solicitor who, when unexpectedly called upon to defend five officers accused of murder in South Africa in January 1902, acquitted himself well before the Courts Martial notwithstanding his lack of experience in military trials, in criminal trials in general and in trials for capital offences in particular.
(f) He was overcome by the outcome of the trials and during the rest of his life appears to have been unable to come to terms with it. He died a lonely and somewhat embittered man on Armistice Day (11th November) 1942.
(g) He was, however, when all is said and done, a "gentleman". May he rest in peace.

Appendix A

Below are excerpts from NSW Parliamentary Debates and a series of letters from Thomas relating to the reasons for and circumstances of his return to South Africa in August 1902.

'12 Castlereagh Street
18/07/1901
Private
Hon. John Lee
Chief Secretary's Office
Dear Mr Lee,
Regarding returned soldiers, I am getting heaps of applications from men who want to go back to South Africa — and heaps of them will get back somehow. I have notified Victoria Barracks that I am ready to go back, if required, with a new detachment. Failing my being required to go over officially, I shall probably go privately on a plan of my own. Plenty of men would go over with me privately to enrol in South Africa, but I don't want to be party to anything of the sort except with Government approval. But with men that want to go over for civil and other employment it is different and I have a proposal before me which I am considering and which I need not refer to now.

'My suggestion re Land grants may or may not be one which would be attended with success. As far as I can gauge, there is a general inclination amongst "unemployed" returned soldiers to go back to South Africa to try their fortunes. After all, it does not matter much if they do — they will advertise Australia and Australian products — and most of them will come back by -------. But, I do think it would be politic (if you will pardon me for saying so) for our Government to say, "… if you returned soldiers, most of you from country districts, want to stop in New South Wales, we are prepared to offer you every reasonable inducement to settle on the land. We will propose to Parliament to give each of you who desire *it and who fulfil the settlement conditions, a free grant of crown land, and in other ways will help you become settlers".*

'How would it go to appoint a small parliamentary committee of three to report on the matter and an advertisement might be published in the metropolitan and provincial newspapers asking for men, who desire to be granted a land concession, to send in their names at once to such a committee. This would be a guide as to whether it was worth while pursuing the matter further, or bringing in legislation for military settlers.

'If nothing comes of it, then the Government will have done its part and no man would have a right to complain — for really the Government has no moral obligation to find civil service billets for all returned soldiers.

'Pardon me if I appear to presume, but I conceive it to be in a ------ my duty as a Commanding Officer to interest myself in the matter.'

Yours faithfully,
J.F. Thomas'
To:
'Under Secretary Federal Defence
20th July, 1901

'Will minister disapprove my offering Lord Kitchener privately raise another Bushmens regiment without expense. Commonwealth are receiving numerous applications daily from returned soldiers seeking re- enlistment and am myself returning South Africa.

please-----reply.
J.F. Thomas'

(Source; Australian Archives Victoria Department of
Defence (1) Central Administration; Correspondence Files Annual single number
series Accession No B168 File No 1901/1734
See also Daily Telegraph 15th August, 1901, Page 5

'No 12 Castlereagh Street
Sydney
New South Wales

23rd July, 1901
From J.F. Thomas (Late Major New South Wales Citizen Bushmen)
To Captain Robert Collins Federal Defence Department.

'*Referring to my telegram of 20th instant, and your reply thereto of yesterday- I think it proper to write to you as to the occasion of my telegram, for the information of the Federal Minister of Defence.*

'*I returned from South Africa a few weeks ago in command of the Citizens Bushmen Regiment from this State.*

'*I returned as a matter of duty to the Regiment as no-one above the rank of a 1st Lieutenant was accompanying them and there was a great deal of regimental work and returns to be attended to. I mean to go back to the Cape for at least a few months.*

'*Large numbers of the men who returned with me have been utterly unable to find employment of any kind, and many are absolutely stranded. The same remarks apply to other returned soldiers to this State.*

'*I have been asked by my men to try to get them back to South Africa where they will try their fortunes on the gold fields — and whilst the war continues they are willing to enlist again.*

'*Lord Kitchener according to --------- says he wants more men- and here are plenty of experienced soldiers destitute of employment, who are willing to enrol. I have been interviewed by over 100 men (returned soldiers) during the last few days, all from the city. Many of them will go back privately and others are going back on promises of re-enrolment made in South Africa. Thousands of Australians will flock to Cape Colony, and those who go nowhere snapped up by the British Regiments and lose their Australian identity.*

'*Fifty men were to leave today by the Orient to join the Canadian Scouts. The men say "If we can go as Australians we would prefer it, but if we cannot we will join anything that offers".*

'*I am forming an Australian Association amongst those who are going to South Africa, to keep up their Australian identities and interests.*

'*I do not want to act behind the back of the Government, but if my late comrades want help to better themselves, then in my civil capacity I will do so; and I am sorry that there is a disinclination to give me any* assistance in furthering the ardent desires of those men to go to South Africa as Australians for more service- if

they are wanted and at no expense to the Commonwealth. They merely wish to offer their services and be given any reasonable facilities to go.

Great inducements were offered them to settle in South Africa- but our Government opposed — yet have done almost nothing to induce our Australians to settle in Australia.

I think I may reasonably ask for reasonable countenance from the Federal authorities in assisting these men.

Personally I have no special inducements for another period of hard service, but I like the men and I think they like me, and I am willing to go with them.

I have the honour to be your obedient servant,
James Francis Thomas'

'12 Castlereagh Str
Sydney
New South Wales
26th August/ July 1901
From Major J.F. Thomas;
New South Wales Citizens Bushmen
To Captain Collins — Minister for Defence;
'I have telegraphed you today that there are over 150 returned soldiers in and about this city who have given me their names and asked for passages back to South Africa. There is absolutely no employment in town or country for a large number of men and they say "let us go back to South Africa". The position may give rise to trouble — but I have asked the men not to call a meeting or anything of that kind.

'They want to go back as a body and as Queensland is sending a draft there seems no reason why these New South Wales men should not go in that capacity.

'A Corporal has been recruiting for the Canadian Scouts, and 50 of the men were to go by the "Orient", but a hitch occurred and they could *not get passages, which were to be indulgence passages). Why is not this matter done on the same system? I have merely registered the names of Citizen Bushmen (who are joined by others now) who cannot get employment — but I want to get them back to South Africa — as my actions are open.*

J.F. Thomas'

To Major Thomas
  12 Castlereay Street
  Sydney
  New South Wales
  30 July, 1901
'Re your letters twenty third and twenty sixth instant, also your telegram.

'Minister is cabling Lord Kitchener informing him number of men, Australia wish to return to South Africa, and enquiring whether he desires them to have permission; also whether indulgence passages will be granted. Minister however points out that in case of Officers or men of Commonwealth Forces wishing to take advantage of any such permission they would have to obtain leave through Military Commandant.

'Even though Thomas' actions contravene the policy of the NSW and Victorian Governments it is clear that there is alternative. The Government wished to retain its men, but could offer them no way of supporting themselves. It is a clash of policy vs reality rather than ideology over the war.

'Nonetheless, it was a hot-potato politically because NSW had made it policy not to actively recruit or bear the costs of any more men to go to SA. The long and short of the argument is summed up in the following exchange:
  'Mr See "...
I was astonished the other night when the Hon. member referred to a Captain Thomas as advertising for soldiers disposed to proceed to South Africa in the interests of the Government. Of course I have given no authority for the publication of the advertisement. I was communicated with by the Federal Premier, Mr Barton, as to the disposition of this Government on the subject; and I at once stated that I thought the

Appendix A

Government had gone far enough, and that we were not prepared to give Government sanction to any further enlistment here. Upon enquiry, I find that a gentlemen named Major Thomas, late of the Citizens Bushmens Contingent, is in Sydney, and has advertised for returned soldiers who desire to re-enlist for service in South Africa. The Government have nothing whatever to do with Major Thomas.

'Mr Gayness; Cannot the Government stop it?

'Mr See; As far as the Government are concerned, it has stopped; but I do not think the Government can prevent men going to South Africa if they desire to do so.

'Mr Moore; Why should the Government prevent them?

'Mr See; I do not think that the Government can prevent them.

'Mr Gayness; We want men in New South Wales, that is all.

'Mr See; The fact has been communicated to me that provision has been made by the Imperial Government for the conveyance of troops in a steamer called the Britannic. This information was furnished to me by the Federal Premier. The Imperial Government give the men a free passage on the condition that they pay for their own food on board, and also on condition that the respective State Governments pay the expenses of bringing to the port the various members of the contingent who desire to leave. I at once stated that I would not give my approval to that. The Government are not responsible for the advertisement which has been published, nor for any effort which is being made to obtain men, nor will they incur any expense in the matter. Of course I do not see my way clear to interfere with the rights of our subjects. If they feel inclined to go to South Africa upon a mission of the kind referred to, I do not see how we can stop them. Under the circumstances the Government have done all they can be expected to do...'

Source: New South Wales Parliamentary Debates VL pages 451 — 452 1901 13 Aug. 1901)

Appendix B

Opinions of Senior Lawyers, Judicial Officers and Community Leaders

- **The House of Representatives Petitions Committee** in March 2010 that stated the case for review as, *strong and compelling*. Alex Hawke, MP a member of the Committee addressed the House of Representatives on 15 March, *'the fact that the trial was not conducted properly means there is an avenue for redress of those convictions. There is in my view serious and compelling evidence that some form of redress should be given all these years later to those men executed by the British'*;

- In 2013, **Robert McClelland**, former Attorney General stated, *'I think there is cause for such an inquiry, an independent inquiry as recommended by Geoffrey Robertson. I've focused in particular on those flaws in the process. We're not seeking to be judgmental on the British Government as it exists today or the British people as they exist today, but the facts of the matter are there were fundamental flaws in the criminal process that resulted in these people being executed, and when that injustice occurs I think it needs to be revisited, and certainly it is a matter of public interest that that occur'*;

- **Dr Brendan Nelson**, Director Australian War Memorial, in a letter to me dated 21 July; *'I concur with your statement that your research should now be assessed by a competent and independent inquiry'*;

- **Geoffrey Robertson, QC**, (extract of legal opinion 2013): *'They were treated monstrously. The case of Morant and Handcock, the two men who were executed, is a disgrace. Certainly by today's standards* *they were not given any of the human rights that international treaties require men facing the death penalty to be given. But even by the standards of 1902 they were treated improperly, unlawfully';*

- **Gerry Nash, QC**, (analysis and written legal opinion of 14 October 2013): *'Clearly, in my opinion, the executions were unlawful and motivated otherwise than by a concern for justice. The descendants and relatives of the executed men have legitimate grounds for seeking a review 'The Australian Government could conduct its own low key judicial inquiry, to flesh out, so far as is possible, the true facts and then to present to the British Government the findings of that inquiry with a request that the British Government formally pardon each of Lieutenants Morant, Handcock and Witton';*

- **Greg Hunt, MP**, Minister: *'Well my view is that any Australian Government at any time should seek final resolution, and if we are elected then I will continue to work within the parliament to see that outcome. Well I think the concern is that two Australians were executed in a summary fashion without justice. Now none of this excuses what was clearly a heinous act in relation to the prisoners under care, but it is time, in my judgment, for a proper independent inquiry. That may not change the decision of the court, it may reverse the decision, or it may say that there were mitigating circumstances that these were actions taken under orders. But there was no justice, there was a summary execution after a sham trial and there deserves to be a full trial. This will not ever excuse their actions, but similarly it is clear that the actions of the colonial administration of those who were running the Boer conflict were equally reprehensible. And if there is a stain on the historic record we need to address it';*

- **Alex Hawke, MP**, (Hansard 15 March 2010 & 27 February 2012): *'I would support an inquiry. I would support an inquiry into this matter, because there are outstanding issues to be resolved. I think it's so important to Australia's future that we have our own legends, our own myths,* our own history, and that we have it thoroughly discussed, explored and dealt with, and it's so important not just for now but for future generations.' The executions were conducted with extreme haste and without appeal, I am convinced that some form of redress is necessary in this matter and could provide the current generations with some relief after decades of controversy. The passing of time does not diminish any injustice. There is in my view serious and compelling evidence that some form of redress should be given all these years later to those men executed by the British. It is the case that the executions were conducted with extreme haste and without appeal';

- **Mrs Julia Irwin, MP**, Chair of the House of Representatives Petitions committee. Copy of Hansard transcript dated 26 October 2009;[209] 'there appears to be some level of agreement across these two camps that the accused men had little opportunity to prepare a defence against the charges. This petition argues that there are indeed 'questions and concerns' over 'fairness, legal process and sentencing' at the court martial, and it is on these grounds, the petition suggests, that the cases against Morant, Handcock and Witton should be reviewed.'

- **Mr Tony Smith, MP**, now speaker of the House of Representatives, Copy of Hansard transcript dated 26th October 2009;[210]
  'He is asking that what he has researched be inquired into, be examined, be reviewed, and he has, in the best traditions of the parliament, presented that as a petition to the parliament.'

- **Mr Julian McGauran**, former Senator for Victoria. Senate Notice 'Calls on the Government to petition directly the British Government for a review of the case with the aim to quash the harsh sentence of death for Harry 'Breaker' Morant and Peter Handcock.'[211];

- **David Denton, QC**, (extract of legal opinion 2013):
  'In my ultimate opinion, based upon the foregoing, there are good grounds for the Australian Government itself to convene a public

enquiry into the circumstances affecting the convening, arraigning and conduct of the court martial of the Australian military veterans and to the subsequent conduct of the military authorities having authority over the Australian military veterans in their handling of the rights of the prisoners once they were found guilty of certain offences which carried a death penalty. In my opinion the issues raised by descendants of Morant, Handcock and Witton should be assessed with the assistance of a public inquiry. A public inquiry will also assist in finishing what the House of Representatives Petitions 'Committee considered in March 2010 and described as a compelling and strong case for pardons.'

- **Alexander Street, SC**, Judge Federal Court: Judge Street appeared at the Moot court in 2013 and successfully argued that on the evidence the men had been denied procedural fairness in their trials and the errors of law according to military law of 1902 were fatal to the administration of justice. Judge Street remains committed to having this case reviewed and believes Defence Inquiry is appropriate and lawful.

- **Sir Laurence Street, QC**, former Chief Justice NSWs (extract of legal opinion 2013):
  '*I think the British Government should intervene and appoint an enquiry, the outcome of which I'm sure would be that the conviction should not be allowed to stand and would quash the convictions.' This is an appalling affront to any general notions of justice, and an appalling injustice to the remaining living man. This was an exercise of the administration of criminal justice which sadly miscarried. No judge with any ownership of the criminal justice system in his jurisdiction, or her jurisdiction, could tolerate a... something of this sort going unremedied. This is crying out for judicial intervention.*'

- **Dr Howard Zelling**, (deceased) former Chief Justice of South Australia.
  '*The major faults (which are the same in both summings-up) are;*

- neither Morant nor his co-accused received a proper trial which the law says every accused person, and a fortiori an accused person on trial for his life, shall have;
- The summings-up were so appallingly bad that no proper trial was had on either charge on which the accused were convicted.
- There is no direction on onus of proof;
- There is no direction on the standard of proof where an onus lay on the accused (as it did on some issues in those days);
- There is no definition of what constitutes provocation at law;
- There is a misdirection as to intending the natural consequences of one's acts;
- There is no direction on the defence of honest and reasonable but mistaken belief in facts which if true might have afforded a defence;
- The defence case on any defence is never put in either summing-up;
- The so-called summing-up was, in short, a speech for the prosecution in each case;
- Neither summing-up would survive for one minute before a Court of Criminal Appeal (or a Court Martial Appeal Court for that matter).'[212]

- **Mr Charles Francis,** QC (deceased).

'While expressing no views on the facts that gave rise to the court martial of Breaker Morant and Peter Handcock ("Morant deserves a break," February 6), their conviction was clearly wrong in law. Early in the 19th century the Duke of Wellington propounded the military legal principle of condonation. No soldier facing court martial could be required to perform military duties until his trial ended. If he were placed on military duties, that was a condonation of any offence previously committed and thereafter he could not be tried for it. During the process of Morant and Handcock's trial, the Boers attacked the unit where they were imprisoned. They were temporarily released to fight valiantly in a successful defence action. Consequently, when the trial resumed, the court had an express duty immediately to discharge *them, as their offence, if any, had been condoned. Lord Kitchener would well have known their conviction was wrongful. Because of these executions, the Australian Government in the first days of World War I made Australian participation conditional upon no British court martial having the right to execute an Australian.*'[213]

- **Tim Fischer**, former Deputy PM (extract of interview 2013):
  'Because two great wrongs were done to both Breaker Morant and Peter Handcock — absolute wrongs — and also a wrong towards George Witton. And this goes to the moral values and fabric of a nation. We know these wrongs were done, do we do nothing about it, or do we in fact seek to at least... we can't reinstate life, correct the formal record by one method or another here or in Great Britain.'

- **Victorian Supreme** on 20 July 2013, Moot court:
  The decision of the Moot court determined Morant, Handcock and Witton were not tried according to law and suffered a serious and fatal injustice. Presiding judges, Andrew Kirkham, QC, RFD and Gary Hevey, RFD concluded after considering all available admissible evidence and hearing submissions from legal counsel:
  'considering the effect of the irregularity upon the Court's Martial verdict, that the Applicants have not had a proper trial and there has been a substantial miscarriage of justice. Where an irregularity has occurred which is such a departure from the essential requirements of the law that it goes to the root of the proceedings.'

Appendix C

Courts Martial Charges

VISSER CASE
Count one
G.C.M., Pietersburg, 16/1/1902.
President:
Lt.-Col. H.C. Denny, C.B. 2/Northampton R.
Members:
Bt.-Major J. Little, 2/Northampton R.
Bt.-Major H.M. Thomas, R.F.A.
Major Ouseley (D.S.O.), R.F.A.
Capt. A.D. Nicholson, 1/Cameron Hrs.
Capt. W.S. Brown, 2/Wilts. R.
Capt. W.M.K. Marshall, 1/Gordon Hrs.
Lieut. H.H. Morant, Lieut. H. Picton, Lieut. P.J. Handcock, and
Lieut. G.R. Witton, Bushveldt Carbineers.

When on active service, committing the offence of murder, in that they, each and all, or one or more of them, did, at or near Reuter's Mission Station, in the District Zoutpansberg, Transvaal, on or about the 11th day of August, 1901, wilfully, feloniously, and with malice aforethought, incite, instigate, and command Troopers Silke, Thomson, Botha, and Honey, Bushveldt Carbineers, then and there under the command of the said prisoners, each and all or one or more of them, to kill and murder one Visser, an unarmed prisoner of war then and there in the custody of the said prisoners; whereupon the said Troopers, Silke, Thomson, Botha, and Honey, being then incited, instigated, and commanded as aforesaid, did, each and all or one or more of them, kill and murder the said Visser.
    Plea   Not Guilty

Finding   Lieut. Morant. Guilty.
Lieut. Picton. Not guilty of murder; guilty of manslaughter.
Lieut. Handcock. Not guilty of murder; guilty of manslaughter.
Lieut. Witton. Not guilty of murder; guilty of manslaughter.
Sentence Lieut. Morant. Death by being shot. Recommended to mercy.
Lieut. Picton. To be cashiered.
Lieut. Handcock. Six (6) c.n. I.H.L.
Lieut. Witton. To be cashiered.
Dated 29th January, 1902

RECOMMENDATION TO MERCY.

The court strongly recommend Lieut. H. H. Morant to mercy on the following grounds: -

1. Extreme provocation by the mutilation of the body of Capt. Hunt, who was his intimate personal friend.

2. His good service during the war, including his capture of Field-Cornet T. Kelly in the Spelonken.

3. The difficult position in which he was suddenly placed, with no previous military experience and no one of experience to consult.

Confirmation   Lieut. Morant. Confirmed.
Lieut. Picton. Confirmed.
Lieut. Handcock. Finding confirmed.
Lieut. Witton. Confirmed.
Dated 25th February, 1902.[3]

---

3   *Australian Archives. Sentences on Officers in South Africa. 15 April 1902. House of Representatives in CRS 78/1. Carnegie pp. 191-192. Witton pp 157-160*

8 BOERS CASE
Count two

G.C.M., Pietersburg, 3/2/1902.

President:

Lt.-Col. H.C. Denny, C.B., 2/Northampton R.

Members:

Bt.-Major J. Little, 2/Northumberland R.

Bt.-Major H.M. Thomas, R.F.A.

Capt. W.E. Matcham, 2/Wilts. R.

Capt. H.R. Brown, 1/Cameron H.

Capt. A.D. Nicholson, 1/Cameron H.

Capt. W.S. Brown, 2/Wilts. R.

Lieuts. H.H. Morant, P.J. Handcock, and G.R. Witton, Bushveldt Carbineers,

When on active service committing the offence of murder, in that they, each and all or one or more of them, at or near Fort Edward, in the District of Zoutpansberg, Transvaal, on or about the 23rd day of August, 1901, did, when on active service, wilfully, feloniously, and of malice aforethought, instigate, incite, and command Squadron Sergeant-Major Hammett, Troopers Thomson and Duckett, Bushveldt Carbineers, then and there serving under the command of the said prisoners, each and all or one or more of them, to kill and murder eight men, names unknown, unarmed prisoners of war then and there in the custody of the said prisoners; whereupon the said Squadron Sergeant Hammett, Troopers Thomson and Duckett, being thereto incited, instigated and commanded as said, did, each and all or one or more of them, kill and murder the said eight men, names unknown.

Plea	Not guilty.
Finding	Lieut. Morant. Guilty.
	Lieut. Handcock. Guilty
	Lieut. Witton. Guilty.
Sentence	All death by being shot. Dated 4th February, 1902.

Appendix C

RECOMMENDATION TO MERCY.

The court recommend Lieut. H. H. Morant to mercy on the following grounds: -

1. Provocation received by the maltreatment of the body of his intimate friend, Capt. Hunt.

2. Want of previous military experience and complete ignorance of military law and military procedure.

3. His good service throughout the war.

The court recommend Lieut. P. J. Handcock and Lieut. G. R. Witton to mercy on the following grounds: -

1. The court consider both were influenced by Lieut. Morant's orders, and thought they were doing their duty in obeying them.

2. Their complete ignorance of military law and custom.

3. Their good service throughout the war.

Confirmation: Lieuts. Morant Handcock. Finding and Sentence confirmed.
Lieut. Witton. Commuted to Penal Servitude for Life.
Dated 25th February, 1902.[4]

---

4   *Australian Archives. Sentences on Officers in South Africa. 15 April 1902. House of Representatives in CRS 78/1. Carnegie pp. 192-193. Witton pp 157-160*

3 BOERS CASE
Count three

G.C.M., Pietersburg, 5th 2.1902.

President:

Lt.-Col. H.C. Denny, C.B., 2/Northampton R.

Members:

Bt.-Major J. Little, 2/ Northampton R.

Bt.-Major H.M. Thomas, R.F.A.

Capt. W.H. Matcham, 2/Wilts. R.

Capt. H.R. Brown, 1/Cameron H.

Capt. A.D. Nicholson, 1/Cameron H.

Capt. W. S. Brown, 2/Wilts. R.

Major-Thomas, R.F.A., objected to.

Capt. J.G. Lecky, A.S.C., replaces him.

Lieuts. H.H. Morant and P.J. Handcock, B.V.C.

Second Charge Sheet.

When on active service committing the offence of murder, in that they, at or near Sweetwater Farm, in the District of Zoutpansberg, Transvaal, on or about the 7th day of Sept., 1901, did, when on active service, wilfully, feloniously, and of malice aforethought, incite, instigate, and command Troopers Thomson and Botha and Corporal McMahon, B.V.C., then and there serving under the command of the said prisoners, each and all or one or more of them, to kill and murder two men and one boy, names unknown; whereupon the said Troopers Thomson and Both and Corporal McMahon, being thereto incited, instigated and commanded as aforesaid, did, each and all or one or more of them, kill and murder the said two men and one boy, names unknown.

Plea   Not Guilty.

Finding   Guilty,

Sentence   Death by being shot. **Recommended to mercy.**

Dated 6/2/02

Both confirmed. Dated 25/2/02.

Appendix C

HEESE CASE

G.C.M., Pietersburg, 17/2/1902.

President:

Lt.-Col. F. Macbean, C.B., 1/Gordon H.

Members:

Major L.L. Nicol, 2/Rifle Brigade.

Major E. Brereton, 2/Northampton R.

Capt. E. Comerwell, 1/York R.

Capt. E.J.C. Stapylton, R.F.A.

Capt. W.J.B. Rhodes, 1/Welsh R.

Capt. T.W.S. Kent, 2/Northampton R.

Lieuts. H.H. Morant and P.J. Handcock, Bushveldt Carb.

First Charge Sheet.

When on active service committing the offence of murder, the prisoner,

Lieut. Handcock,

in that he,

at or near Bandolier Kop, in the district of Zoutspansberg, Transvaal, on or about the 23rd day of August, 1901, when on active service, wilfully, feloniously, and of malice aforethought, did kill and murder one C.A.D. Heese, a missionary.

The prisoner Lieut. Morant,

in that he, at or near Fort Edward, in the district of Zoutpansberg, Transvaal, on or about the said day and date, when on active service, did wilfully, feloniously, and of malice aforethought, incite, instigate, and command the aforesaid Lieut. P.J. Handcock, B.V.C., then and there serving under his command, to kill and murder the said C.A.D. Heese; whereupon the said Lieut. Handcock, being thereto incited, instigated, and commanded as aforesaid, did there and then kill and murder as aforesaid the said C.A.D. Heese.

Plea	Not Guilty
Finding	Not Guilty. Dated 19th February, 1902.[5]

---

5   *Australian Archives. Sentences on Officers in South Africa. 15 April 1902. House of Representatives in CRS 78/1. Carnegie pp. 191-192, Witton pp 157-160*

Appendix D

Parliamentary Motion and transcript of addresses made by Scott Buchholz, MP, Mike Kelly, MP and Michael Danby, MP, 12th February 2018[214]

HOUSE OF REPRESENTATIVES

NOTICE OF MOTION

MEMBER FOR WRIGHT: I give notice that on the next day of sitting I shall move that this House:

Notes that:

A) Approximately 16,000 Australians fought in the Boer War in contingents raised by the Australian colonies or the Commonwealth Government (after 1901), or joined British and South African colonial units.

B) Australians, Lieutenants Harry 'Breaker' Morant, Peter Handcock and George Witton served as volunteers in a South African irregular unit, the Bushveldt Carbineers under British Military Command.

C) Morant, Handcock and Witton were found guilty at their courts martial for the death of 12 Boer prisoners even though they pleaded their actions were in accordance with orders of their British superiors.

D) Morant and Handock were executed on 27th of February 1902, with Witton's sentence commuted to life imprisonment. He was released from prison in 1904 after representations from the then Australian Government and British Parliamentarians, including Winston Churchill.

Acknowledges that:

A) Morant, Handcock and Witton were convicted of committing a serious crime.

B) Serious deficiencies in the handling of the legal case against the three men, including the right to appeal their sentences by their legal advocate, Major James Francis Thomas, the opportunity to seek intervention by the Australian Government and to contact their families to inform them of their plight.

C). The failure of British Military Command to implement the recommendations for mercy made by the courts martial to be applied equally to these men.

D). Findings of respected legal figures and community leaders who support this assessment.

E). The ongoing emotional suffering this case has caused the descendants of Harry Morant, Peter Handcock and George Witton.

Appendix D

Expresses;

A) Sincere regret that Harry Morant, Peter Handcock and George Witton were denied procedural fairness contrary to law and this had cruel and unjust consequences.

B) Sympathy to the descendants of these men as they were not tried and sentenced in accordance with the law of 1902.

_____ (signed)
Mover

_____ (signed)
Seconder, Member for Menzies

SPEECH

Date Monday, 12 February 2018
Page 28
Questioner
Speaker Buchholz, Scott, MP

Source House
Proof Yes
Responder
Question No.

Mr BUCHHOLZ (Wright) (10:13): I move:

That this House:

(1) notes that:

(a) approximately 16,000 Australians fought in the Boer War in contingents raised by the Australian colonies or the Commonwealth Government (after 1901), or joined British and South African colonial units;

(b) Australians, Lieutenants Harry 'Breaker' Morant, Peter Handcock and George Witton served as volunteers in a South African irregular unit, the Bushveldt Carbineers, under British Military Command;

(c) Lieutenants Morant, Handcock and Witton were found guilty at their courts martial for the death of 12 Boer prisoners even though they pleaded their actions were in accordance with orders of their British superiors; and

(d) Lieutenants Morant and Handcock were executed on 27 February 1902, and Lieutenant Witton's sentence commuted to life imprisonment, but he was released from prison in 1904 after representations from the then Australian Government and British parliamentarians, including Winston Churchill;

(2) acknowledges:

(a) that Lieutenants Morant, Handcock and Witton were convicted of committing a serious crime;

(b) the serious deficiencies in the handling of the legal case against the three men, including the right to appeal their sentences by their legal advocate, Major James Francis Thomas, the opportunity to seek intervention by the Australian Government and the ability to contact their families to inform them of their plight;

(c) the failure of British Military Command to implement the recommendations for mercy made by the courts martial to be applied equally to these men;

(d) the findings of respected legal figures and community leaders who support this assessment; and

(e) the ongoing emotional suffering this case has caused the descendants of Lieutenants Morant, Handcock and Witton; and

(3) expresses:

(a) sincere regret that Lieutenants Morant, Handcock and Witton were denied procedural fairness contrary to law and acknowledges that this had cruel and unjust consequences; and

(b) sympathy to the descendants of these men as they were not tried and sentenced in accordance with the law of 1902.

Harry 'Breaker' Morant is a name which is familiar to all Australians, but maybe not for the right reasons. In the movie *Breaker Morant*, produced in 1980, Edward Woodward, Bryan Brown and Lewis Fitz-Gerald depicted the three Army personnel. It spoke of the executions of Lieutenants Harry 'Breaker' Morant and Peter Handcock on 27 February 1902—some 116 years ago—and the sentencing of Lieutenant George Witton to life imprisonment. The issue continues to ignite passionate debate about the guilt or innocence of these men and calls for the acknowledgement of and relief for their descendants.

I wish to acknowledge some of the descendants of Lieutenant Harry 'Breaker' Morant, Peter Handcock and George Witton, as they sit in the chamber today: Michael and Lesley Handcock; Merrill Urban and Richard

Appendix D

Williams; Beverley Little, Tony Little and Lynette Pont—all descendants of Harry; Jennifer Witton-Sand, a descendant of George Witton; Ann and Cathy Morant, descendants of Harry 'Breaker' Morant; and Beach Thomas, a descendant of Major James Thomas, their defence counsel. I acknowledge and welcome you here today to the Australian parliament. And I acknowledge their advocate, James Unkles, and his wife, Maries, and the historians Shane and Melissa Williams, who are in this chamber to witness this moment. James, thank you so much for the work that you've done to date in preparing this auspicious motion.

Today, I acknowledge that Lieutenants Morant, Handcock and Witton were not tried in accordance with military law of 1902 and suffered great injustice as a result. The convictions were unsafe and unlawful and the sentences illegal as appeal was denied. This provides an opportunity for the parliament to discuss this.

The war between Britain and the two Dutch South African republics—the Boer War—began on 11 October 1899, where the Boers declared war on the British, and lasted until 31 May in the year 1902. During the Boer War, approximately 16,000 Australians served under British command and about 600 Australians died during the conflict. It was the first major conflict involving Australians overseas.

Harry Morant, Peter Handcock and George Witton, like so many other volunteers from Australia and other Commonwealth countries, joined up to support the Empire. The three men became commissioned officers and joined a volunteer unit called the Bushveldt Carbineers. These men shot 12 Boer prisoners while acting under the orders of senior British regular army officers—this fact is not in dispute. The court martial made significant recommendations for the three accused with respect to shooting the Boer prisoners. The court strongly recommended that, due to mitigating circumstances, including their lack of previous military experience, their ignorance of military law and their good military service during the war, mercy should be shown during the trial and their sentences. The court martial and Lord Kitchener, the military Commander-in-Chief, confirmed their sentences on 25 February 1902. He commuted Witton's sentence to penal servitude and ignored the court's recommendations for mercy for Handcock and Morant. Following the trial in 1902, Lieutenants Moran and Handcock were executed and Lieutenant Witton was imprisoned but released from prison following representation from Australian and British parliamentarians.

Today, I acknowledge that the process used to try these men was flawed and that they were not afforded the rights of an accused person facing serious criminal charges enshrined in military law in the year 1902. The prosecution had three months to prepare cases against the accused before trials commenced in January 1902. That was in stark contrast to Morant, Handcock and Witton, who were denied the right to consult legal counsel until 15 January 1902, leaving one day's preparation before trial to seek legal advice on serious allegations and complex issues with their defence counsel, Major James Francis Thomas, with whom they had had no previous contact. Their confinement and their limited time to prepare a defence, including locating and interviewing witnesses, prevented or frustrated them from mounting a defence to charges of murder. The circumstances that led to the execution of Morant and Handcock and the sentencing of Witton to penal servitude were characterised by indecent haste and a disregard for the rule of law and the appeals process.

This is what this motion speaks to. It speaks to the fact that these officers in the Australian Army, serving as volunteers, were not afforded their right to an appeals process. They were also prevented from communicating with their relatives, the Australian government and, most importantly, the sovereign king, who could have examined their pleas for clemency. Had their verdicts been stayed for a few days, Handcock, Morant and Witton could have discussed their options with legal counsel. They could have sought advice from the Australian government, as the military standards would have normally provided. Lord Kitchener made himself unavailable when the sentences were announced and could not be contacted, denying an opportunity for the accused to seek his reconsideration of the sentences. Lord Kitchener's actions ignored due process and denied an opportunity for an appeal or allow the men to exercise their right to a state or military redress of grievance. The sentences were carried out within two days of convictions and the sentences being announced. The accused were denied the opportunity to consider all avenues of review, including appeal action, with this unnecessary haste.

The laws of war prior to 1928 permitted reprisal against prisoners. 'Take no prisoners' was then a lawful order and was construed as such by Morant, Handcock and Witton, demonstrating that the British military had to take decisive action in fighting a devious guerrilla campaign waged by the Boers. Kitchener's decision to issue such orders was considered lawful according to the law in 1901, and one that had to be obeyed by the men. At the time of the offences, the law of reliance on superior orders was recognised as a legal defence in certain circumstances.

Sir Isaac Isaacs, Witton's second defence counsel, who eventually served as Governor-General and Chief Justice of the High Court, entered a submission on Witton's culpability, obedience to superior officers, limited military experience and disproportionate sentence. This could also be applied to the cases of both Morant and Handcock. Following a petition signed by over 80,000 Australians and support from the Australian and British parliaments, Witton was released from prison. Several members of the legal community have also supported the expression that we have here today, and I mention David Denton QC; Robert McClelland, former Attorney-General; Sir Laurence Street QC, former Chief Justice of the New South Wales Supreme Court; Geoffrey Robertson QC; and Gerard Nash QC.

I acknowledge the descendants of Lieutenant Harry 'Breaker' Morant, Peter Handcock and George Witton. The treatment of these men has caused them much grief and shame. Over the years, their families have had to try to deal with the guilt of the way in which these men were treated. Their collective grieving has been in secret, fearful that they would be shamed for the events of all those years ago. I'd like to express my deepest sympathy to all those in the chamber here as descendants and hope that this motion will go some way to easing your pain from 116 years ago. The Australian support for the British during the Boer War was significant for an emerging nation. This motion regarding Handcock, Morant and Witton recognises their service, respecting that duty to obey the orders of British superiors and be loyal to the Crown.

Lieutenants Morant and Handcock were the first and last Australians executed for war crimes, on 27 February 1902. The process used to try these men was fundamentally flawed. They were not afforded the rights of an accused person facing serious criminal charges enshrined in military law in 1902. Today, I recognise the cruel and unjust consequences and express my deepest sympathy to the descendants and thank their advocate, James Unkles, for his ongoing work. Today, I acknowledge the Morant and Handcock descendants and I note that this appeals process, again, will help bring some closure to what is an oversight and a travesty of military justice. It is through these few words in this chamber that I hope you find relief and that the history books will reprieve you.

Appendix D

SPEECH

Date	Monday, 12 February 2018	**Source**	House
Page	30	**Proof**	Yes
Questioner		**Responder**	
Speaker	Kelly, Mike, MP	**Question No.**	

Dr MIKE KELLY (Eden-Monaro) (10:24): I rise to thank my good friend the member for Wright for raising this motion. I salute his support for men and women in the Australian Defence Force and the interest he's taken in this issue. I also acknowledge the descendants who are in the chamber with us today on what has been an issue that has been a deep scar on and deep trauma of the Australian experience over many years. It was in the context of one of the more traumatic conflicts that our men and women in the Australian Defence Force have been involved in—the guerrilla warfare counterinsurgency environment is the most challenging circumstance that serving men and women can be involved in. We all know the stories that there have been through the years of being unable to identify the enemy clearly in that environment, the severe tension and trauma that is put upon those people in working through difficult environments of being sniped at and, in more modern times, attacked by improvised explosive devices. The incident that comes to mind too, most recently, was the killing of the cook in Afghanistan, Private Jones, and the emphasis that that then places on leadership in these circumstances, where we have to ensure that we're wrapping around our personnel, that there are no revenge or retaliation motivations, and also that people that we identify who are experiencing the stresses and traumas of these environments are properly identified and provided with support.

One thing that really jumps out at you if you look back at the history of this war, as I have. In also drawing on my own personal experiences in many deployments, I've noted that your standards start to get brutalised and can decline. This first happened to me in Somalia. It really came as a shock to me when I identified this happening. I understood then that one of my biggest roles as an officer was to maintain standards, to identify these kinds of pressures and problems that can arise. Many times in my own deployments there were circumstances where it would have been quite easy—no-one would have known—to fudge issues and problems in a way that would have been completely counter to the long-term strategic objectives we had and the interests of our soldiers in both their safety and their mental health in subsequent years.

Coming back to that experience in the Boer War, one of the things that really jumps out at me is the issue of the mental health of Breaker Morant himself. When his good mate Captain Hunt was killed and his body mutilated, something clearly snapped in him. It was identified by all the observers who were there that he was a completely changed person after that. Because this was an irregular unit, there were clearly failures of leadership about managing those personal matters in that brutal environment. Of course different standards applied at that time about how prisoners who were wearing uniforms were dealt with. The circumstances in which these people found themselves created this massive mental trauma that should have been better managed.

As has been alluded to, the issue of the 'justice' process was the greatest heinous issue of all. When you look back and think that we became a nation during the course of this war, and our government was not even informed for a couple of months about the process that took place and that these men were executed and Witton imprisoned, that led to the fact that we weren't going to let that ever happen again. So, if there's anything positive that we can say came out of this, it was that Australians on all sides of politics, and in our national approach to these issues, were never going to be subject to military justice again. And just as well, because in the First World War there was a lot of intense pressure to bring Australian military personnel under military justice. The British executed over 300 people—306 people, including Canadians and New Zealanders and Irish—but no Australian was executed. We were subject to our own discipline system. The reason that happened was the experience that occurred in this unfortunate and tragic circumstance.

So it's important and it's great that we've learned these lessons. I might also say, to the great credit of the Australians serving in the Boer War at that time, that many of them identified and were ashamed and disgusted by some of the practices that were going on there, given, obviously, signals by higher command, and actually raised this issue en masse in a petition to say, 'These need to be investigated and dealt with.' We've learned that lesson. We need to maintain that standard. If we take any lesson out of this, we need to preserve the integrity and the reputation of the slouch hat. Obviously these injustices of the past need to be remembered.

Ready Aim Fire | James Unkles

SPEECH

Date Monday, 12 February 2018	**Source** House
Page 31	**Proof** Yes
Questioner	**Responder**
Speaker Danby, Michael, MP	**Question No.**

Mr DANBY (Melbourne Ports) (10:29): I commend the member for Wright and the member for Eden-Monaro for their remarks. The injustice suffered by Harry 'Breaker' Morant is something that is in the Australian imagination. I commend the members of his family that are here in the gallery, and particularly Jim Unkles, for his long campaign for justice on their behalf. This is not an issue, as the member for Eden-Monaro pointed out, of whether some wrong act was committed; it's an issue of whether Australian servicemen serving in the Boer War were treated differently to British troops fighting in the same conflict. It's not just clear from the legend of the film but from all of the research that has been done since that that was the case.

I really think the member for Eden-Monaro made a great point: because of this great injustice, perhaps Australian troops were not executed during World War I, which came so soon afterwards. That's a very important step. It was a step that Australia took in seeing that we were more independent of Britain—not that we want to disassociate ourselves from the great Westminster system or anything like that, but there were circumstances where the imperial interests of Great Britain, prior to the First World War, were trying to be friendly with the German kaiser. Lord Kitchener felt, therefore, that the Australian colonials could be treated differently to British troops. These kinds of incidents happened after, as the member for Eden-Monaro said—and I'm sure the member for Wright did too—the mutilation of members of the Bushveldt Carbineers by the Boers. It was a very vicious conflict. Breaker Morant and his associates were treated differently to British troops. I think the idea of Lord Kitchener, in making himself absent from any ability to appeal the court martial, was that this would appease the Germans. After all, a German minister had been killed in that conflict. If one looks at even the geostrategic aims of what was attempted to be achieved, no appeasement was raised with Germany. The kaiser was determined to have his Great War; he was determined to show that Germany was the great power in Europe. And such foolish efforts by Lord Kitchener to appease, in anticipation, the Germans by executing colonials was unethical and a mistaken idea.

Jim Unkles, in his wonderful piece recently in *The Australian*, explained that this is a debate not about the execution of prisoners during the Boer War but about whether they were denied justice. He details the scandalous point that Lord Kitchener left Pretoria and told his staff he was uncontactable, thereby denying the Australians their legal right to appeal to King Edward and seek the assistance of the Australian government. That was a calculated perversion of the course of justice. He may have been told to do that by higher-ups in the British government, but, whatever it was, it was an example of treating Australians differently. I think this country has developed independently since then. That was a key point in the breaking of the commonality between Australia and Britain. If one looks at *The Bulletin* or any of the magazines that were published in all of the intervening years, they were very strongly aware of this injustice, and it sort of helped develop the independent Australian psyche that we have now, particularly when we're involved in military conflict. It's commendable that we continue to raise this with the British. I don't think any justice will be done until the capital punishment suffered by those two poor men is overturned.

The **SPEAKER**: The time allotted for this debate has expired. The debate is adjourned and the resumption of the debate will be made an order of the day for the next sitting. At a personal level, I welcome the descendants of the Morant, Handcock and Witton families to the gallery today and also James Unkles and his wife. Jim is a very passionate and dedicated member of my constituency and I want to welcome him here today.

Appendix E

Speech by George Christensen to the Australian Parliament, House debates, Thursday, 2 December 2021

Morant, Lieutenant Harry (Breaker)

Handcock, Lieutenant Peter

Witton, Lieutenant George

Mr CHRISTENSEN (Dawson) (11:17): Apart from the last sentence, I concur with the previous speaker. We should never have had lockdowns.

If justice were a meal, it would be better served cold than not served at all, and in a country where belief in a fair go is in our DNA the quest for justice should never fade. That's why, 120 years after the fact, there remains a strong desire amongst many people, some of my parliamentary colleagues included, for one of our national legends to receive long-overdue justice. In February it will be 120 years since the execution of Harry Morant—better known as Breaker Morant—and Peter Handcock, as well as the sentencing of their colleague George Witton to life imprisonment. Their trials and execution have been the subject of great conjecture in Australian history as well as the subject of stories, books, ballads, a screenplay and the 1980 movie titled *Breaker Morant*.

Harry Morant established himself as quite a character from very early on in life. He was undoubtedly an expert horseman, reportedly a womaniser and perhaps a little loose with the truth about his past and legendary exploits. Depending on which stories you believe, he may even have been a bit of a scoundrel. But being larger than life or, indeed, being a scoundrel does not make justice any less deserved. Even in times of conflict on foreign soil, everyone should be entitled to due process and equality before the law. Morant, Handcock and Witton were not tried in accordance with the military law of the time—1902 we're talking about. Their convictions were likely unlawful and their sentences likely illegal, as the men were not afforded an opportunity to appeal, which was a right enshrined in law in 1902. There was a failure to implement the courts martial recommendations of mercy, and there were denials of a proper opportunity to consult legal counsel before trial, the right to communicate with witnesses and next of kin and the right to communicate with the Australian government of 1902 to seek intervention and support.

Australians have always held in high regard the men and women putting their lives on the line by defending our freedoms on foreign soil. But not all Australians show the same respect today that they once did. There are those in the media and amongst the elites who despise our nation and those who fight to protect it. In 2016 some rumours were enough to launch an investigation conducted by New South Wales Supreme Court judge Paul Brereton to answer questions of unlawful conduct concerning the Special Operations Task Group in Afghanistan. What followed was a media and antimilitary pile-on besmirching not only the subjects of the rumours but an entire class of people.

You might recall that Chinese foreign ministry official Lijian Zhao posted to Twitter a photoshopped image depicting an Australian soldier holding a knife to the neck of an Afghani child. When the Brereton report was released the entire Special Air Service's second squadron was completely disbanded, tarnishing the reputation of every single member, whether they were a subject of that report or not.

When you read the report, it found that the rumours, the allegations and the suspicions around 39 alleged incidents were 'not substantiated'. While the inquiry found 'credible information' about 23 incidents, it said about that credible information:

There can of course be credible information of a matter warranting further investigation, even if there is also credible information to the contrary. A finding that there is credible information of a matter is not a finding that the matter is proved ...

But the trial by media and public persecution of our soldiers had already been conducted. A whole squadron was treated as if it were guilty and sentenced to a tarnished reputation, regardless of what outcomes may yet come out of any legal proceedings, so 120 years on we still have Australian soldiers being judged unfairly and not being afforded due process. But, as I said, justice is better served cold than never served at all. We can still afford Breaker Morant, Peter Handcock and George Witton the legal processes they deserved at that time. That's why I'm calling on the government to initiate an independent review into those allegations, the evidence, the trial and the legal processes to determine whether justice was properly served and whether those three Australian soldiers really were just scapegoats. I know many people have spoken about a pardon, and descendants of these men would be extremely happy to have their ancestors exonerated. At the very least we should give them the courtesy of proper due process and properly investigate the circumstances that led to the execution of Morant and Handcock. If an independent review finds grounds for an exoneration, then a pardon from the Australian government for those men who served their country in the Boer War would be the appropriate course of action.

Appendix F

GEORGE CHRISTENSEN MP
Federal Member for Dawson

26 May 2021

Hon Darren Chester MP
Minister for Veterans Affairs
PO Box 6022
Canberra ACT 2600

Via e-mail:
cc: Defence Minister Peter Dutton via email

Dear Minister,

I write to ask that you give further consideration to an issue which has been raised by a number of our past and present colleagues as well as many other leading legal minds over the past 12 years, and that is the perceived injustices regarding the trial and subsequent punishments meted out to three Australian Boer War veterans.

I do not seek the standard response explaining that this matter falls under the jurisdiction of the British Government.

What I do seek, on behalf of the many descendants of the affected men, is a commitment from the Australian Government to establish a short and independent inquiry or review of the material gathered by people such as lawyer and former commissioned RAN officer James Unkles, and considered by senior legal minds in this country (attachment provided) to determine once and for all, if there was a grave miscarriage of justice in their cases.

This is not a case of seeking pardons, but merely an assessment of the evidence, in the manner similar to that carried out by the New Zealand Government in 2000 in relation to the execution of five WWI soldiers. (Please see NZ Pardons case attachment). It is also the recommendation of QC Geoffrey Robertson that an independent inquiry or review be undertaken.

The circumstances surrounding the trial and execution of Lieutenants Harry 'Breaker' Morant and Peter Handcock, as well as the imprisonment of George Witton, are well known in this country and a number of books and films have told the story of these mounted riflemen from the colonies who volunteered to fight the Boers in Africa after they declared war on the British.

Though these events took place more than a century ago, there is considerable feeling about a grave miscarriage of justice and a lack of lawful due process in the treatment of these men, who were serving as Australians under the command of the British.

You may well be aware (and will see in the material attached) that the matter has been raised over the past 12 years by the Member for Casey Tony Smith, the Member for Mitchell Alex Hawke, the Member for Wright Scott Buchholz, the Member for Flinders Greg Hunt, the Member for New England Barnaby Joyce, NSW Senator Jim Molan and others.

Please also note the numerous expressions of support about these cases from eminent community leaders and the legal fraternity.

I write to support the call of the descendants of these men for an independent inquiry and assessment noting the work of Mr James Unkles who has requested "an independent inquiry … to bring a conclusion on the facts and matters in dispute and provide reassurance to Commonwealth countries that democratic traditions and the rule of law are paramount in reviewing cases in which there is credible evidence of a miscarriage of justice."

Appendix F

Please note the following attachments:
- Briefing on issue
- Support for a review
- Motion put by Member for Wright
- NZ Pardons case

I thank you for your consideration and advise that I will seek a meeting in the near future to discuss this matter in person.

Yours sincerely

[signature]

George Christensen MP
Federal Member for Dawson

Appendix G

Letter and Statement of Thomas to the Premier of Western Australia dated 2 May 1902

Pretoria.
C o p y.
2nd May 1902.

The Hon. the Premier,
Perth, West Australia.

Sir/,

It is rather taking a liberty to write to you perhaps, but I hope you will not think it so, as I really do not know to whom else to write at Perth, unless it be to the Editor of the "Perth Advertiser" (which I believe is your leading daily paper.

West Australia, being the nearest port of call from South Africa, it has occurred to me in reference to the deplorable shooting of Officers here on 27th Feby., that an item of news for the Australian press would best be sent from Perth, and that probably the proprietors of one of the leading Perth newspapers would telegraph it--if it appears necessary--to the ether metropolitan State newspapers, or otherwise use it for general public opinion information. That I would therefore like, if you will, would be that you would cause this to be handed to the Perth press. I acted as Counsel for the late Lieutenants Morant and Handcock and for Lt. Witton, who are the officers Australia is mainly concerned with.

I have the honour to be, Sir, Your
obedient servant, (Sgd) J. F. Thomas.

Appendix G

(1)

Major J. F. Thomas, of the New South Wales Mounted Rifles, who acted as Counsel for the late Lieutenants Morant and Handcock, and for Lieutenant Witton, now in imprisonment, during the Pietersburg court-martial cases says (writing from Pretoria on 2nd May): Although Lieutenants Morant and Handcock were shot here on 27th February, I have refrained from writing to the Australian Press upon the subject, because I assumed that an official report would be made at once to the Australian Government, seeing that Lieutenants Handcock and Witton are both native-born Australians--the former of New South Wales and the latter of Victoria. Lieutenant Morant, their senior and commanding officer, I may remark, was an Englishman who had served for a time in the Navy and afterwards knocked about Australia a good deal, coming to South Africa with one of the South Australian Contingents.

It would now appear that the first intimation the Australian Government received was from a returned Australian soldier, and, at the time of my writing, some of the Australian newspapers seem to have got hold of some very incorrect news--apparently from English sources.

I fully expected that the military authorities here, either directly or through the War Office, would have advised the Australian Government of the whole situation, because they were well aware of these Officers' nationality and that they were sent over to South Africa with contingents raised by the Australian States. I refer especially to Lieutenants Handcock and Witton, who besides being Australian-born soldiers, originally enrolled in recognised Australian contingents, took commissions, immediately their terms of service expired in those contingents, in a Corps commanded by an Australian officer--Major Lenehan--himself commissioned by the Government of New South Wales.

I put in a special plea for Lieutenant Handcock for this reason. It will be a great surprise to many Australians to learn that the Premier of the Australian Commonwealth apparently disowns any res-

(2)

responsibility for Australians merely because they re-enrol in a corps raised in South Africa; because some of these South African Irregular Corps are composed very largely of time-expired Australian soldiers from State Corps.

There is no Australian national corps (locally raised) in South Africa, and therefore Australian soldiers who wish to continue serving here have to seek some South African carps, or latterly they can join one of their own State corps (often a very unsatisfactory thing as they cannot take rank over the heads of the men already in the corps).

We have tried several times to get permission to raise locally a corps of Australian Scouts, but this is viewed with disfavour by the military authorities, who, it is said, want the Australians to be scattered through the South African Irregular corps. Surely these men, if they get into serious trouble, should be allowed, if only out of courtesy to appeal to their own Government to guard their welfare. Especially should not this be so in the case of those who have been promoted to officers' appointments? The military authorities here were most anxious to secure the services of experienced Australians, and being Colonials they should, in my opinion, have always the privilege of appealing to their own Government/ a fortiori before the dreadful penalty of death is inflicted by the authorities of the Regular Army.

Personally, I think it almost an insult to our nationality, when the same is distinctly pointed out, to put one of our soldiers to death without any reference whatever (as appears to be the case with Lieutenant Handcock) to his Government.

However, this is a question which need not be further touched upon here.

All that I desire at present to say is that I sincerely hope that the Australian press and people will not give credence to the infamously false allegations made by a certain section of the English press, detailing horrors and enormities which never took place. The whole thing lies in a nutshell. Lieutenant Morant, as senior and responsible

(3)

responsible officer of a detachment of the Bush Veldt Carbineers, ordered certain reprisals to be carried out against some Boers, and under his orders Lieutenants Handcock and Witton were present. They were all court-martialled and all sentenced to death, but Lieutenant Witton's sentence was commuted to penal servitude for life, whilst the 2 others were forthwith shot, in spite of appeals.

I can assure the Australian public that these reprisals were not made a cover for gain, and it was never even insinuated so by the prosecution. Neither is it true that these officers accumulated large sums of money. Handcock and Witton certainly did not, because they were practically moneyless.

Some very unfit aspersions have been thrown on the Bush Veldt Carbineers as a whole. It is quite true that there were some most undesirable and unscrupulous men enrolled in that corps (as poor old Handcock found to his cost), but the bulk of them were excellent men and numbers of them gentlemen by birth and education. They did most excellent work, and the fact that every effort was made to retain their services in the new (phoenix-like) corps, the Pietersburg Light horse, proves that they were thought highly of.

There is a great deal yet to be told, and which will in due course be forthcoming, but until the official reports are made public I

do not care to say more. But this much I can say, that both Handcock and Witton were under the orders of Morant, and though the conduct of the latter was undoubtedly in some respects very irregular, yet there is a great deal to be said on his behalf which at date of writing I have not seen published.

It must be remembered that both Handcock and Witton were subordinates; and I do not think that, when all the facts are made known, the latter will be kept long a prisoner. As for Handcock, I shall only say now that I think his execution is most deeply to be deprecated and deplored-- for he was a most estimable man, of previous unblemished character, and the most that can be urged against him is that

(4)

he had an exaggerated idea of patriotism and soldierly duty.

He simply obeyed the orders of Morant, who alleged that the reprisals were legal and justifiable. I shall never cease to grieve for him and I feel his death very, very bitterly. Pending fullest particulars, I would ask the public, especially those of his own State, to believe what I say about him; and as he left three young children unprovided for, I pray my fellow countrymen or their kindheartedness, not to forget these poor little ones thus INS by a hard misfortune left fatherless. I pledged myself to poor Handcock that Australia would not forget the children of a brave soldier torn from them by severely (too severely) hard luck.

I hope before long to return to Australia, when much can be explained that now and here I cannot enter upon.

(Sgd) J. F. Thomas.

Pretoria,
6th June 1902.

Appendix G

Sir/,

I have the honour by direction of the Honourable the Premier to acknowledge the receipt of a letter addressed to him by yourself on the 2nd May last, This letter has reference to the death penalty inflicted upon Lieutenants Morant and Handcock and encloses a written communication from yourself which the Premier is asked to hand to the local press.

The Premier is, however, unable to comply with your request as he cannot be in any way associated with the publication of a statement which might be considered a reflection upon the Military Authorities in South Africa. He will, however, forward your communication to the Prime Minister of the Commonwealth, who acting upon the advice of the General commanding will no doubt use his discretion with regard to the publication of whet you have sent.

I may inform you that the chief daily papers in circulation. in Perth are the "West Australian" and the "Morning Herald". There is no such paper as the Perth Advertiser.

Minn APRI CA.

Under Secretary, Premier's Department

COMMONWEALTH OF AUSTRALIA
DEPARTMENT OF EXTERNAL AFFAIRS.
IN REPLY
PLEASE QUOTE   Melbourne, 21st. June. 1902.

Sir: -
I have the honour to acknowledge the receipt
of your letter of the 11th June, forwarding a letter sent to
you by Major Thomas of South Africa and a copy of your reply
thereto.
I hate forwarded the correspondence to my
colleague the Acting Minister of State for Defence.
I have the honour to be,
Sir,
Your Obedient Servant,

The Honourable,
The Premier of Western Australia,
PERTH.

Appendix H

Press Reports:

The Bathurst Free Press and Mining Journal (NSW: 1851 — 1904), Wednesday 2 April 1902.

The Advertiser (Adelaide SA) 4 June 1901.

The Advertiser (Adelaide SA) 8 May 1902.

The British Times newspaper, *The Trial of Officers for murder of Boer prisoners*, Reuters correspondent, 17 April 1902.

Execution of Officers.

STATEMENT BY THEIR ADVOCATE.

Melbourne, Tuesday.

The most reliable information concerning the shooting, after court-martial sentence, of Lieutenants Morant and Handcock at Pretoria on February 27 is contained in a letter received by Mr. D. W. Witton, of Gippsland, father of Lieutenant Witton, who was court martialled at the same time. The letter is from Mr. J. E. Thomas, solicitor, who appeared at the court-martial to defend the prisoners, and is dated from Pretoria, March 1902. It reads as follows:—" Dear Sir,—I have a painful duty—though I am glad it is not so painful as it might have been—to perform, in giving you some particulars of his conviction, for instigating to murder, of your son, of the Bushveldt Carbineers. I may say at once that I believe, when the facts become known to your Government, it will not be long before your son is released. But, in any case, I anticipate he will be kept prisoner till the war is over, or, possibly, till the King's Coronation I am seriously dissatisfied with the severe punishment meted out. It was astounded, I think, every unbiassed person. I cannot say much here, but to one, at least, of the officers who were shot—a New South Wales man—I owe a sacred duty, and that is to let Australia know all the circumstances.

" Lieutenants Morant and Handcock, who were shot here on the 27th ult., were convicted, together with your son, by a court-martial, consisting of Imperial officers, of ordering their men to murder, as the charge alleges, several Boers, who had been captured under the following circumstances: Briefly stated, the evidence distinctly shows that their senior officer, Captain Hunt, formerly a Hussar officer, gave his junior officers and his sergeants orders that after a train-wrecking episode, in which an officer and a number of men were killed near Pietersburg, they were to take no prisoners. Hunt was soon afterwards killed himself, and Lieutenant Morant, his personal friend for years, succeeded to the command of the detachment. Hunt's body was badly maltreated by the Boers. Morant swore vengeance, and swore to carry out Hunt's orders. He pursued the party of Boers, who had done this to Hunt, and captured one who was shot through the head, and had portion of Hunt's clothing in his possession. It was decided to hold a drumhead court martial, and the Boer was found guilty of wearing khaki, and of being implicated in the barbarities to Hunt. He was shot by a firing party. Subsequently eight Boers, who had been captured in some outlying place, were, under Morant's order, all shot for being wreckers, bandits, and concerned in Hunt's maltreatment. Your son was present, and a Boer rushed at him was shot by him.

" It was considered by the court martial these executions were illegal, and that all the officers present were equally to blame for the shooting of these Boers by their men. The defence maintained was that under the customs of war the shooting of these Boers was allowable as they were merely roaming bandits or marauders. It was proved that in other cases exactly the same procedure was adopted and approved of by other officers. Consequently you will see that from a soldier's point of view, as any rate, the crime was not so dreadful as might appear, although technically it was a crime. I only regret that poor Morant and Handcock did not receive a sentence of penal servitude, but poor fellows, they were shot at about 18 hours' notice. Over Handcock's death I have suffered the deepest grief. It may be that before long I shall be back in Australia, when I shall make it my business to let the Government know the position. Your son has been sent a prisoner to England, and I think it will be wise to defer any active steps concerning him till the Australian Commonwealth Government is in possession of the facts.

" As counsel for your son and other officers I should like to see that all the facts from the prisoners' point of view are fairly brought forward. When everything is known you will not think the disgrace amounts to much or anything. War is war, and rough things have to be done. Only yesterday news came in of horrible barbarities on the part of the Boers towards some of our colonials. I say they deserve all they (the Boers) get, and with less nonsense and sentiment the war would be over.—(Signed) J. F. Thomas, Army Post-office, Pretoria. March, 1902."

215

MAJOR THOMAS'S EXPERIENCES.

Major Thomas, of the New South Wales Bushmen's Contingent, said he had witnessed some exciting scenes in South Africa. He left Australia as a captain, but had since been promoted to the rank of major. The squadron to which he belonged had been 540 strong, but soon after reaching the front it had been split up, through force of circumstances, into four sections of about equal strength. At one time they concentrated at Marandellas, in Rhodesia. A company of them, 100 strong, then made for Bulawayo, with a view of being present at the relief of Mafeking, but they were just two days too late to assist in the relief. The rest of the contingent put in an appearance later. The first hundred men had an opportunity, however, of witnessing the jubilation which followed. The major speaks with enthusiasm of the reception given to the hero of the event, Major-General Baden-Powell, at Bulawayo. The town, which was gay with bunting, was delirious with excitement, and festivities in honor of the occasion were made as attractive as possible under the circumstances. The Bushmen never met again in one band until Worcester was reached, some time afterwards. Portion of the contingent was with General Plumer, when he occupied Zeerust, the first town captured in the Transvaal. They patrolled the district, and did good work in clearing the rough country of the enemy. For the kind of fighting necessary in the circumstances there could be no question that the Australians were especially well adapted. They made themselves useful in the siege from August 4 to August 20 at Eland's River. Major Thomas and his men were a good deal in company with Canadians, especially with the Artillery. They found them pleasant and agreeable companions, thoroughly good bushmen, rough riders, and courageous soldiers. "But," added the major, "they are a very rough lot of fellows." The New South Wales men did an immense amount of work in the Eland's River district, mostly scouting. It was in this kind of service that the Australians mostly shine. "Although," says the major, "they did good work all round." Many of the men suffered from enteric fever, but they pulled through in most instances wonderfully. In all the contingent lost ten men from the fever.

The following is a copy of the report of the trials of the BVC officers on page 6 of The Times, 17 April, 1902.

THE TRIAL OF OFFICERS FOR THE MURDER OF BOER PRISONERS

Reuter's correspondent at Durban writes under date March 22:-

At Pietersburg on January 17 the trial by general Court-martial of Lieutenants H.H. Morant, P.J. Handcock, Picton, and Wilton, all of the Bushveld Carbineers, was begun. The Court was composed of Lieutenant-Colonel Denny (president) and five other officers. Major Copland was Judge Advocate, and Captain Burns-Begg, Public Prosecutor.

The prisoners were charged with the murder of a wounded Boer prisoner named Visser. They pleaded "Not Guilty", and were defended by Major Thomas, New South Wales Mounted Rifles.

The prosecution called Sergeant S. Robertson, who stated that he remembered the fight at Devil's Kloof, when Captain Hunt and Sergeant

Hunt were killed. Captain Hunt's body was found to have been stripped. He took the bodies back to Reuter's farm, where the party was reinforced by Lieutenants Morant, Handcock, Picton and Wilton.

Next morning they went in pursuit of the Boers, overtook them, and captured their laager, finding one wounded Boer there. Next day the Boer accompanied the force some distance. During the dinner hour the accused held a conversation in which the Boer prisoner, who was in a Cape cart six yards away, appeared to take no part. Morant and an Intelligence officer named Ladybore went to Visser (the Boer prisoner) telling him that they were sorry, but he had been found guilty of being in possession of the late Captain Hunt's clothing, and also of wearing khaki. The witness did not catch what further was said, but was told to warn two men for duty. He refused, asking Picton by whose orders this man was to be shot. Lieutenant Picton replied that the orders were by Lord Kitchener, naming a certain date, and were to the effect that all Boers wearing khaki from that date were to be shot. The witness said he had never seen any such orders, which should have been posted or read regimentally.

Cross-examined, he said that Captain Hunt's body bore marks of ill-treatment. The prisoner had a kind of khaki jacket on. Captain Hunt had previously told the witness that he had direct orders that no prisoners were to be taken. On one occasion Captain Hunt abused him for bringing in three prisoners against orders. The outrage on the train when Best was killed had embittered the men very much. Morant had previously been considerate to prisoners. He was in charge of the firing party that executed Visser.

Trooper Botha corroborated the previous witness, and said he was one of the firing party who carried out the sentence on Visser, who was carried down to a river and shot. The witness had previously lived with Visser on the same farm. He objected to forming one of the firing party.

Corporal Sharpe gave corroborative evidence, and said that after the firing party had fired Picton discharged his revolver apparently at the dead man's head.

L. Ledeboer deposed that on August 10 last year he translated the sentence of a Court-martial that condemned Visser to be shot. Morant, Picton, Handcock, and Wilton formed the Court-martial.

The prisoners elected to give evidence on their own behalf.

Morant stated that he was under Captain Hunt with the force charged with clearing the northern district of Boers. It was regular guerilla warfare. Captain Hunt acted on orders he brought from Pretoria. On one occasion he brought in 30 prisoners, when Captain Hunt reprimanded him for bringing them in at all, and told him not to do it again. The witness took command after Captain Hunt was killed and went with reinforcements. When he learnt the circumstances of Captain Hunt's death, and the way he had been maltreated, he followed the Boers and attacked their laager. The Boers cleared, leaving Visser, who had on a soldier's shirt, and was using Captain Hunt's trousers as a pillow. He was court-martialled and shot on this account. The others knew of Captain Hunt's orders. Morant told them he had previously disregarded them, but after the way the Boers had treated Captain Hunt, he would carry out the orders which he regarded as lawful.

Cross-examined, the prisoner said that Captain Hunt's orders were to clear Spelonken and take no prisoners. He had never seen these orders in writing. Captain Hunt quoted the action of Lord Kitchener's and Strathcona's Horse as precedents. The prisoner had not previously carried out the orders because his captures were "a good lot." He had shot no prisoners prior to Visser. No witnesses were called, as they were all eye-witnesses. Picton raised an objection to Visser being shot, on the ground that he should have been shot the night before. Captain Hunt told the witness not to take prisoners. He never questioned their validity.

The prisoner was asked whether he knew who gave the orders, but the Judge-Advocate protested against the question, and was upheld by the Court after consultation.

On the resumption of the trial next day, however, the Court allowed the question, and the prisoner Morant stated that Colonel Hamilton, Military Secretary, was the one who had given Captain Hunt the orders that no prisoners were to be taken. Others, including Handcock, received these orders from Captain Hunt. The Court-martial was reported to Colonel Hall within a fortnight after it was held. A report was also sent to Captain Taylor. The prisoner had only Captain Hunt's word for it that

Colonel Hamilton had given these orders. He had made no attempt to get his report of the Court-martial as evidence.

Picton, another of the accused, deposed that he had previously done two years' service in this war, and gained a D.C.M. under Le Gallais. After the capture of Visser, Morant said he was perfectly justified in shooting him. The prisoner said it would be hard lines to shoot him, and asked Morant to call the other officers together. A meeting was held, and it was decided to shoot Visser. Picton corroborated the statement that he had also received orders from Captain Hunt not to take prisoners. He never questioned the orders, and had been reprimanded by Hunt for bringing in prisoners. Captain Hunt was very bitter about the death of a friend of his, a lieutenant in the Gordon Highlanders, who had been killed in a train wrecked by Boers. The prisoner reported the execution of Visser to Major Lenehan verbally immediately after, and then to Colonel Hall. Morant and Hunt had been old friends, and after Hunt's death Morant was inclined to be more severe on the enemy. He had never previously shot a prisoner or seen one shot. Visser was not informed of the nature of the trial that was taking place. Prisoner opposed the shooting of Visser at the Court-martial. He had never obeyed the orders to take no prisoners, because he did not like the idea. He was in command of the firing party, and merely obeyed orders. On the whole Visser would be aware of the charge against him, as the prisoner had previously told him of the seriousness of his position. Hunt never had any chance to carry out his own orders about taking no prisoners.

Major Neatson, staff officer to Colonel Hall, Officer Commanding Lines of Communications, deposed that he had received certain reports from Captain Taylor with regard to engagements with Boers, but remembered nothing about a summary of a Court-martial.

P.J. Handcock, another of the prisoners, deposed that he had attended the trial of Visser at Morant's request. He corroborated the previous evidence as to the reasons for executing Visser and the orders not to take prisoners.

Prisoner Wilton gave corroborative evidence, and said he was present at a conversation with a Mr. Reuter, from which he gathered that Hunt had been murdered. Reuter said Hunt's neck was broken, and his eyes gouged out. The prisoner was guided by his superior officers in regard to the finding of the Court-martial. He believed Visser knew that he was being tried, but he was given no opportunity to speak or make a defence.

F. L. Reuter, missionary in charge of the German Berlin Mission station, deposed that Captain Hunt's and Sergeant Eland's bodies were brought to his place. Hunt's body was much mutilated. The neck appeared to have been broken, and the face bore marks of boot nails.

Civil Surgeon Johnston testified that he heard Hunt reprimand Morant for bringing in prisoners. He was of opinion from the evidence that the injuries to Hunt's body were caused before death.

Captain Taylor stated that he had received a message from the Boers through natives that if he were caught he would be given four days to die, which meant torture, because he had previously been hunting in the country. The Boers in that part of the country were more outlaws than part of a legal commando. He had heard Hunt reprimand Morant for bringing in prisoners. Morant had always behaved well to the Boers. He had transmitted a report of the expedition in which Hunt was killed, but did not know what was in it. Field Cornet Tom Kelly sent him a message saying that the first Englishman who came near his wagon would be shot.

Major Lenehan, in command of the Bushveld Carbineers, was next called. He said he had no direct control over the corps, which acted under headquarters at Pretoria. Captain Hunt took over the command from Robertson and got orders from the officer commanding the line of communication. From his knowledge of Morant he thought him incapable of murder or inciting thereto. Picton reported the shooting of Visser, and the witness reported it to Colonel Hall. He knew nothing of any order not to take prisoners.

Major Bolton denied any knowledge of a proclamation that Boers taken in khaki were to be shot.

Major Lenehan had never heard of orders that no prisoners were to be taken.

The evidence of Colonel Hamilton, taken in Pretoria, emphatically denied the issue of any order that no prisoners were to be taken.

On the 23rd the Court sat to hear the case against Major Lenehan.

The charge against him was that, being on active service, he culpably neglected his duty by failing to report the shooting by men of his regiment, the Bushveld Carbineers, of one man and two boys, these being prisoners and unarmed. The prisoner pleaded "Not Guilty."

Trooper Botha deposed that three Boers were being brought in by Captain Taylor's Police, and were shot at close quarters by five of his own corps. He reported what had been done to Morant in the presence of Lenehan.

Trooper Bonny testified to hearing the last witness make his report to Morant.

In his defence the accused denied having heard any such report made to Morant. He had heard Morant say to Taylor that he had had a scrap with the Boers and got three. The accused told them that he had come down to Spelonken expressly to make inquiries concerning rumours of the shooting of prisoners, and statements were taken. He had never had any reason to believe that these three Boers had not been killed in fair fight.

Lieutenant Edwards, who took down the evidence in connexion with the inquiry made by Lenehan, said that the report on the shooting of these three Boers was included in papers sent in on the subject.

Civil Surgeon Leonard deposed that Morant and Taylor were having an argument regarding the trustworthiness of the Boers, Morant maintaining the affirmative. He sent for Botha, who, in reply to questions by Morant, said he was a good soldier and had done his duty and shot Boers. There was no special mention of any particular Boers being shot.

The accused was further charged with having failed to report that a trooper of the Bushveld Carbineers had been shot by Lieutenant Handcock. He pleaded "Not Guilty."

Lieutenant Edwards deposed that he received a confidential letter from Captain Hunt, of which a copy was made, the original being forwarded to Pretoria. A postscript to the original had since been torn off. The postscript read:-"Will also write details of death of Van Burend; Handcock shot him." The detachment in which Van Burend was was only nominally a detachment of the corps. No details of van Burend's death were ever received. Lenehan sent word by witness that he would make a confidential report. It was Handcock who reported the death of van Burend.

Major Bolton gave evidence as to the searching of the prisoner's kit and finding of the letter produced, minus the footnote.

Ex-Captain Robertson said he knew Van Burend, who was shot on July 4 last. The witness had been warned about van Burend as one who was not to be trusted and was suspected of thefts of whisky from an officer and of money from Kaffirs; and men refused to go on duty with him. He was always creating disturbances and abusing khakis. The witness, Taylor, arid Handcock had a talk over the man and it was decided he was to be shot. Handcock and four men went out on the left flank, and when it was finished the witness told Lenehan he was prepared to stand a Court-martial, as he had 30 prisoners, and Boers were near, and the man might give them the slip and give them away. The witness was superseded by Hunt. He made a report of this occurrence and of the shooting of six men to the accused. The report made to Lenehan of Van Burend's death was not a true one. He concealed the true facts in the interests of the corps. Taylor also knew the true facts. The witness also reported the true facts to Hunt. Lenehan had come down to inquire into the charges against the witness.

The prosecution was closed, and the defence claimed the discharge of the prisoner on the ground that it had not been shown who was the superior authority to whom the prisoner should have reported, and it was not shown, therefore, that a report had not been sent.

The Court decided that the case should proceed. The accused in his defence denied that Robertson had ever informed him of the manner of van Burend's death. It never occurred to him that the postscript in Hunt's letter indicated anything suspicious.

Captain Taylor denied that he was a party to the conversation when it was agreed that van Burend must be shot. Robertson mentioned casually that he would have to shoot him, but the witness never heard till afterwards that he was shot. The accused asked the witness if he knew anything about van Burend's death. The witness replied "Not personally." The accused said he would have to report the murder when he returned to Pietersburg.

Lieutenant Handcock denied that a meeting was held which decided on the shooting of van Burend. The witness carried out Robertson's instructions in this matter, and Robertson ordered him to make a report, making it appear that van Burend had been shot in a brush with the Boers. The report which he prepared did not suit Robertson, who wrote one himself. The witness reported the true facts to Hunt, asking him to inform Lenehan. He told Robertson, who said he was a fool to have anything put in black and white. Robertson's evidence was all a fabrication.

The counsel for the defence referred to the fact that the prisoner had already been under arrest for three months and protested against an officer's being kept so long without trial. The prisoner was commander of the corps in name only. Robertson was the man who should have reported, and he had done so falsely. He and Taylor were the men who should have been prosecuted, but Robertson had been allowed to resign unconditionally.

The prosecution maintained that, Robertson having reported to the accused, the latter should have reported to his superior.

Lieutenants Morant, P.J. Handcock, and G. Wilton were then charged with having murdered, or instigated others to murder, eight men whose names were unknown. They pleaded "Not guilty."

Major Bolton prosecuted.

L.H. Ledeboer deposed that about August 20 last he was in charge of a party who captured eight Boers. He handed the prisoners over to a patrol, and did not know what became of them.

Trooper Thompson stated that he and Troopers Duckett and Lucas were sent for by Morant, who asked them if they were friends of the late Frank Eland; if they knew the late Captain Hunt; and if they had seen Lord Kitchener's proclamation to the effect that "those who take up the sword shall perish by the sword." The Lord, he added, had delivered eight Boers into their hands, and they were going to shoot them. Lucas objected, but Morant said, "I have orders and must obey them, and you are making a mistake if you think you are going to run the show." On the morning of the 23rd the witness saw a party with eight Boers. Morant gave orders, and the prisoners were taken off the road and shot, Handcock killing two with his revolver. Morant afterwards told the witness that they had to play into his hands, or else they would know what to expect. The witness said that the evidence which he had given at the Court of Inquiry was given under pressure and was untrue. He only knew about Hunt's orders by hearsay. Wilton was present at the execution.

Sergeant-Major Hammett corroborated the evidence as to the shooting of the prisoners. Morant informed him on the previous evening that prisoners were being brought in and were to be shot. The witness asked Morant if he was sure he was not exceeding orders. Morant replied that he had hitherto disregarded them, and would do so no longer. The Boer prisoners were first asked to give information about Tom Kelly, and one of them made a rush at Wilton and caught him by the jacket, whereupon he was shot dead, and all the rest afterwards. Morant had always treated prisoners well till Hunt's death, and then he became a different man altogether. Wilton shot the prisoner who seized hold of him.

Sergeant Wrench said it afterwards appeared that some objected to the shooting. Morant told him to find out who did not agree, and he would soon get rid of them, adding that he had been congratulated by headquarters over the last affair, and meant to go on with it.

The prosecution was then closed.

The counsel for the defence claimed the discharge of the prisoners on the ground that the charge was not proven, arguing that they should, if charged with anything, be charge with conspiracy.

The court overruled the objection.

The counsel for the defence then said he did not dispute the facts, but would call evidence to show — (1) the orders received; (2) the prevailing custom, having regard to the enemy they were fighting; (3) the practices adopted by other irregular corps against an enemy breaking the usages of war.

The prisoners having handed in their statements of defence, Civil Surgeon Johnson deposed to reprimands administered by Captain Hunt to men who brought in prisoners.

Lieutenant Hannam stated that when he was a trooper in the Queensland Mounted Infantry on one occasion at Bronkhorst Spruit in 1900 his squadron took some prisoners, and was reprimanded by Colonel Craddock for taking them.

Lieutenant B.F. Guy, R.S.O., handed in a statement as to trains wrecked on the Pietersburg line by Boers.

J.E. Tucker testified to Boers breaking into refugee camp and carrying off 141 of the inmates.

Other evidence showed that Captain Hunt gave distinct orders to sergeants not to take prisoners.

Sergeant Waller Ashton deposed to Brabant's Horse receiving orders to take no prisoners in consequence of specific acts of treachery on the part of the Boers.

The Judge Advocate objected to such evidence as irrelevant.

Sergeant McArthur testified to seeing one Boer summarily shot for being caught in khaki.

Lieutenant Colin Philip said the Queensland Mounted Infantry were in disgrace on one occasion for bringing in prisoners caught sniping. Boers caught breaking the customs of war were shot summarily. Instructions were published in the orders in Colonel Garrett's column that Boers caught in khaki were to be shot.

Captain King, of the Canadian Scouts, stated in evidence that Boers guilty of wearing British uniforms, train wrecking, or murdering soldiers were dealt with summarily.

Another witness deposed that Hunt's and Eland's bodies were found stripped and maltreated.

Sergeant Roberts said that on one occasion Hunt gave him orders to lead a false attack on a fort, during which some prisoners were to be shot. The witness objected, and the orders were not carried out.

Further testimony as to the good character of all the prisoners and their kindheartedness was given, and the case then closed.

The counsel for the defence pleaded justification, on the ground that the Boers in that district were gangs of train wreckers without a head, and their conduct had brought reprisals.

The prosecution submitted that the evidence was not denied. The eight men had been shot.

The Judge Advocate refused the plea of justification. The contention that other corps had done similarly did not make two wrongs right.

The court was cleared and on its reopening Major Lenehan was asked if he could give evidence regarding the character of the prisoners. He gave an excellent account of the pluck and good services of Morant, who was responsible for the capture of Tom Kelly. Handcock, he said, had an excellent record and was a simple-minded man with a strong sense of duty, obeying orders implicitly. Wilton was also a good soldier and officer.

Lieutenants Morant and Handcock were next charged with murder in instigating the killing of two Boers and one boy, names unknown. They again pleaded "Not guilty."

Sergeant-Major Hammett deposed that he was one of the patrol which the prisoners accompanied in search of three Boers. It was reported that the Boers were discovered, and it was then agreed that when Morant asked, "Do you know Captain Hunt?" that was to be the signal for shooting them. This was done. The youngest Boer was about 17.

Other members of the patrol corroborated this evidence. The Boers, they stated, were discovered at a native kraal, were sent on, and at the signal shot. It was understood that no prisoners were to be taken.

For the defence, Morant deposed that he went out to look for the three Dutchmen. He found them, and never asked them to surrender. As they were Dutchmen with whom they were at war and belonged to a party which had stripped and mutilated a brother officer, who was a friend of his, he had them shot.

Handcock gave evidence as to Hunt's orders that no prisoners were to be taken. The Boers in that district were simply a scattered band of marauders.

The counsel for the defence urged that it must have been a matter of military knowledge that the Boers in this district made no pretence whatever of being under a leader or carrying on recognized warfare.

On February 7 the Military Court then sat to hear the charges against Alfred Taylor, who was accused of murder in inciting Sergeant-Major Morison, Sergeant Oldham, and others to kill and murder six men, names unknown. The prisoners pleaded "Not guilty."

Sergeant-Major Morison, Bushveld Carbineers, deposed that on a certain day in July last he paraded his patrol and reported to Captain

Robertson. The accused was present, and said he had intelligence that six Boers with two wagons were coming in to surrender, but that he would have no prisoners. The witness asked Captain Robertson if he should take orders from Taylor. Captain Robertson said, "Certainly, as he is commanding officer at Spelonken." Morison asked Taylor to repeat his order, which he did, saying that, if the Boers showed the white flag, the witness was not to see it. The witness repeated these orders to Sergeant Oldham, and warned six men and a corporal to accompany Oldham as an advance party. Six Boers were shot by the advance guard. These were the only ones met with that day. The patrol went on, and the following day a larger party of Boers with women and children was brought in, Taylor and Picton going to meet them.

Sergeant Oldham stated that the previous witness warned him of six Boers, and told him he was to make them fight, and on no account bring them in alive. The Boers were ambushed. There was a man in front of a wagon holding a white flag, and a great noise in the wagon. Oldham stopped the fire, thinking there might be women and children, but since he found only six men, as described in the orders, they were taken out and shot. He believed the flag was put up after the firing commenced. The Boers were armed, and their rifles loaded. A good many prisoners were afterwards taken and sent into Pietersburg. The witness addressed his report of the affair to Captain Taylor, by Morison's orders. Captain Robertson complained, and the report was readdressed to him. Neither Taylor nor Robertson was present at the shooting of the Boers.

Trooper Heath corroborated this. He said the Boers were disarmed, lined out on the road, and shot.

Ex-Captain Robertson corroborated and said that he had told Morison he must take his orders from the accused. Oldham reported, "All correct; they are all shot," and the witness saw the bodies.

Cross-examined, the witness admitted having had to resign and having been refused admission to any other corps. Morison reported that he was threatened with arrest. Morison demanded an inquiry, but broke his arrest and went to Pietersburg. Taylor asked for the patrol, as six armed Boers with two wagons were reported. Morison did not receive instructions from Taylor in the witness's presence. It was usual for patrols to get orders from Taylor

Major Lenehan deposed to receiving orders to supply 50 officers and men to proceed to Spelonken with Taylor. An inquiry was held in regard to charges in which Robertson and Morison were mixed up. Colonel Hall decided that it was better that Morison should go. This closed the case for the prosecution

The accused elected to give evidence in his own defence. He said that during July last year he was in charge of natives and intelligence work. He was formerly a lieutenant in Plumer's Scouts and came down on special service. No part of his instructions authorized him not to take prisoners. He had no military command. His instructions went to the officer commanding the detachment of Bushveld Carbineers. Colonel Hall's instructions were that a detachment of 60 men were to assist him in the Zoutpansberg. He gave instructions to the officers, telling the number of men required for patrols if any Boers had to be fought or captured. He never interfered with non-commissioned officers but once, when Lieutenant Picton placed Morison under arrest, and the witness refused the latter permission to go to Pietersburg, although he nevertheless broke his arrest and went. The witness received intelligence of certain Boers coming in to surrender, but never of the party of six. He never gave Morison any orders, and knew nothing about the six Boers, nor had he asked for a patrol to meet them. That patrol took three days' rations with it. The patrol afterwards brought in parties of Boers of which the witness had been advised. The first intimation he had received of the charge of six Boers having been shot was made yesterday in court.

Davidson, clerk to the accused, deposed to the fact that letters addressed to the latter giving intelligence of the Boers were missing from the office after some one else took the witness's place. The empty file was found at his successor's office.

Otto Schwatz, an intelligence agent, spoke to having reported to Taylor the intention of two parties of Boers to surrender, but said he had never mentioned a party of six. Taylor was angry about the shooting of these Boers.

Further evidence for the defence was taken to show animus on the part of Morison.

The counsel having addressed the Court, a second charge was preferred against the same prisoner in respect of the murder of a native.

Corporal McMahon deposed to being out on patrol when he sighted some Boers, but the latter evidently had wind of his coming, for when the place where they had been seen was rushed no Boers were there, but some opened fire from a Kaffir kraal. The Boers were driven off. The witness heard a report and somebody said, "Taylor's shot a nigger." He walked over and saw a Kaffir, and Taylor standing by with a pistol in his hand.

Trooper Lucas stated that after the engagement with the Boers he rode to the kraal. Captain Taylor questioned a native, who said "I kona." The witness heard a report, and the native fell dead. Taylor had a pistol in his hand.

Trooper Sheridan corroborated this.

The accused stated in his defence that he had received his appointment as Native Commissioner in the north on account of his knowledge of the natives, and went on condition that he should have a free hand. On this occasion the natives had warned the Boers of the approach of the party, and one native was brought in and recognized as one of them who had been assisting the Boers. He refused to give any information and was threatened with trial as a spy. He refused to show or say anything, and was going off when he was called back, but would not return. Witness then fired, meaning to frighten him, but unfortunately fired too low, and the native was killed. The shooting of this native had a salutary effect.

Corroborative evidence was called, and the counsel for the defence pleaded justification.

The Court deliberated, and on its reopening the prisoner was informed that he was acquitted of both charges.

On February 17 the Court-martial sat to hear a charge of murder preferred against Lieutenant Handcock in having killed Mr. Heese, a German missionary, while Lieutenant Morant was charged with the offence of inciting to murder.

The prosecution stated that witnesses would be called to prove that on August 23, 1901, Missionary Heese left Fort Edward for Pietersburg, and the motive for killing him was that he had got to know of the killing of eight Boers, and was on his way to Pietersburg to report the occurrence when he was shot by Handcock under orders from Morant.

Trooper Phillip deposed that on 23rd August last he was on duty at Cossack Post when a Cape cart containing the missionary and a Cape boy was going in the direction of Pietersburg. The missionary showed a pass signed by Captain Taylor. He was greatly agitated, saying there had been a fight that morning and several had been killed, but he did not say whether they were British or Boers.

Corporal Sharp said that he had seen Morant addressing Heese, and had afterwards seen Handcock riding in the same direction as the missionary. It was about 10 or 11 a.m. when the missionary went past, and Handcock went about 12. The latter had a carbine. He did not take the same road as the missionary.

Cross-examined, the witness admitted that he had gone a long way to fetch one Van Roozen, who, he thought, was an eye-witness of the killing of the missionary. He did tell Hodd that he would walk barefooted from Spelonken to Pietersburg to be of the firing party to shoot Morant. He admitted that Handcock had issued an order against soldiers selling their uniforms in consequence of the witness's having done so. He had made it his business to collect notes of what was going on at Spelonken.

Two witnesses said that Handcock had left the fort that day with a rifle. He was on a chestnut horse. It was no unusual for an officer to carry a rifle.

A native deposed to having seen an armed man on horseback following the missionary. The man was on a brown horse. The witness afterwards heard shots, and then saw the dead body of a coloured boy. He took fright and fled. This was about 2 p.m.

Trooper Thompson testified to having seen the missionary speaking to the eight Boers who were shot.

Other witnesses gave evidence as to having seen Heese speak to Taylor, while Morant was present after the shooting of eight men

H. van Roozen gave evidence as to having spoken to the Rev. Mr. Heese on the road about 2 p.m. The witness trekked on with his wagon till sundown, when he saw a man on horseback coming from the direction of Pietersburg. The man turned off the road. Afterwards a man came on foot to the witness. He could not say if it was the same man that he had seen on horseback. The man on foot was Handcock, who advised the witness to push on, as Boers were about.

Trooper Botha deposed that he was one of the patrol of which Handcock had charge, and which found the missionary's body.

The case for the prosecution then closed.

The accused Morant deposed that on August 23 eight Boers guilty of train-wrecking and other crimes were shot by his orders. Heese spoke to these Boers and was told not to do so. Afterwards the witness saw Heese in a cart. He produced a pass signed by Taylor. The witness advised him not to go on to Pietersburg because of the Boers. Heese said he would chance it, and by the witness's advice he tied a white flag to the cart. The prisoner returned to the fort and then went to Taylor's, and he afterwards saw Handcock at Bristowe's. Handcock went on to Schiel's. The prisoner never made any suggestion about killing the missionary. He was on good terms with him.

The accused Handcock made a statement as to his doings on that day. He said he left on foot for Schiels' in the morning, taking the road which branched off to the Pietersburg road, and then across country. He lunched at Schiel's, and then went to Bristowe's till dusk, then back to the fort.

Further witnesses proved that Handcock was at Schiel's and Bristowe's when the missionary was shot.

The Court returned a verdict of "Not Guilty" in the case of both prisoners.

The result of the trials is that Morant, Handcock, Wilton, and Picton were found *Guilty* in connexion with the charges of murdering prisoners. Morant and Handcock were sentenced to be shot, and the sentence was duly carried out in Pretoria Gaol on February 27. Lieut. Picton was cashiered, and Major Lenehan reprimanded.

Appendix I

MEDIA RELEASE

Wednesday, 25 September 2019

TENTERFIELD SOLICITOR THE 4TH VICTIM IN 'BREAKER' MORANT TRIAL

Former Senator and Major-General (ret'd) Australian Army, Jim Molan AO, DSC, will officially launch "Ready, Aim, Fire", a book dedicated to the memory of the late Major James Francis Thomas – known as the fourth victim in the execution of Lieutenant Harry 'Breaker' Morant, in Sydney on 30 September 2019.

Thomas was the defence lawyer in the 1902 Courts Martial of Lieutenants Harry Morant, Peter Handcock, and George Witton who were tried and sentenced for executing 12 Boer prisoners, one of the first war crime prosecutions in British military history. Morant and Handcock were executed on 27 February 1902 and Witton's death sentence was commuted to life imprisonment.

117 years since the Courts Martial, military lawyer and the book's author, James Unkles, is still fighting on behalf of the men's descendants for the Commonwealth Government to hold a judicial inquiry into the trial and sentencing of the three men and seeking their posthumous pardons.

Like many, Unkles believes the men were scapegoats for the war crimes of their British superiors – who were not prosecuted for similar offences and giving illegal orders to shoot prisoners. Critics of the accused say they were lawfully convicted of serious war crimes and deserved the sentences they received

According to Unkles, the book acknowledges the sacrifice Major Thomas made in acting as the defence lawyer for these three men, a task that took a terrible toll on his mental and physical health and his life in Tenterfield.

"Major Thomas inadvertently found himself the centre of this controversy when he was asked to defend the accused - he was given only one day to prepare the defence of the accused of serious charges tried over a period of about one month," Unkles said.

"While the prosecution had three months to prepare its cases and unlimited resources to assist in their preparation, Major Thomas had no such assistance.

"He had to act as both solicitor and counsel and was refused an adjournment so he could better prepare a proper defence. He also protested that following the sentencing; his clients were illegally denied the opportunity to seek assistance from the Australian Government, exercise their right of appeal and lodge a petition for mercy to the Crown, a decision that sealed their fate as the sentences were carried out within hours."

As Unkles explains, Major Thomas was a colourful character; bachelor, poet, lawyer, soldier, war reporter, newspaper owner and editor of the "Tenterfield Star", cheese maker, grazier, gardener, local historian, bankrupt, resident of Long Bay goal for 20 months, and lobbyist for Federation.

The book's author, James Unkles, has been a lawyer for 35 years and a former Crown and Police Prosecutor. He is a serving Officer in the Royal Australian Navy Reserve.

INTERVIEW REQUESTS & MEDIA CONTACT:
Sue Finn | Media and Public Relations Manager
The Law Society of New South Wales
T: +61 2 9926 0288 | M: +61 413 440 699 | E: media@lawsociety.com.au

Appendix J

COUNCIL   27 NOVEMBER 2019

MAYORAL MINUTE

(ITEM MM8/19) REQUEST FOR REVIEW INTO THE EXECUTION OF LIEUTENANTS HARRY "BREAKER" MORANT, PETER HANDCOCK & LIFE SENTENCE OF GEORGE WITTON - BOER WAR 1902

SUMMARY
During the Anglo Boer War of 1901, James Francis Thomas from Tenterfield, New South Wales joined thousands of other Australians and travelled to South Africa as a volunteer to support England in its fight against the Boer population between 1899 and 1902. Approximately 16,000 Australians fought in the Boer War in contingents raised by the Australian colonies or the Commonwealth Government (after 1901), or joined British and South African colonial units.

BACKGROUND
Australians, Lieutenants Harry 'Breaker' Morant, Peter Handcock and George Witton served as volunteers in a South African irregular unit, the Bushveldt Carbineers, under British Military Command. These men were tried for shooting Boer prisoners and were found guilty at their Court Martial even though they pleaded their actions were in accordance with orders of their British superiors and lawful under the principle of reprisal.

Lieutenants Morant and Handcock were executed on 27 February 1902, and Witton's sentence commuted to life imprisonment, but he was released from prison in 1904.

Major James Thomas served with distinction as an infantry officer, but was also appointed to defend Morant, Handcock and Witton.

Major Thomas protested the innocence of his clients and insisted that an inquiry should have been convened to review the manner in which the arrest, trial and sentencing of these men was conducted by the British Military. Major Thomas raised serious doubts that they were not tried in accordance with the law of 1902.

Military and civilian lawyer, James Unkles has advocated for an enquiry and posthumous pardons. His work in this regard has included petitions to the British Crown, the Parliament of Australia and Government Ministers.

On 12 February 2018, a motion was tabled in the House of Representatives by Mr Scott Buchholz, MP. Of significance is the motion that expressed:

(a) sincere regret that Lieutenants Morant, Handcock and Witton were denied procedural fairness contrary to law and acknowledges that this had cruel and unjust consequences; and
(b) sympathy to the descendants of these men as they were not tried and sentenced in accordance with the law of 1902.

Mr Buchholz also stated:

'The process used to try these men was fundamentally flawed. They were not afforded the rights of an accused person facing serious criminal charges enshrined in military law in 1902. Today, I recognise the cruel and unjust consequences and express my deepest sympathy to the descendants'.

20 November 2019

Appendix J

COUNCIL 27 NOVEMBER 2019

Mayoral Minute No. 8 Cont...

COMMENT

These Australian veterans served the interest of the Crown and should be recognised and respected. If doubts exist as to the manner in which they were treated by the British Military Command this should be examined by an independent authority.

The descendants of these men seek an independent Australian Government review after decades of doubt that their relatives were tried fairly. They are seeking posthumous pardons.

The case continues to be controversial in Australian history. It has drawn concerned comments from community leaders, judicial figures, MPs, and the House of Representatives Petitions Committee who have reviewed the matter.

Posthumous pardons will bring a conclusion and provide reassurance that democratic traditions and the rule of law are paramount when reviewing cases in which there is credible evidence of a miscarriage of justice.

It is an appropriate time for posthumous pardons be extended to Lieutenants Morant, Handcock and Witton and accept that:

- due process taken to investigate and try the accused failed to meet the standards of the Military Law of 1902;
- the trials and sentences were not conducted in strict accordance with the judicial procedures and regulations of the time;
- the veterans were denied the right of appeal and petition to the King for clemency;
- they were held in isolation during the trials and were denied the opportunity to contact their families in Australia;
- their Counsel, Major Thomas was denied the use of the telegraph to seek intervention from the Australian Government that was unaware that these men were on trial and were facing capital punishment;
- The British military's decision not to consult the Australian Government about the arrest and trials was an appalling tactic to ensure these men were tried and sentenced without Australian intervention;
- the execution of Morant and Handcock was carried out with indecent haste, within a few hours of the sentences being proclaimed. This was a cruel decision and one that prevented any judicial or Australian Government intervention.

The lack of consultation with the Australian Government and denial of appeal were aggravating features that ensured that the accused were sentenced without any form of review, which they were entitled to seek. Pardons will address this injustice:

Mr Unkles has made a submission about this matter on behalf of the descendants to The Honourable Scott Morrison, MP, Prime Minister. I have reviewed this submission and believe it is compelling and should be supported by Council.

Taking action in this case reflects Australian values and ethics enshrined in respect for rule of law and due process. While the Morant matter occurred 117 years ago, the principles of due legal process and fairness remain as relevant today as they did in 1902.

Securing an inquiry will bring satisfaction to the descendants and if pardons are granted, would remove the stigma that the descendants have endured. Pardons would also

COUNCIL	27 NOVEMBER 2019

Mayoral Minute No. 8 Cont...

provide relief after 117 years of stress, anxiety, and recognition that Major Thomas' dedication to try to secure a fair trial and sentencing process was not in vain and will be vindicated by an independent inquiry.

RECOMMENDATION

I, Councillor Peter Petty hereby move the following Mayoral Minute at the Ordinary Council Meeting held on Wednesday, 27 November 2019.

That Council supports Mr Unkles' submission to the Prime Minster, The Honourable Scott Morrison MP as follows:

'The Tenterfield Council supports the proposal that the Australian Government appoints a suitably qualified person, such as a former Judge, to review the evidence and submission that three (3) Australian veterans, Lieutenants Harry 'Breaker' Morant, Peter Handcock and George Witton were not tried and sentenced by Courts Marital according to the law of 1902 and suffered a terrible injustice as a consequence.

The descendants of these men seek redress to mitigate the adverse effects the trials and executions have had and continue to have on the families of these men. Aggravating aspects include:

- The veterans, individually and through Major Thomas, were denied the right of appeal and petition to the King for clemency;

- They were held in isolation during the trials and were denied the opportunity to contact their families in Australia;

- Major Thomas had one day to prepare complex trials on charges, which carried the death penalty. The prosecution had 3 months and unlimited resources to assist in preparing the cases. Major Thomas had no such support and was denied the opportunity to contact the Australian Government;

- The British Military's decision not to consult the Australian Government about the arrest and trials was an appalling tactic to ensure these men were tried and sentenced without Australia's intervention;

- The execution of Morant and Handcock was carried out with indecent haste, within a few hours of the sentences being proclaimed. This was a cruel decision and one that prevented any judicial or Australian Government intervention

The granting of statutory pardons, will remove the stigma associated with the military service of these veterans and the dishonour to Australia's history.

Pardons will also acknowledge that the executions of Morant and Handcock and imprisonment for life of Witton were penalties they did not deserve noting the significant mitigating circumstances and recommendations for mercy that were made by the trial officers but not implemented by the British authorities'.

20 November 2019

Appendix K

From the Office of the Mayor

5 December 2019
OCR20199661

The Hon Scott Morrison MP
Prime Minister
PO Box 6022
House of Representatives
Parliament House
CANBERRA ACT 2600

Dear Prime Minister

Re: Letter of Support – Submission by Mr James Unkles – Request for Review

In support of Mr Unkles, and in consideration of Tenterfield resident Major Thomas who never recovered from his experience in this case, dying a sad and lonely death, Major Thomas exerted a considerable influence in the early development of Tenterfield and his grave in the Tenterfield Cemetery is still much visited.

Tenterfield Shire Councillors, at the Ordinary Meeting of 27 November 2019, voted unanimously as follows:

Resolution 239/19
Resolved that Council supports Mr Unkles' submission to the Prime Minster, The Honourable Scott Morrison MP as follows:

'The Tenterfield Council supports the proposal that the Australian Government appoints a suitably qualified person, such as a former Judge, to review the evidence and submission that three (3) Australian veterans, Lieutenants Harry 'Breaker' Morant, Peter Handcock and George Witton were not tried and sentenced by Courts Marital according to the law of 1902 and suffered a terrible injustice as a consequence.

The descendants of these men seek redress to mitigate the adverse effects the trials and executions have had and continue to have on the families of these men.

Aggravating aspects include:

.. 2/ ...

All correspondence should be addressed to:
The General Manager
Tenterfield Shire Council
247 Rouse Street (PO Box 214) TENTERFIELD NSW 2372

Telephone: (02) 6736 1744 Facsimile: (02) 6736 2669 email: council@tenterfield.nsw.gov.au website: www.tenterfield.nsw.gov.au
ABN 85 010 810 083

Page 2

- The veterans, individually and through Major Thomas, were denied the right of appeal and petition to the King for clemency;

- They were held in isolation during the trials and were denied the opportunity to contact their families in Australia;

- Major Thomas had one day to prepare complex trials on charges, which carried the death penalty. The prosecution had 3 months and unlimited resources to assist in preparing the cases. Major Thomas had no such support and was denied the opportunity to contact the Australian Government;

- The British Military's decision not to consult the Australian Government about the arrest and trials was an appalling tactic to ensure these men were tried and sentenced without Australia's intervention;

- The execution of Morant and Handcock was carried out with indecent haste, within a few hours of the sentences being proclaimed. This was a cruel decision and one that prevented any judicial or Australian Government intervention

The granting of statutory pardons, will remove the stigma associated with the military service of these veterans and the dishonour to Australia's history.

Pardons will also acknowledge that the executions of Morant and Handcock and imprisonment for life of Witton were penalties they did not deserve noting the significant mitigating circumstances and recommendations for mercy that were made by the trial officers but not implemented by the British authorities".

Council looks for to your consideration and action in this matter.

Yours sincerely

Peter Petty
Mayor

Cc   The Hon Barnaby Joyce MP

Endnotes

    Petition for clemency, pardon, and the immediate release from incarceration of George Ramsdale Witton, addressed to King Edward VII, and signed by 37 citizens of Colebrook, Tasmania, c.1904

1. William Woolmore, *The Bushveldt Carbineers and the Pietersburg Light Horse*, 2002, p 130, reference to a quote from Major Thomas in his letter of 6 June 1921
2. http://www.lighthorse.org.au/james-francis-thomas/
3. Bruce Oswald and Jim Waddell, Justice *In Arms, Military Lawyers in the Australian Army's First Hundred Years*, Big Sky Publishing, 2014
4. Oswald and Waddell, Op Cit, p. 1
5. Bennett, J.M. '*Doubting Thomas*' New South Wales Law Society Journal October 2001.
6. Chief Justice Robert French, book launch, *Justice In Arms, Military Lawyers in the Australian Army's First Hundred Years*, 2 Oct 2013, p 3
7. F. M. Cutlack, *Breaker Morant, A Horseman Who Made History*, Ure Smith Pty Lyd, 1962
8. Lieutenant G. Witton, *Scapegoats of the British Empire, the true story of Breaker Morant's Bushveldt Carbineers*, Angus &Robertson 1982 p. 244
9. G.A Embleton, afterword of, Lieutenant G. Witton, *Scapegoats of the British Empire, the true story of Breaker Morant's Bushveldt Carbineers* 1982, p. 245
10. WO 81/135B 1902 Jan. - Judge Advocate General's Office: letter book Jan 1902 — Aug 1903, applications for trial records
11. Lieutenant G. Witton, op cit pp. 93, 9-100, 118 — 124
12. Manual of Military Law, 4th edition, 1899
13. Lieutenant G. Witton, op cit p 124
14. https://www.smh.com.au/national/get-it-right-you-bastards-the-fight-to-clear-breaker-morants-name-20091019-h382.html & https://www.smh.com.au/national/rest-in-peace-20091019-h38b.html
15. James Unkles 2010 — 2018 *research, documentary, political agitation*
16. Mitchell Library ML Doc3274
17. Stubbs, J. Northern Star (Lismore) '*Victim of the Trial of Breaker Morant*' 16th August, 1980 Page 16
18. *http://www.lighthorse.org.au/james-francis-thomas/*
19. http://www.lighthorse.org.au/james-francis-thomas/*Article courtesy of Anthony Hoy, taken from 'The Bulletin', April 4, 2000*
20. Breaker Morant, film, South Australian Film Corporation, 1980
21. *On revisiting The Kings' School Parramatta in Australian Poets 1788-1888*, published by Griffith, Farran, Okended & Welsh 1888 p.553-554
22. Arthur Davey, *Breaker Morant and the Bushveldt Carbineers* Cape Town, 1987
23. *To a silver eyes and May O'The South* in Australian Poets published by Griffith, Farran, Okended & Welsh 1888 p.553-554
24. https://en.wikipedia.org/wiki/William_Barclay_(theologian);https://www.brainyquote.com/quotes/william_barclay_186927
25. James Francis Thomas, New South Wales Registrar of Births Deaths and Marriages

	Birth extract of 25 Aug 1861
26	New South Wales Registrar of Births Deaths and Marriages Entry 26908/1948
27	New South Wales Registrar of Births Deaths and Marriages Entry 8519-1897
28	Free BDM December Quarter 3b 593
29	Kings School magazine, Vol 98 article dated December 1911
30	Sladen, D.B.W Australian poets 1788-1888: being a selection of poems London: Griffith, Farran
31	K. Denton, *Closed File, The true story behind the execution of Breaker Morant and Peter Handcock*, 1983, p.61
32	K. Denton, op cit, p.62
33	https://en.wikipedia.org/wiki/The_Boy_from_Oz
34	K. Denton, K. Closed File Rigby Sydney 1983 Page 146
35	K. Denton, op cit, p. 35
36	http://www.labuschagne.info/anglo-boer-war.htm
37	Mark Weber, *The Boer War Remembered*, The Institute for Historical Review, http://www.ihr.org/jhr/v18/v18n3p14_Weber.html
38	K. Denton, *Closed File, The true story behind the execution of Breaker Morant and Peter Handcock*, 1983, p.20
39	https://www.goodreads.com/work/quotes/284013-la-guerra-de-guerrillas
40	Mark Weber, *The Boer War Remembered*, The Institute for Historical Review, http://www.ihr.org/jhr/v18/v18n3p14_Weber.html
41	K. Denton, *Closed File, The true story behind the execution of Breaker Morant and Peter Handcock*, 1983, p.31
42	Sir Henry Campbell-Bannerman, Leader of the Liberal Opposition Party in Britain: at a meeting of the National Reform Union, June, 14. 1901
43	Mark Weber, *The Boer War Remembered*, The Institute for Historical Review http://www.ihr.org/jhr/v18/v18n3p14_Weber.html
44	K. Denton, *Closed File, The true story behind the execution of Breaker Morant and Peter Handcock*, 1983, p.34
45	LTCOL N.C. Smith, *The Odd Blemish, Australian and Military Justice In The Boer War 1899 — 1902, 1999*, p.2
46	Lord Roberts, Commander-in-Chief, South African War (1899-1901), http://www.pinetreeweb.com/roberts-bio.htm
47	Mark Weber, *The Boer War Remembered*, The Institute for Historical Review, http://www.ihr.org/jhr/v18/v18n3p14_Weber.html
48	House of Commons Hansard *26 February 1901 vol 89 cc1239-91* <u>1239</u>
49	House of Commons Hansard *26 February 1901 vol 89 cc1239-91*1247
50	John Dillon, MP, House of Commons Hansard *26 February 1901 vol 89 cc1239-91*
51	John Dillon, MP House of Commons Hansard *26 February 1901 vol 89 cc1239-91*
52	Stephen Miller in his article *Duty or Crime, Acceptable Behavior in the British Army in South Africa, pp 311-331*
53	Deneys Reitz, Commando: *A Boer Journal Of The Boer War*, 1929
54	Lieutenant G. Witton, op cit P.76
55	Lieutenant G. Witton, op cit P 81
56	Kelly's Handbook To The Titled, Landed And Official Classes. 1906 32nd Edition London Page 1321
57	Colonel. J. St Clair, A legal opinion dated 22 November 1901 *JA821- Confidential*
58	Mark Weber, *The Boer War Remembered*, The Institute for Historical Review, http://www.ihr.org/jhr/v18/v18n3p14_Weber.html

Endnotes

59 Treaty of Vereeniging, https://www.britannica.com/event/Peace-of-Vereeniging
60 SJP Kruger. As quoted in *Rhodes of Africa*, Gross, F., Cassel & Company Ltd., London., 1956,pp. 379-380
61 https://www.azquotes.com/quote/557570
62 A.Davey, *Breaker Morant and the Bushveldt Carabineers*, second series no 18, Van Riebeeck Society 1987, p.55
63 Wallace, R.L. *The Circumstances Surrounding the Siege of Elands River Post: A Boer War study* Wollstonecraft N.S.W., 1992
64 The Tenterfield Star 23rd October, 1900
65 Craig Wilcox historical researcher of Dee Why mentions this in a letter to me on 1/6/01 and refers to the Public Record Office (London) War Office 32/8033 Court of Inquiry into Thomas' Loss of a Convoy
66 Public Record Office (London) War Office file W032/8033 Court of Inquiry into loss of convoy by Thomas, January 1901
67 Australian War Memorial in Canberra — Kenneth Mackay papers PR87/207 Box 1 Item 10
68 William Reid, Lord Mayor address Tenterfield 1901
69 R Wallace, op cit
70 Gavin Souter, *Lion and kangaroo : the initiation of Australia*, Text Publishing, 2000
71 R Wallace, *Australians at the Boer War: the story of the Australians who served in the South African War 1899 to 1902*, 1976
72 The Advertiser SA, *Major Thomas Experiences*, 4 June 1901, P 5
73 Thomas Walker letter dated 15 June 1901
74 Barry Bridges, "Lord Kitchener and the Morant/Handcock Executions", *Journal of the Australian Historical Society* 73 (June 1987): 37
75 *The British Times* newspaper, *The Trial of Officers for murder of Boer prisoners*, Reuters correspondent, 17 April 1902
76 Witton, G.R. *Scapegoats of the Empire: the story of the Bushveldt Carbineers* Angus and Robertson 1982
77 Judge Advocate General's Office: Minute Books, 1871-1953, WO 83/12 1902 Mar. Vol. 12, 10 — 1903, Nov. 13
78 K. Denton, *Breaker Morant File — Bush Lawyer*, p.4
79 Denton, K. Closed File, Rigby Sydney 1983, P 94,
80 Bleszynski, op cit, p. 318
81 Bleszynski, op cit, p. 318
82 Charge Sheets 1902
83 Lieutenant G. Witton, op cit p.63
84 Charles Clode, *Military Forces of the Crown*, 1869, p. 173
85
86 *Australian Archives. Sentences on Officers in South Africa. 15 April 1902, House of Representatives in CRS 78/1. Carnegie pp.190-191*
87 Lieutenant G. Witton, op cit
88 Manual of Military Law, 4th edition, 1899, p.112
89 Manual of Military Law, 4th edition, 1899, ps. 199 and 200
90 Bleszynski, op cit, p.578
91 Manual of Military Law, 4th edition, 1899, p 3
92 Bleszynski, op cit, p.574
93 MML op cit, p. 583
94 MML op cit, p. 51

95   MML op cit, p. 553
96   LTCOL E. Gunter, *Outlines of Military Law In Accordance with Manual of Military Law* 1900
97   LTCOL.E. Gunter op cit
98   Bleszynski, op cit, p. 577
99   MML op cit, p. 46
100   Bleszynski, op cit, p. 575
101   A. F.Tytler, *An Essay on Military Law,* 3rd edition 1814, p. 243
102   MML op cit, p. 53
103   MML op cit, p. 44
104   MML op cit, p. 46
105   MML op cit, p. 159
106   Clode, *Military Forces of the Crown* 1869, p.176
107   MML op cit, p. 55
108   Lieutenant G. Witton, op cit, p.70
109   K. Denton, op cit, p. 101-102
110   K. Denton, op cit, p. 113-114
111   William Woolmore op cit, p.123
112   William Woolmore op cit, p. 118
113   Renar, Frank, Bushman and Buccaneers H.T. Dunn & C, Sydney 1902, p.28
114   Lieutenant G Witton, op cit, p. 155
115   Clode, op cit, p.173
116   C.Clode, op cit, p. 173
117   Isaac Isaacs, op cit
118   Bleszynski, op cit, p.614
119   Bleszynski, op cit, p. 628
120   Lieutenant G. Witton, op cit p. 151
121   Lieutenant G. Witton, op cit p. 151
122   Lieutenant G. Witton, op cit p. 151
123   MML op cit, p. 619
124   Charles Clode, *Military Forces of the Crown,* 1869, p.175
125   MML op cit, p. 363
126   William Woolmore op cit, p. 129
127   27thFebruary 1902 Thomas to Major Lenehan
128   J.F. Thomas letter to Premier of WA dated 2 May 1902
129   William Woolmore op cit, p.130
130   F. Shields and M. Carnegie *In search of Breaker Morant: balladist and Bushveldt Carbineer,* H.H. Stephenson 1979
131   A.Davey, op cit 108
132   K. Denton, op cit, p 109
133   J. Unkles Aug 2018
134   K. Denton, op cit, p.145
135   K. Denton, op cit, p. 145
136   The British Times newspaper, op cit
137   William Woolmore, op cit, p.309
138   J. Unkles opinion 2013
139   Alexander Street, SC (now Federal Court Judge) submission moot court 20 July 2013
140   Moot court decision, transcript 20 July 2013, p.16
141   Gerard Nash, QC legal opinion of 13 Oct 13, p 32-34

Endnotes

142 Bleszynski, op cit, p.627
143 Geoffrey Robertson, QC interview with Jim Unkles 2013
144 https://www.screenaustralia.gov.au/the-screen-guide/t/breaker-morant-the-retrial-2013/31500/
145 Jim Unkles, video interview of Greg Hunt June 2013
146 http://www.lighthorse.org.au/the-bushveldt-carbineers/ & https://www.alexhawke.com.au/node/741
147 Bleszynski, op cit, p. 178
148 http://http://www.smh.com.au/nsw/breaker-morant-relics-found-on-rubbish-tip-20160422-gocn1a.html,
149 J. Unkles, www.breakermorant.com
150 See also Cutlack,F.M. Breaker Morant: A Horseman that Made History, Ure Smith 1962
151 Witton, G.R. op cit, Page 151
152 Witton, G.R. op cit, P 154-5
153 Witton, G.R. op cit, P 112, -114
154 Witton, G.R. op cit, P 98
155 Witton, G.R. op cit, P 102-3
156 The Sydney Morning Herald (NSW : 1842-1954), Saturday 25 February 1939, page 21
157 Roderick, C. Banjo Paterson — Poet by Accident Allen and Unwin 1993 Pages 164
158 Bathurst Free Press and Mining Journal (NSW: 1851 — 1904), Wednesday 2 April 1902, Clarence and Richmond Examiner (Grafton, NSW: 1889 — 1915), Saturday 5 April 1902, page 8
159 Bleszynski, op cit, p. 180
160 Bleszynski, op cit, p. 180
161 William Woolmore, op cit, p. 130
162 The Adelaide Advertiser, *The Bushveldt Carabineers, Statement by an Ex Trooper*, 8 May 1902
163 Bleszynski, op cit, p.628 & Lord Kitchener letter to Secretary of State dated 6 April 1902
164 Thomas letter dated 17 Aug 1901
165 Julian Putkowski, Shot at Dawn: Executions in World War One by Authority of the British Army Act, p.68
166 Julian Putkowski op cit P.69
167 Lord Kitchener telegram reproduced in F.M.Cutlack op cit p. 103
168 University of England and Regional Archives A186 V3098/18
169 The *Tenterfield Star* newspaper Centenary Edition 1870 — 1970
170 National Library of Australia. Letter in the George Mackaness Collection MS554/855/1
171 Evidence of the Royal Commission of Inquiry into Proposals for the Establishment of a New State or New States Formed Wholly or in Part Out of the Territory of New South Wales NSW Government Printer Volume II 1925 Page 1287
172 The *Tenterfield Star* "Confidence Tricksters — Mr. J.F. Thomas Victimised — Retired Manager Also Duped".
173 University of New England and Regional Archives V3095/2
174 The High Court appeal was reported in The Australian Law Journal page 32 15th May, 1929. He argued that the High Court had jurisdiction because he had been guilty of misappropriating over £300, and therefore the High Court had jurisdiction because it

	involved a civil right of more than that magnitude
175	Mother Teresa — quote https://www.goodreads.com/author/quotes/838305. Mother_Teresa
176	Robert Robertson Museum and Archive, Kings School Parramatta, Old Boys File No 1348
177	Stubbs, J. Northern Star (Lismore) 'Victim of the Trial of Breaker Morant' 16th August, 1980 Page 16
178	Mitchell Library ML Doc3274
179	Stubbs, J Northern Star (Lismore) 'Victim of the Trial of Breaker Morant' 16th August, 1980 Page 16
180	The *Tenterfield Star* 12th November, 1942
181	James Thomas, New South Wales Registrar of Births Deaths and Marriages Birth extract 12 Nov 1942
182	John Stubbs *Major who defended Morant spent a year in Long Bay gaol,*
183	K. Denton, op cit, p.124
184	*Thomas v The Incorporated Law Institute of New South Wales, High* Court 18 April 1929
185	K. Denton, op cit, p.129
186	K. Denton, op cit, p.130
187	K. Denton, op cit, p.131
188	K. Denton, op cit, p.134
189	Robert Wallace, *Australians at the Boer War: the story of the Australians who served in the South African War 1899 to 1902* Paddington, NSW: National Boer War Memorial Association
190	K. Denton, op cit, p.139
191	K. Denton, op cit, p.130
192	K. Denton, op cit, p.145
193	https://www.findagrave.com/memorial/189853584/james-francis-thomas
194	Beach Thomas address speech for moot dinner 20 July 2013
195	The Australian newspaper, *Breaker Morant lawyer's relative takes up case for a judicial commission,* 5 Aug 2011
196	Motion House of Representatives 12 February 2018, Hansard p. 28
197	Photograph at Parliament House 12 February 2108
198	Appendix B
199	Appendix E https://www.aph.gov.au/Parliamentary_Business/Hansard/Hansard_Display?bid=chamber/hansardr/25177/&sid=0271 https://youtu.be/OzZ7IRLyD2k https://www.contactairlandandsea.com/2021/12/03/nationals-mp-calls-for-breaker-morant-inquiry/
200	(G.Christensen letter to Darren Chester, MP dated 26 May 2021)
201	Bleszynski, op cit, p.627
202	Sladen, D.B.W *Australian poets 1788-1888: being a selection of poems* London: Griffith, Farran
203	http://samilitaryhistory.org/vol054ed.html
204	Alex Hawke, MP. *Grievance Debate: Harry 'Breaker' Morant,* March 15 2010
205	Thomas to the Editor of the Sydney Morning Herald, Sydney 14th June 1923
206	UK Ministry of Defence email of 26 June 2018
207	Australian Department of Defence letter DH&A 18/648999 of 14 June 2018

Endnotes

208 The Fourth Victim by Jack Drake 2002
209 Mrs Julia Irwin, MP, Extract from Hansard, House of Representatives, 26 October, 2009
210 Mr Tony Smith, MP, (Mrs Julia Irwin, MP), Extract from Hansard, House of Representatives, 26 October, 2009
211 Senator McGauran, Senate Notice Paper No 83 of 25 June 2003, Senate Notice Papers
212 Dr Howard Zelling comments in Adelaide Advertiser newspaper, June 7 1988
213 C. Francis QC, letter to Herald Sun newspaper, Copyright News Limited Feb 13, 2002
214 House of Representatives Hansard — motion and transcript, 12 February 2018, p.28 — 30.
215 Law Society of New South Wales, *A Country Lawyer at War*, issue 60 Oct 2019 36-39
216 Senator Jim Molan Facebook entry October 9 2019
217 Jim Molan entry on Facebook 9 Oct 2019
218 Mayoral Minute - *Request For Review Into The Execution of Lieutenants Harry Breaker Morant, Peter Handcock and life sentence of George Witton – Boer War 1902*, 20 November 2019
219 Office of the Mayor, *Letter of support – Submission by Mr james Unkles-request for review* dated 5 December 2019
220 Richard Williams email to Peter Petty 2 December 2019

www.ingramcontent.com/pod-product-compliance
Lightning Source LLC
Chambersburg PA
CBHW021057080526
44587CB00010B/283